Guide to
Lump Sum
Investment

www.iii.co.uk

FINANCIAL SHOPPING MADE EASY ONLINE.

interactive investor international is your website
for everything from mortgages to insurance,
pensions to share dealing. choose with confidence.
there's no pressure and no jargon,
but there is all the information you need,
as well as comments from investors like yourself.
take financial control online, go to **www.iii.co.uk**

interactive
investor
international
financial power is changing hands™

Guide to
Lump Sum
Investment

TWELFTH
EDITION

Liz Walkington

**KOGAN
PAGE**

Throughout this book, 'he' etc has been used where 'he' or 'she' etc should properly have been. This is to avoid clumsy language and no discrimination, prejudice or bias is intended.

First published in 1985
by Telegraph Publications
Author: Diana Wright

Twelfth edition published in 2000
Author: Liz Walkington

Kogan Page Limited
120 Pentonville Road
London N1 9JN

British Library Cataloguing in Publication Data

A CIP record for this book is available from the British Library.

ISBN 0 7494 3311 6

Typeset by Saxon Graphics Ltd, Derby
Printed and bound in Great Britain by Thanet Press Ltd, Margate, Kent

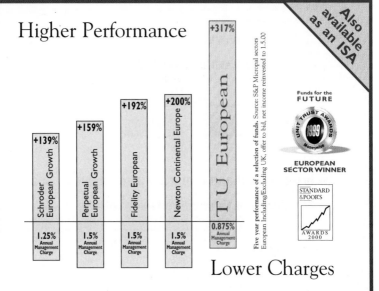

Contents

Investing a lump sum –
Do you have more questions than answers?

Having a lump sum to invest sounds straight forward enough. But to make the most of your money, there are a wealth of important considerations to take into account before you decide which of the many investment opportunities is right for you...

The most appropriate and productive investment of a lump sum depends entirely on your circumstances now and when they are likely to change in the future – as they probably will.

In other words, it's important to establish just what it is you are trying to achieve – are you looking to generate income, growth or a combination of the two? If you need your investment to produce income, when do you want it to start and how frequently do you want it paid?

Are you additionally looking to improve your overall returns by cutting your tax bill or that of your spouse? If you are working, are you making full use of potential pension contributions? If you are self-employed, this should include involving your spouse in the business and building up a pension fund for them too.

If you are retired, are you eligible for Age Allowance benefits? And if so, have you arranged your 'income' (made up perhaps from PEPs, ISAs, Investment Bonds and full use of the annual capital gains tax exemption) in such a way as to maximise your entitlement? It's important to remember too, that because of the Age Allowance 'trap', some people over 65 on total incomes between £17,000 and £19,810 are paying marginal rates of over 30%, when they probably think 22% is their top rate.

And what about any inheritance tax liability? Your investment could be arranged in such a way that any potential liability could be progressively reduced, but still providing you with a flow of regular payments. Or, in an alternative arrangement, leaving you with access to capital.

And yet another aim might be to remain in your own home for as long as possible in later life. After all, that is where you are likely to be happiest and most comfortable, with your family around you and friends and local facilities close at hand. But you may need to buy in services to fulfil this ambition in order to keep your independence for as long as possible.

Naturally none of these investment aims is necessarily exclusive. Each requirement can be addressed, as appropriate, as part of an overall strategy based on the priorities you set yourself.

Lincoln recommends that you find an adviser to help you make the most effective use of your net assets and help you through the complexities of finding tax-effective solutions.

Rob Merrick,
Investment Marketing Manager,
Lincoln Financial Group

Lincoln is a marketing group regulated by the Personal Investment Authority providing life assurance, pensions, unit trusts and ISAs. Any regulated advice offered will relate only to the products of Lincoln.

Figures correct for the tax year 2000/2001.

Investments?

I've got more important things to worry about.

True. There are more pressing issues on your mind than where to put your money. But perhaps we can offer a little sound financial advice. And leave you with more time for the things matter most.

For further information or to arrange an appointment, please telephone **free** on

0800 783 0222

Clear solutions in a complex world

Lincoln
Financial Group®

DISCOUNT ISAS AND UNIT TRUSTS THROUGH BETTER INVEST DIRECT

Saving you money, and helping you make money

As a buyer of the Daily Telegraph Lump Sum Investment Guide, you are undoubtedly one of the growing number of people throughout the UK who wish to gain greater control over their financial destiny. And that means you can also save yourself hundreds of pounds in set-up charges, commission payments and fees.

Many people seek advice from Independent Financial Advisers. And, in return for that advice, when you buy a financial product the IFA is entitled to commission from the investment company that supplies the product. For ISAs and unit trusts, this generally equates to around 3% of the amount invested.

Reduce costly set-up charges

If you have spent time carrying out your own research, you may decide that you do not need independent advice, and you may want to go direct to the investment company in an attempt to avoid commission payments… not a good move. All that happens is that the investment company pockets the commission. What's more, whether you go through an IFA or you go direct to the investment company, you will expect to lose a further 2% or more in initial set-up charges. On an ISA investment of £7,000, these commission and set-up charges will equate to as much as £367, in effect making your investment worth only £6,633 on Day One.

Benefit from commission rebates and extra discounts

But, by buying your ISA or unit trust through Better Invest Direct, you can save between 3% and more than 5% - Better Invest Direct rebates all initial commission to which it is entitled as an IFA, and it is able to negotiate further discounts with investment companies. In some cases, this can mean no initial charges at all. And, importantly, Better Invest Direct does not charge handling fees.

Not only does this mean that your investment is working harder for you from the start, it also gives you the ability to change from one investment to another without reducing the value of your investment. This is ideal for PEP transfers if you feel that your current PEP is not performing well.

So, how does Better Invest Direct earn a living? Investment companies generally make an annual charge of around 1.5% on your ISA or unit trust, irrespective of whether you go through an IFA or go direct to the investment company. We have simply agreed to receive 0.5% of this amount, which would normally be retained by the investment company anyway.

The normal value of your investment, therefore, is unaffected by what Better Invest Direct earns from the investment company. And just think about the long term benefits, say over five years, of saving, for example, £350 on set-up charges in Year One! That saving could be worth significantly more after just a few years.

A wide range of financial products from all leading investment companies

Better Invest Direct has saved thousands of investors hundreds of thousands of pounds in the last year. To find out more about how we can help you save money on literally thousands of ISAs, unit trusts, OEICs and PEP transfers from all of the leading investment companies, simply call our Investor Hotline on 0800 169 3604 or visit our web site at www.betterinvestdirect.co.uk.

Richard Wood

Richard Wood is Managing Director of independent financial advisers Better Invest Direct Limited, a member of Investment Strategies (UK) Limited which is regulated by the Personal Investment Authority. Call Better Invest Direct's Investor Hotline free on 0800 169 3604 for further information.

i|Shares™

The way you invest now. Only better.

The UK's first Exchange Traded Fund

Find out more at:

www.ishares.net
or call 0845 357 7000

The iShares revolution – Simplicity, efficiency, clarity

by John G Demaine, Director iShares plc

Using pooled funds as part of an investment portfolio is widely accepted as an intelligent and sensible way to diversify risk and capture market returns without the need to buy dozens of shares. But, there are now more pooled funds than there are individual listed equities in the UK. Choosing the right ones to make up the core of an equity based investment portfolio is as hard as choosing the right mobile phone tariff.

In fact, the similarities between grappling with mobile telephony and choosing a pooled vehicle are uncanny. What's the coverage? How safe is it? Will I be able to use it when I need it? And how much are those intricate fee structures going to relieve me of?

So the question is: do we really need a new type of "Exchange Traded Fund" called iShares, to be launched in the UK? If you want to do some or all of the following, then the answer is a resounding "yes":

- Have a well-diversified investment
- Buy or sell quickly at a price you know through any stockbroker
- Invest at low cost
- Pay no stamp duty on trading
- Hold an investment that is ideal for a long term buy & hold strategy and which provides flexibility to be traded when you need to

SIMPLE

iShares are bought and sold exactly like normal stock market shares through a stockbroker. They are also like well-diversified pooled funds because by buying an iShare you are, with one trade, buying the contents of an index such as the FTSE 100. You will therefore know exactly what you have bought without having to wait for a fund manager to release their asset allocation in a report.

INSTANT ACCESS AND TRANSPARENT PRICING

Isn't this just like buying an index fund? Yes it is, but because iShares are listed on a stock market, investors have instant access to their investment at transparent prices throughout the trading day. It is more flexible than buying into a regular index fund. The only charge for buying or selling iShares is the fee charged by your stockbroker because the first iShares, such as iFTSE100, are not currently liable for stamp duty.

So taking into account the total costs of buying iShares - narrow spreads and execution-only fees - these products are excellent value for money, whether you are a short-term trader or are looking to buy and hold for the long term.

Liberation from stamp duty is not the end of the story. Qualifying investors can include iShares in their ISAs and also hold them in existing PEPs, so capital gains and income arising from lump sum investments through iShares can benefit from significant tax advantages.

WHY iSHARES ARE DIFFERENT

The bugbear of investors in the UK's Investment Trust sector is the problem of discounts to net asset value. In brief, this is where the shares of an investment company command a lower price than the value of their underlying assets.

iShares are different, because, while similar to Unit Trusts and OEICs in that they are open-ended funds - they are available to be traded in real time. Furthermore, as a result of partnership with some of the City's largest securities houses, they should not suffer the discounts and premiums to net asset value, that can affect Investment Trusts. The creation/redemption mechanism ensures that the supply of iShares expands and contracts to meet market demand. For iShareholders this means that the price of iShares on the stock market should always be very close to the underlying price of the fund's assets.

By comparison with Unit Trusts or OEICs, iShares offer greater ease of access (via any stockbroker) greater transparency (of both fees and the price at which you buy or sell, which is not known when you place an order for a Unit Trust or OEIC) and greater flexibility.

BORN IN THE USA

Hoovers, indexing, corn flakes- just a few of the great ideas that sprouted in the US and then ran tendrils across the Atlantic to take root here. Exchange Traded Funds are not a new invention. They were first launched in the US in 1993, where investors of all hues from both institutional and private camps now use them. Now, for the first time, similar products are being made available in Europe.

Within a few years, I anticipate that investors will be able to decide which parts of the world's economies they like and then buy or sell the relevant equity index easily and cheaply.

Since the majority of professional investment managers do not outperform the index, now private investors have a chance to outperform the professionals. This is a nice choice to have - and a simple one.

iSHARES IN BRIEF

What do they cover?

The iFTSE 100 covers its namesake index. Coverage will extend to a range of important equity indices over time.

What can I use them for?

iShares give you rapid exposure to an entire market or a sub-sector of that market, so they are an excellent way of implementing your asset allocation, whether as a stable core for your portfolio or to beef up your presence in sectors or markets you like.

How liquid are they?

About as liquid as they come. You can deal throughout normal market opening hours. The price changes throughout the day.

How much will I pay?

Low cost investing is the name of the game. Management fees are 0.35% and there's no stamp duty currently payable on iShares.

Is it a share?

It trades and settles like a share, but you are buying an investment company similar to a Unit Trust or OEIC which provides exposure to a lot of shares.

So is it an investment trust?

No. iShares are open-ended funds and do not suffer from sustained discounts or premiums to NAV

It's a unit trust, isn't it?

No, although there are some similarities. The differences are quite complex, but the main ones are that there is a real time price at which you can trade and the bid-offer spread is much narrower than with most unit trusts.

Where do I get them?

Call your stockbroker to deal in them. And for background information take a look at www.ishares.net, or call 0845 357 7000.

The Willis Owen difference

For 15 years Willis Owen has been providing independent investment advice to private clients and companies. It was however only three years ago we opened up our doors to investors wanting the benefit of Willis Owen research and analysis through the increasingly popular 'discount broker' route.

Discount brokers come in a variety of guises but fall mainly into two camps, being either 'Execution Only' (the majority) or 'Advisory'.

Willis Owen are advisory brokers but we offer a different way for people to invest by making 'product specific' recommendations based on varying degrees of risk/reward (for which we take no initial commission), rather than 'client specific' recommendations (which would necessitate the taking of initial commission).

We do this because we believe that the majority of people are quite capable of making their own investment choices when given information and guidance on where to invest and a selection of well researched funds from which to choose.

Our research and analysis into every sector (with unit trusts alone there are over 1,600 to choose from) produces a handful of Willis Owen recommended funds. These funds are then carefully monitored and form the basis of our selections for investment advice and review services.

The Complete ISA Guides

The Willis Owen Complete ISA Guide series has recently offered these funds to readers of The Daily Telegraph. So far over 60,000 people have taken advantage of our recommendations and invested nearly one half of a billion pounds. All of this has been transacted with full discounts or no initial charges. Already our clients have saved around twenty million pounds in commission and charges.

It goes without saying that we often have the financial muscle to negotiate further discounts from the investment houses.

How do the Willis Owen discounts work?

When you invest you will normally pay an initial charge. This initial charge is either kept in its entirety by the investment company, or if you use a broker or adviser a proportion of this charge is paid to them.

When you invest through Willis Owen this amount (typically 3%) is paid to you – usually back into your investment together with any further discounts we have been able to negotiate on your behalf. This ensures you will always receive the best discounts available and pay less to invest, making more of your money work harder for you from day one.

To find out more, call us on 0115 947 2595. Or ask to receive regular copies of *'objective'* – our client magazine.

Some people pay
full initial charges.

Others don't.

Telephone 0115 947 2595
www.willisowen.co.uk

willisOwen.

...investment solutions for everyday life

Willis Owen is regulated by the Personal Investment Authority.

xx

FLEET STREET PUBLICATIONS LTD

Penny shares are viewed as a white-knuckle-ride even by high-risk investors. But, chosen carefully, they can be an essential part of a diversified portfolio.

If a blue-chip stock was a film it would be Star Wars. Expensive, solid and guaranteed to earn you a return on your investment. The penny share, however, would be The Full Monty. An outside punt that, against the odds, bagged Oscars. In holiday terms it's two weeks in a Borneo jungle, compared to a fortnight at Centre Parks. And, obviously, they attract different types of investor. According to Tom Winnifrith, editor of the monthly tip sheet Red Hot Penny Shares and co-host of Channel Four's Show Me The Money, the penny shares investor is a dreamer. But it's the Klondiker in everyone who believes that with the next sift he'll find that golden nugget. Winnifrith is not alone in his affection for the penny share.

"Safer than the 3.30 at Chepstow, more fun than the football pools, better than breaking the bank at Monte Carlo," writes renowned penny share guru Michael Walters in his book How To Make A Killing In Penny Shares. His view, along with other investors, is that the penny share is a flutter, pure and simple. But why shouldn't the rules that make blue-chip companies successful equally apply to the smaller caps? One thing is certain. If you know the rules of the penny share then there must be a fortune to be made.

The rewards can be staggering - if you'd put £1,000 in Glaxo shares when they were just 2p they would have made you a stunning £809,000. £2,000 in Pentland Industries would have made £300,000 and if you'd put £5,000 into the ordinary shares of First National Finance Corporation near the bottom in 1975, you'd have made your first million by 1986.

According to Winnifrith, who has been a penny share devotee since 1992, the reason is common sense. It's easier for a company worth £10m to become a company worth £100m than a company worth £2bn to double.

"Elephants don't gallop," he says. "Small companies can grow faster than big ones." Another advantage is that the City analysts will overlook them. Added to which the recent booming market in tracker funds and personal pensions has thrown up some real bargains in the smaller company sector.

Winnifrith confirms, "This is why the penny share can be such a great investment for the private investor" - because investors can pile in at a time when the City institutions cannot.

The advantages are obvious. Walters writes: "Not every investor wants to play a conservative investment game. Not everyone wants a solid, blue-chip portfolio which will let them sleep at night. Many want a fling, to play for double or quits and are quite prepared to make an outright gamble. If you only have £1,000 or £2,000 and can afford to lose it, what is the point in earning a solid 10% return each year? What you need is a gamble, something which will make worthwhile winnings if you get it right."

The recent bull market has seen an unparalleled boom in penny share investing, with cheap tech stocks and cash shells hitting dizzying heights. The promise of the penny share is based on leverage. Investors can purchase many shares for their money, so even a slight price rise can have a significant effect.

According to Walters, the penny share is alive and kicking and the shrewd, or lucky, penny shares players can multiply their money eight, nine or tenfold in a year or two. In the current climate however, Winnifrith is not quite so bullish. He said: "I would alter my advice depending on the economic conditions. A year ago I might have considered investing 40 or 50% of a portfolio into smaller companies, now I might keep it at 10 or 20%. Even though penny shares may attract all sorts - including dreamers - it is still a sensible long-term investment approach. A well diversified portfolio must include small companies."

But there is a way to minimise the risk of the penny share. Despite their perceived high risk status, company fundamentals are similar, no matter what the market capitalisation. Winnifrith's filter system follows a ten-point check list which includes the quality of the company's management and how many shares are held by the directors. He added: "Be wary of companies where the management changes often To lose one non-executive director or one key adviser is acceptable, to lose two is careless, to lose more is terrifying."

He also believes in 'letting the trend be your friend'. In other words, investing in shares that are on an upward track. The reverse may mean that someone somewhere knows something is amiss.

Financially, Winnifrith will not invest in a company with any outstanding litigation, or one that is not generating a steadily increasing EPS (earnings per share). The balance sheet is vital and gearing (debts expressed as a percentage of net assets) should generally be low.

And it has to be said that the results of Winnifrith's regular tips in the Red Hot Penny Shares newsletter are impressive. As of May 2000, 10 of his 59 tips have made gains of over 100% in less than 12 months. As Winnifrith says: "With the right guidance you can make significant money from penny shares."

A PERSONAL SHAREDEALING SERVICE: THE VIEW FROM THE SMALLER BROKER

How good a service do you get from your stockbroker?

The Government's privatisations during the eighties and nineties opened up share ownership to the general public in a huge way for the first time. Thousands of individuals became shareholders overnight with the flotations of British Telecom, British Gas, the Water and Electricity companies. This was followed by the demutualisations of some building societies and insurance companies.

More recently popularity of internet and technology stocks has encouraged more and more people to invest money into the stockmarket. A number of new brokers have entered the UK market over the past year, accompanied by huge advertising campaigns offering cheaper commission on buying and selling shares.

Sharedealing has also been made easier by a new generation of stockbrokers who act for investors on an execution only basis rather than offering advice on what to invest in. Most of the recent growth in individual sharedealing has been fuelled by the growing amount of financial information available, both in the press and on the internet, and by more investors taking charge of their own finances. Now all you have to do is pick up the phone or click onto the internet and place your order.

But is it really all that easy, and what happens if you need to talk to a stockbroker? When we deal with our personal finances we expect a personal service from a qualified professional and sharedealing is no exception. However, with more and more financial services being conducted via telephone call centres and the internet, where do you go to get a personal service?

The answer lies with the smaller broker. At Norwich and Peterborough Sharedealing Services we have found that, although investors know that they want to buy and sell shares and which shares they want to buy and sell, they don't necessarily know how to go about it. Not only do we provide a range of sharedealing services, but we also pride ourselves on offering a personal and professional service at all times. We have nine sharedealing branches across the East of England, where clients can speak to qualified staff either in person or by phone. In addition, we also operate a share-dealing service throughout 62 branches of Norwich and Peterborough Building Society.

Our branch offices offer personal, face to face service and assistance in transacting sharedeals with the minimum of fuss. Whilst we cannot guarantee the financial success of the individual shares bought or sold, we can give our clients peace of mind that their transaction has been dealt with properly. In our experience, investors buying and selling shares for the first time are grateful for assistance, not only in completing their transactions but also for an explanation of how the sharedealing process works.

Not everyone wants to deal in shares in person and for more experienced investors, a telephone dealing account is essential. This allows investors to ring up and place orders over the phone. But even the most experienced investor sometimes wants to speak to someone they know, rather than a call centre operative, with a query or to find out some background information. With a personal sharedealing service, individuals can speak to a qualified representative (and generally the same one) each time they deal.

However, even with a telephone dealing service, the next question is how to hold your shares. There is a choice of holding them in certificate (paper) form or asking your broker hold them for you in a Nominee account. Having paper certificates has always been the traditional way to hold shares. Just like a bank note in your wallet, some investors feel that they can keep better track of their investments if they are in paper.

Of course, paper certificates can make it hard to deal quickly with your broker and more expensive. Buying shares through a stockbroker can mean having to wait as long as six weeks to get the share certificate from the company registrars. This can lead to problems if you wish to sell the same shares quickly, as many stockbrokers will not allow you to sell shares if you do not have the relevant certificate and this is where a nominee dealing account can help.

The introduction of the CREST settlement system has seen a change in both the way shares are held and the way that they are traded. The CREST system allows shares to be held electronically with no need for a paper certificate, and shares can be traded and settled automatically without the need for certificates to change hands. All of which means that the share-dealing process can be made quicker, more efficient and less costly.

Holding shares with stockbrokers in a nominee account allows them to settle transactions through the CREST system on the investors behalf. Individuals do not then get bogged down with paperwork nor do they have to worry about losing certificates, or delays in reaching them from company registrars. The standard period for settling a paper certificate share transaction is now ten working days. When you buy shares, the transaction only takes the same time but you can expect to wait another couple of weeks before you receive a paper certificate.

The standard settlement period for a nominee account is five working days, so for sale transactions, proceeds are available on the fifth day. With a purchase transaction, the shares are deposited automatically into nominee accounts on the settlement date. Already it is being planned that the standard settlement period will move from five days to three days early next year with the long term goal being automatic same day settlement.

All of this is good news for the private investor as it will make shares easier to trade and should open share ownership to an even wider audience. However, as with any fast-moving market place, investors will still need assistance and a 'personal service' whatever their sharedealing needs.

NET SAVINGS

The very latest news and sport, unbeatable travel and shopping offers and the ability to send messages anywhere in the world in an instant - plus of course fast, free and reliable Internet access and Free Internet calls 24 hours a day, 7 days a week!*

These are just some of the many reasons why people are joining the Internet through LineOne every day.

But did you know it's also possible to harness the power of the Internet to save hundreds or even thousands of pounds a year on your mortgage, loan and insurance payments, tax bill, legal fees and even your pension?

Find the best deals in seconds

The Internet enables the provision of formidably effective new services to help you save money – services which would simply not be possible without the power of the Internet. Such services can quickly and easily compare your current mortgage, credit card and savings account rates, etc, with the best on offer anywhere in the country. Plus, you can also get quotes for house,

motor and travel insurance in seconds, ensuring you get the best possible deals - and all instantly at your fingertips!

Best ISP 1999

One of the best fully comprehensive Money sites on the Internet is LineOne's Money section. LineOne was voted Best Internet Service Provider 1999 by PC Plus and is Britain's second largest free ISP with over 1,000,000 members.

LineOne's Money section is a vast storehouse of information, services, advice and exclusive deals divided into sub-sections such as Pensions, Mortgages, Tax and Insurance, making it easy to find the information and services you need.

Slash interest and insurance costs

A house is probably one of the biggest purchases most people ever make and LineOne's Mortgage section is packed with valuable resources whether you've already got a mortgage or whether you're in the process of looking for the best deals before taking one out. You'll find interest rate tables from lenders around the country showing you exactly who is offering the best deal on a home loan and whether you're currently paying too much. There's also an exclusive LineOne Mortgage Calculator. Just enter a few details such as the amount you want to borrow, over what length of time, the current interest rate, etc, and the Mortgage Calculator will give you a rough feel for the mortgage amount you can qualify for and how much the mortgage repayments would be each month. Plus there's a comprehensive mortgage guide, Jargon Buster and even a property search to help you find the ideal home to buy or rent.

LineOne's Money section doesn't just save you money on your mortgage though. You'll also find regularly updated tables showing the very best rates on credit cards, pension annuities and loans, and instant insurance quotes so you can see in seconds if you're paying over the odds - and where to go to get a better deal. Getting this sort of comprehensive information without the Internet can be tedious and time consuming. So LineOne is a breath of fresh air when it comes to finding all the information you want in one place - and at any time of the day or night in just seconds!

Cut your utility bills

The Internet can also be a powerful tool to help cut your electricity, gas and other utility bills and LineOne's Cut Your Bills feature exploits this very effectively. Most people don't realise they can shop around for utilities, yet by simply entering a few details such as your post code, LineOne's Cut Your Bills will find out which alternative utility providers serve your area, discern whether or not they provide a cheaper service, and calculate the estimated annual savings you could make by switching supplier. It also provides the necessary forms for you to fill in to make the switching process quick and painless.

Save on legal fees

The Desktop Lawyer service in LineOne's Money section provides an innovative and effective way to slash legal fees on straightforward matters. From buying a house to making a will, you'll find all the relevant documents that you need available to download instantly ready for you to complete at a fraction of the cost of engaging a lawyer to draw up the documents for you. For more complex legal situations LineOne provides web links to a "Find a lawyer" service and to the Law Society's Web site for additional legal resources if you need them.

As well as providing you with the information and tools to save a great deal of money, LineOne's Money Section is a first class source of financial information, tips and advice including comprehensive directories of finance organisations and the latest news on pensions, mortgages and tax issues. You can also compare experiences with and put financial questions to other LineOne members in the Personal Finance forum, track your share portfolio with LineOne's Portfolio Manager and enter regular online competitions to win some valuable prizes.

And best of all, LineOne membership and access to LineOne's Money section is absolutely free! Can you afford not to join today?

It's no wonder LineOne has rapidly become the second largest free Internet Service Provider in the UK, with over 1,000,000 members and growing fast. Get more from the Internet with LineOne.

Just spend £5 or more a month on national or international phone calls with Quip! - the new low cost telephone company which can save you up to 60% on national and international calls. There is no need to change your current phone line or number, simply pay a one-off charge of £20 for a telephone adapter that plugs into your existing phone socket.* It's that easy! To get your free calls simply join LineOne and go to www.lineone.net/freeinternet

*Subject to availability and the terms and conditions stated at www.lineone.net/freeinternet This offer is not available to business users. *Savings compared to BT daytime standard rates. Non Offer calls charged at local rates.

1 Introduction

Money makes the world go around, or so the song says, and it is a valid point of view. But from another angle, the world makes money go around, and many of us, in different ways, are playing catch-as-catch-can trying to get a share of it. This book is, in very broad terms, about making the most of that share.

Given the chance, most people like to save money, whether it is for a short-term purpose, such as a holiday, a long-term purpose, such as retirement, or simply for unspecified 'emergencies'. Saving is effectively deferred consumption: you save today to spend tomorrow. This is true even if your savings pass on to a future generation and 'tomorrow' is 50 years hence; sooner or later, the savings will be spent.

While savings could be simply money stuffed under the mattress, investment implies some added value – either actual or potential. Generally, this would take the form of a monetary reward; *Chambers English Dictionary*, for example, defines investment as 'the placing of money to secure income or profit'.

But for some people, the actual rewards may be secondary in importance to the pleasure of going after them. Just as there is enjoyment to be had from horse-racing, so there is in, say, playing the stock market, and there are similar opportunities to study 'form' and look for attractive odds. Of course, it is always good to win, but there can be pleasure in taking part even if some ventures fail.

So before you can decide how to invest, you need first to be clear why you want to. It may be to fulfil a particular need at a specific time, for example to meet expected school fees; it may be a less definite saving for retirement or for the future in general; it may be that you have spare money you feel should be put to good use; or it may be simply for the fun of it.

Having settled the why, you should then have some idea of what you expect to achieve from the investment, which is a first step to deciding the how. Other factors to take into account are:

☐ the amount of money you have available;
☐ your attitude to risk;
☐ your tax position;
☐ the time you are prepared or able to devote to managing your investments.

As regards the size of investment, there are few limits in either direction. Much of the information in this book could be as well used by someone with just a few hundred pounds to invest as someone right at the other end of the scale, although the majority of readers will perhaps fall into the middle band, with somewhere between a few thousand and a six-figure sum.

RISK AND PROTECTION

As to risk, again the book aims to cover a wide range. To start with, Chapters 2 and 3 look at various types of investment that provide capital security. Those who prefer rather more spice to life may want to skip these and move straight on to unit trusts or shares. Nevertheless, most people will find some use for this type of investment.

As well as short-term cash-flow management – putting aside money for bills and so on – vehicles such as bank and building society deposits can be useful over the longer term for 'emergency' cash. Most of us like to feel we have some money that is not only safe, but also readily accessible; fixed capital investments can provide this security while also offering some return.

The drawback is that security can become a habit. The amount of safe money that it is sensible to have will differ from person to person: single people with no dependants may need less than families, while those whose only recourse for loans is the bank manager may want to tuck aside rather more than those who have obliging relatives. Deciding when you have enough and can start to move up the risk scale can be like letting go of the side of the swimming pool.

The other important point to remember is that 'safe' investments that guarantee capital security are almost always open to a different kind of danger – inflation. An investment that is not growing in money terms will be shrinking in real terms, as measured by its purchasing power.

To get an idea by how much, you need only look at Table 1.1, which shows how much £1000 would come to be worth, valued in today's terms, given different rates of inflation. Even at the modest rate of 3 per cent, more than a quarter of the value would be eroded over 10 years. At 8 per cent, more than half would be lost.

The 1990s saw reduced inflation and the predictions are that it will remain low in at least the near future. But the long-term record, as shown in Table 1.2, should act as a warning. After the extreme levels seen in the 1970s and at the beginning of the 1980s, inflation reached a low point in 1986 not far above the current level. Yet four years later it had climbed back up to 9.5 per cent, and

Table 1.1 *Inflation*

What £1000 would be worth in the future, in today's terms

Years ahead	Annual rate of inflation		
	3%	5%	8%
1	971	952	926
2	943	907	857
3	915	864	794
4	888	823	735
5	863	784	681
6	837	746	630
7	813	711	583
8	789	677	540
9	766	645	500
10	744	614	463
15	642	481	315
20	554	377	215
25	478	295	146

Table 1.2   *Average annual inflation rates*

Year	%
1980	15.1
1981	12.0
1982	5.4
1983	5.3
1984	4.6
1985	5.7
1986	3.6
1987	4.1
1988	4.9
1989	7.8
1990	9.5
1991	5.9
1992	3.7
1993	1.6
1994	2.5
1995	3.4
1996	2.4
1997	3.1
1998	3.4
1999	1.6

there is no guarantee the same thing could not happen again if political priorities were to change.

It is possible to have an inflation-proofed investment, in the shape of index-linked National Savings Certificates (outlined in Chapter 2) or gilts (outlined in Chapter 4). These will guarantee to give you back your capital uprated by inflation, so in real terms you get back what you started with.

The downside is that this security comes at a price. The current 17th issue of index-linked National Savings Certificates pays tax-free interest equivalent to 2.0 per cent a year compound, for five years, on top of the index-linking. This may currently look better than some building society accounts that lack the inflation-proofing, but if inflation rises, so will interest rates, so in neutral-ising the inflation risk you are paying an opportunity cost.

Once you venture beyond the realms of fixed capital invest-ments, you lay yourself open to investment risk. Broadly speaking, this operates on a tit for tat basis – the greater the potential for capital growth, the greater the potential for capital loss. In theory, the upside and downside should be roughly in balance, either in actual amount or when adjusted for likelihood. For example, if an investment is more likely to lose than gain, the possible gain needs to be larger than the possible loss to persuade people into it.

In practice, there are other factors to take into account, not least of which is the investment period. Take, for example, the UK stock market, as measured by the FTSE All-Share Index. Over the long term, the trend is broadly upwards; the 1987 crash, for instance, appears on a long-term graph as only a temporary blip. But for an investor who put money into the market in, say, July 1987 and took it out again at the end of October that year, the loss would have been considerable.

The lesson from this is that the odds improve if you are prepared to commit your money for some time and to be patient. If the market turns down, you may be tempted to cut and run, but if you hold on, the loss is only on paper and may eventually turn round to profit. Conversely, if you have only a short time horizon, the risk becomes much greater and you may be better advised to stick to fixed capital investments. The stock market is not the best home for money that may be needed at short notice.

Another means of controlling risk is to spread your investments around. One of the drawbacks of privatisation issues is that many people who bought them own no other shares. So if the company does badly, they stand to lose a disproportionate amount. At the worst, if you put all your money into a single company that then goes bust, you will lose everything. If, on the other hand, you hold a collection of several different shares, a loss on any one will only be a small part of your investment and may be counteracted by gains elsewhere.

This is the principle behind collective or 'pooled' investments such as unit trusts and investment trusts. Small investors who lack the resources to achieve a wide spread of direct shareholdings can instead buy a stake in a large portfolio. A trust will usually have at least 40 different holdings, so the chances of their all failing together are pretty small.

Again, of course, there is a price for safety. If you hold 10 shares and one doubles in value, you may wish you had backed it to the hilt and not bothered with the other nine. But if one out of the 10 halves in value, you will be grateful for the insurance of the other holdings.

Even with banks and building societies, you should not take safety for granted, bearing in mind the collapse some years ago of the Savings and Investment Bank in the Isle of Man and the more recent crash of the merchant bank Barings. In the UK, and nowadays in several other locations, there is a deposit protection scheme, which guarantees you will get back some, if not all, of your money. But if you are putting money offshore, you should check whether such a scheme applies; if not, only put in as much as you would be prepared to lose, or steer clear altogether.

TAX

Tax is the next factor to consider. A few investments, such as National Savings Certificates and personal equity plans, are tax free; some are subject to income tax, while others are liable to capital gains tax. Depending on your particular tax circumstances, this can influence the net returns you will make and therefore your choice. The main tax rates and allowances are summarised in Table 1.3.

Interest payments and dividends from shares are treated as income and taxed at your highest rate. Interest from bank and building society accounts is normally paid net of 20 per cent tax, although you can register for gross payments if you are a non-taxpayer, while higher rate taxpayers will have to pay the difference. Share dividends are also paid net but non-taxpayers can no longer reclaim what has been paid.

In its first Budget of July 1997, the Labour Government announced an important change to the tax treatment of dividends from UK shares. In April 1999, the Advance Corporation Tax paid by companies on earnings was abolished and the rate of tax credit cut to one-tenth. The way tax is calculated has also changed, so that the net effect for taxpaying investors is just the same. However, non-taxpayers are no longer able to reclaim tax paid on dividends.

Table 1.3 *Income and capital gains tax*

Rates of income tax 2000/2001		
Taxable income (£)	Rate (%)	Cumulative on top of band (£)
0–1520	10	152
1521–28,400	22	6065.60
Over 28,401	40	–

Main tax allowances

Personal allowance	£4385
Personal allowance (age 65–74)	£5790
Personal allowance (age 75+)	£6050
Married couple's allowance (age 65 before 6 April 2000)	£5185*
Married couple's allowance (age 75+)	£5255*
Widow's bereavement allowance	£2000*
Blind person's allowance	£1400
Age allowance income limit	£17,000

*Tax relief is restricted to 10 per cent

Capital gains tax

Annual allowance for individuals	£7200

(The excess, after taper allowance, is charged at 40 per cent for higher rate taxpayers, 20 per cent for basic rate taxpayers.)

Annual allowance for trusts	£3600
Chattel exemption	£6000
Retirement relief (age 55+)	£150,000 plus 50% of gains between £150,000 and £600,000

Major exemptions
- ☐ Principal private residence
- ☐ National Savings Certificates
- ☐ Assets gifted to charity
- ☐ Life assurance policies, for the original owner
- ☐ Betting winnings, including the pools, national lottery and premium bonds

The one concession is that shares held in an Individual Savings Account or a personal equity plan will qualify for a 10 per cent tax credit for the first five years of the scheme (see Chapter 9).

The Government's second Budget, in March 1998, brought another substantial tax reform, this time to capital gains tax. This tax is charged, at the same rate as income tax, on the profit made when assets are sold. In the past, very few people actually paid it because there were two allowances – an annual exempt allowance and an indexation allowance, designed to cancel out gains that were due purely to inflation.

The annual exempt allowance remains and has been increased, in line with inflation, to £7200 for the 2000/01 tax year. But indexation was replaced in April 1998 by a new system of taper relief. Once an asset has been held for three complete years or more, the proportion of the gain that will be taxable is progressively reduced, down to 60 per cent after 10 years. The scale is shown in Table 1.4.

So, for example, if you sell an investment after five years, only 85 per cent of your gain is potentially taxable. If that amount falls within the annual exempt allowance, you will have no tax to pay; if it is more than the allowance (or you have already used your allowance for other gains), you will have to pay tax on the excess amount.

The 2000 Budget brought a further refinement. For business assets, taper relief will operate over four years instead of 10, with the tax rate dropping to 35 per cent after one year, 30 per cent after two years, 20 per cent after three years and finally 10 per cent after four years. Business assets include all shareholdings in unquoted

Table 1.4   *Capital gains tax taper relief (non-business assets)*

Number of complete years of holding asset	Percentage of gain that is taxable
1–2	100
3	95
4	90
5	85
6	80
7	75
8	70
9	65
10	60

companies (including those quoted on the Alternative Investment Market), all shareholdings held by employees in quoted companies and all shareholdings above a 5 per cent threshold held by non-employees in quoted companies.

For assets bought before 5 April 1998, indexation applies up to that date. That is, the purchase price will be scaled up in line with the Retail Price Index up to 5 April 1998 and then frozen at that value for the purposes of calculating the profit when you sell. From then on, the new taper relief will apply and for this purpose all assets held at 5 April 1998 are treated as having already been held for one complete year, regardless of when they were actually bought. Assets acquired after 5 April 1998 qualify only for taper relief, with no indexation.

Whether taper relief is more or less generous than indexation depends partly on inflation – if inflation stays fairly low, most investors should continue to avoid capital gains tax thanks mainly to the annual exempt allowance. But clearly, the longer you hold an asset the more you will benefit from the taper relief and it is just that that the government is aiming to encourage.

The other change relating to capital gains tax was that the Chancellor effectively closed a loophole known as 'bed and break-fasting'. Under this, you would sell shares up to the point that you fully used your exempt allowance and then buy them back the following day. Your portfolio would thus be unchanged but you would have established a new purchase price for the shares you sold, thereby wiping out the gains made to date as far as tax was concerned.

The Chancellor introduced a '30-day rule' under which sales and purchases of the same asset within a 30-day period will be iden-tified with each other. In effect, no gain will be realised and the purchase price (for calculating gains in the future) will not change. Some possible ways around the new rule have already been suggested. You could simply delay buying back the shares for more than 30 days, but the price could move against you in the meantime, possibly costing you more than the tax you save. A better possibility for couples is for, say, the husband to sell shares and the wife to buy them back, although this might be caught by future anti-avoidance rules. Thirdly, you could sell one share and buy another of a similar type.

Tax, of course, should not be the only criterion when choosing an investment, nor even necessarily the prime one. But as a broad rule, the higher rate taxpayer will do better from a growth investment, where he can use the capital gains exempt allowance, than from one that produces income on which he will immediately lose 40 per cent.

There are two other factors that may influence choice. First, since 1990, married couples have been taxed independently, whereas before that all investment income was imputed to the husband.

Since April 2000, the married couple's allowance, previously worth 10 per cent relief, has been phased out altogether for those under 65.

Meanwhile, each of the couple has his or her own personal allowance, capital gains tax exempt allowance and tax rate. As a result, there may be benefits in transferring investments between you and your spouse – particularly as such transfers are exempt from inheritance tax. For example, income-producing investments could be put in the name of whichever partner has the lower tax rate, while those producing capital growth can be split so as to make the most of the annual CGT allowance. Bear in mind, though, that if you give assets away to your partner, you are not entitled to ask for them back if the marriage breaks down.

The other issue is age allowance. Individuals are entitled to a higher personal tax allowance when they pass the age of 65, with another increase when they reach 75, while a higher married couple's allowance is given where either partner reaches 65 or 75 during the tax year. The trap is that there is an annual income limit (based on the husband's income for the married couple's allowance). If income goes above this level, the allowance is reduced by £1 for every £2 of excess income – a heavy penalty. Hence those who are at or near the limit may do better from growth-oriented investments which they can cash in if they need extra income.

Finally, there is inheritance tax. This does not affect an investor directly, since it only comes into play on death, and gifts between husband and wife are exempt. Nevertheless, with the increase in home ownership, many people may find their total assets go beyond the nil rate band, and it may be worth taking note of the exemptions, particularly if your investment plans extend to your heirs. Details are given in Table 1.5.

Table 1.5 *Inheritance tax rates*

Amount of transfer	Tax rate
Up to £234,000	Nil
Over £234,000	40%

Relief on transfers made within 7 years of death

Years between gift and death	*% of full tax charge*
0–3	100
3–4	80
4–5	60
5–6	40
6–7	20

Main exemptions
Transfers between husband and wife
Transfers of up to £3000 a year
Gifts to anyone of up to £250 a year
Gifts out of income forming 'normal expenditure'
Gifts on marriage – up to £5000 for parents, £2500 for grandparents, £1000 for anyone else

LAYOUT OF THE BOOK

Investments can be categorised in a number of different ways: by product type, by what they achieve in terms of income or growth, or by risk factors. For the most part, this book goes by product type, although Chapters 2 and 3, as mentioned above, lump together investments that offer capital security. Chapter 2 covers high street institutions, such as banks, building societies and National Savings products, which are mostly available through post offices; Chapter 3 goes further afield into local authority bonds, insurance company guaranteed bonds and offshore money funds.

Chapter 4 covers gilts, which come halfway between fixed capital and risk investments. If you hold on to a gilt to its maturity date, you will get a fixed return, but meanwhile gilts can be traded, for profit or loss.

Chapters 5 to 9 deal with equity-based investments: shares themselves, unit trusts, offshore funds, investment trusts and

Individual Savings Accounts and personal equity plans, which can be based on individual shares or trusts. While the chapter on equities is largely based on the UK market, a point to bear in mind is that the advantages of spreading your investments can apply equally well on a global scale as on a domestic one.

These days, the major world markets have a tendency to move roughly in line with each other, but there can still be short-term differences, as well as currency factors that will affect the returns. Smaller markets are a law unto themselves, usually displaying significant volatility.

'Smaller', however, is a relative term; the so-called emerging markets currently account for around 5 per cent of total world market capitalisation and the proportion is steadily increasing. While direct investment into these markets – and to some extent, any overseas markets – can be difficult, expensive and risky for the private investor, pooled funds such as unit and investment trusts offer a sensible and accessible route in. A glance at Table 1.6, which

Table 1.6 *World stock markets*

Exchange	Capitalisation (US $bn)	% of world index
Australia	241.0	1.19
Belgium	152.7	0.76
Canada	378.2	1.87
Finland	133.8	0.66
France	731.9	3.63
Germany	748.9	3.71
Hong Kong	216.8	1.07
Italy	435.1	2.16
Japan	2192.9	10.87
Netherlands	481.8	2.39
Spain	238.6	1.18
Sweden	225.8	1.12
Switzerland	567.7	2.81
UK	2099.5	10.41
USA	10,808.3	53.57

Note: Figures are as at 31 March 1999.

Source: The Financial Times

shows the capitalisation of the main markets, provides a clear picture of what you are ignoring if you focus on the UK alone.

Moving on, Chapters 10 and 11 cover investments with life assurance companies, which might more immediately be associated with regular savings. This is particularly true of pension plans, covered in Chapter 11; however, retirement planning can be so important, and so few people can expect the maximum benefits allowed, that topping-up provision should feature high on the list of priorities for investing windfall cash.

Chapter 12 rounds up so-called alternative investments, including tangibles such as precious metals and diamonds, while Chapter 13 looks at charitable giving.

The final criterion for choosing investments that was mentioned at the outset of this chapter is the time you have to devote to your portfolio. While some investments take a while to come good, few selections will be right for all time, particularly as your own circumstances and needs will change over time. Constant chopping and changing will generally lose more in costs than it gains; nevertheless, reviews are an important part of the process.

It is not only your own circumstances that will change; the market is also in constant flux. In the 1980s, there were two major upheavals: Big Bang, which reorganised the operations of the Stock Exchange, and the Financial Services Act, which set up a new system of regulation for the industry.

Neither of these proved conclusive, in that there were several adjustments in subsequent years. In March 1993, the Stock Exchange abandoned the development of Taurus, a proposed electronic dealing system, and has now introduced a different and rather less ambitious system called Crest.

The Financial Services Act has undergone a series of alterations since it was introduced. The Act set up a system of self-regulation under the auspices of the Securities and Investments Board (SIB), which in turn delegated authority to self-regulatory organisations. Before 1994, there were four of these: the Financial Intermediaries, Managers and Brokers Regulatory Association (Fimbra), which looked after independent financial advisers; the Life Assurance and Unit Trust Regulatory Organisation (Lautro), which covered insurance companies and unit trust groups; the Investment Management Regulatory Organisation (Imro), which covered fund management groups (including some unit trust groups); and the Securities and Futures Association (SFA), which covered stock-brokers and the like. In addition, the SIB itself regulated a small number of companies.

In July 1994, a new body, the Personal Investment Authority (PIA), came into operation. This is responsible for all retail investment services, encompassing the operations of former Fimbra and Lautro members, plus Imro firms that primarily deal with private, rather than institutional, investors. Since late 1997, the SIB has been replaced by a new 'super-regulator', the Financial Services Authority (FSA). This will eventually take over the responsibilities of the other bodies and there will also be a single body to handle complaints.

While all these initials may be bemusing, they are not without relevance to private investors in general, and the time factor in particular. The less time you are able to devote to looking after your investments, the more you may need to rely on the services of an adviser, and the Financial Services Act aims to ensure that the advice you will receive is honest and competent. It also provides for redress in the case of malpractice.

Details of how the Act and its various creations operate are given in Chapter 14. This also discusses the various types of advice available and how to choose between different services. For example, one of the main planks of the Act is that advisers are 'polarised' into two categories: completely independent, which means offering advice across the full range of the markets in which they operate, or tied to a single company and able to offer only the products it supplies.

At the outset, one of the cardinal rules for independents was that they should offer 'best advice' – the best possible product, in terms of type and supplier, to fit their customers' needs. This has since been adjusted to read 'good advice', in recognition of the fact that no one can be expected to pick in advance the product that will turn in the best performance in some years' time.

While you may be happy to trust your adviser's judgement, you are likely to get more out of the relationship if you understand the basics of the selection process. This book is designed to help in that, and at the end of each chapter there are suggested sources of further information.

One final word of warning. The book deals only with lump sum investments, hence it does not cover regular savings by way of monthly or annual premiums on life assurance policies or pension plans, or outgoings such as a mortgage. In practice, these may all impinge on your overall financial picture and any part should not be viewed in isolation from the rest.

That said, lump sum investments may arise out of windfall gains such as inheritance and therefore be additional to existing regular, and planned, savings. If you are happy that your basic needs are already catered for, you may be prepared to take a different tack with the lump sum, perhaps involving more risk.

Because the choices are so wide, it is impossible to categorise potential gains. But to whet your appetite, Table 1.7 gives a few key statistics. While there is no guarantee that taking risks will always provide rewards, it does suggest that, over the long term, a little care and imagination can prove fruitful.

Table 1.7 *Past performance comparisons*

Value of £100 invested over periods to 31 March 2000			
	3 years	5 years	10 years
Building society (instant access)	109.1	116.3	159.2
Average investment trust (offer to bid)	157.4	210.1	352.8
Average unit trust (offer to bid)	151.8	206.6	331.3
Retail Price Index (previous month)	108.1	114.0	139.4
FTSE All-Share Index	159.4	231.1	378.5
MSCI World Index (£)	185.1	244.3	364.4

Source: Association of Investment Trust Companies

2 Fixed Capital Investments (1)

As a starting-point, this chapter will look at the more familiar varieties of investment available through high street outlets. In particular, it will deal with fixed capital products: those that guarantee that the capital you get out will be the same as the capital you put in.

This can be reassuring, but the drawback is that old hidden enemy, inflation, which will progressively erode the value. The rate of inflation is one factor that influences the general level of interest rates; they are rarely substantially above inflation for very long, which means that the real rate of return on the investments discussed here is usually pretty small. Indeed, it can even be negative: in October 1990, for example, the gross return on an instant access deposit of £5000 hit a high of 14 per cent, but inflation was then running at 10.9 per cent – above the net return to a basic rate taxpayer. So these investments are suitable chiefly for short periods, 'emergency' money or the extremely cautious.

FIXED VERSUS VARIABLE INTEREST

Most of the investments covered in this chapter pay variable interest, which will move up and down in line with general market rates. But there are a few, including some National Savings products and fixed-term deposits, that pay fixed interest over a predetermined period of time.

Fixed interest rates, like fixed mortgage rates, are something of a gamble: if general rates subsequently go up, you lose; if they go down, you win. As a gambler, you are probably betting on fairly long odds, since the rate offered will ultimately depend on the view of the money market, which has no crystal ball but is generally in a better position to make predictions than the average investor. On the whole, it is better to be guided by your needs and decide whether or not the certainty of a fixed income would outweigh any possible loss.

Variable rates tend to reflect the general economic environment, but different institutions react at varying speeds to underlying changes. It may seem that mortgage rates move up faster than down, while investment rates are sticky in the other direction; in practice the institutions are simply balancing their borrowing and lending against the demand and supply in the market. Broadly, when they are looking to attract investors they will be quicker to raise their interest rates; when they are seeking to increase their lending they will try to hold rates down.

Neither pattern is likely to be consistent for all time, so this should not be a prime factor in deciding where to invest. Of course, it is possible to gain by monitoring all the rates available and switching your investments around accordingly, but this is more valuable if you are locking into a fixed rate; with variable rates, the benefit is likely to be small and short-lived compared with the time and energy you would spend on the research.

THE TAX POSITION

Until April 1991, bank and building society accounts paid interest net of composite rate tax. This was calculated by the Inland Revenue on the basis of the proportion of savers who were non-taxpayers and therefore worked out at slightly less than basic rate income tax, but the major drawback was that it could not be reclaimed by those not liable for tax.

Nowadays, non-taxpayers can register to have interest paid gross by completing the Inland Revenue Form R85, available at banks and building societies. Otherwise, interest will normally be paid net of lower rate tax, which can be reclaimed by those who are not liable to some or all of it. Lower and basic rate taxpayers will have no further liability, while higher rate taxpayers will have to pay the difference.

National Savings Certificates and tax exempt special savings accounts (TESSAs) are free of both income and capital gains tax (CGT), while the return on gilts is liable only to income tax and is normally paid gross if they are registered with the Bank of England (see Chapter 4). A handful of other products pay interest gross, although it will still be liable for tax. These include National Savings accounts, offshore bank and building society accounts (see Chapter 3) and fixed-term bank and building society deposits amounting to £50,000 or more.

Accounts that pay gross have the advantage that you can enjoy the money for a while before the tax falls due, but there is also a potential drawback. In the first year, and the second if you so elect, the tax charged is based on the actual interest received, but thereafter it moves to a 'preceding year' basis. So, for example, in the tax year 2000/01 your tax charge for the account will be based on the interest you actually received in 1999/2000. When interest rates are rising, this means you will effectively pay too little tax, but conversely when they are falling you will be overcharged. In this case there is no right of appeal, because the procedure counts as an actual tax charge, rather than a provisional assessment. The only way around it, if interest rates are dropping and you are therefore losing out, is to close the account, as the tax will be calculated on the interest actually paid in the final year. However, the Inland Revenue is then entitled to reassess the previous year's charge and adjust that to the true amount if it is in its own favour to do so (note that it will not offer a rebate if you paid too much!).

In the long run, the overpayments and underpayments should tend to even out. However, when you decide to close the account, you should try to do so in a year when rates have been falling so that any final swing will be in your favour. If you subsequently open another account, this will not affect the tax assessment of the first.

BANKS

Current accounts

Time was when a current account was simply a convenient alternative to keeping your money under the mattress. You earned no interest on it, but neither did it cost you anything to run, as long as you kept the account in credit. The high street banks, at least, offered services that were more or less identical to each other, so most people picked the one that was nearest to their home or workplace, or possibly the one their parents used, and then stuck with it for life. This had the advantage, in theory at least, that if you established a track record with your bank you were likely to be looked on more favourably if you needed a loan.

Nowadays, competitive pressures have swept all that aside. There are a host of different accounts offering a variety of facilities and there is more point in shopping around to find one that suits your needs. For instance, there are some that offer, within limits, an interest-free overdraft, particularly on student accounts – students being potentially lucrative customers in the future. Others are linked to a savings account, with an automatic sweep between the two, or provide telephone banking through which you can juggle your money between accounts.

Also, since building societies began to provide cash card and cheque-book facilities, banks have introduced interest payments on current accounts. On the basic accounts, however, the rates are very low, so they should be considered as purely for cash-flow purposes, not as investments.

New players

The changing face of banking not only has pushed the traditional banks into offering new services, but also has prompted a host of new players. Chief among these are the supermarkets: Sainsbury's, Tesco and Safeway have all started to offer banking facilities, in conjunction with Bank of Scotland, Royal Bank of Scotland and Abbey National respectively.

Insurance companies have also noted the opportunities – in particular, the potential to retain at least some of a customer's money when a policy matures, instead of seeing it lost to the high street. Standard Life, Prudential, Scottish Widows, Legal & General and Direct Line are all offering savings accounts.

Another innovation is the 'one-stop' bank account, Virgin One, from Virgin Direct. This combines a current account, a credit card facility and a mortgage, all in one. All borrowings are lumped together, secured on the account-holder's home and charged at a single rate. When salary is paid in each month, it immediately reduces the debt, although this will obviously increase again as money is spent during the month. Lump sums can also be paid in at any time to reduce the amount owed. While the account has its attractions, some people may find it harder to keep track of their savings and borrowings when they are all mixed together. Also, while the interest rate is cheap for personal loans and credit, it is relatively expensive for a mortgage, by far the largest part of most people's borrowings. Finally, the account is restricted to minimum mortgage and salary levels.

Internet banking

As well as the new players, there is now a new method of banking: via the Internet. Banks have had an online presence for a while, but the recent trend has been to launch a stand-alone service, available only on the Net. Pioneer services included Egg (from Prudential), Marbles (from HFC Bank) and Smile (from the Co-operative); earlier this year Halifax launched its specialised Net banking operation, IF, which stands for Intelligent Finance. On the other hand, Barclays, which currently claims to be the biggest Internet bank, has chosen to integrate Net banking within traditional services, instead of establishing a separate operation.

One attraction is convenience, especially with the number of bank branches continually shrinking. At the touch of a few buttons, you can carry out most banking transactions – such as paying bills and setting up direct debits and standing orders – as well as accessing full, up-to-the-minute details of your account.

There is also the potential for better interest rates. At launch, Egg was offering much higher rates than other banks and it has remained one of the better payers. Both Egg and Smile are also among the cheapest providers of credit cards.

However, while Internet transactions cost a lot less than traditional methods, not all banks are passing on the savings, so it is worth shopping around. Unfortunately, this may become harder to do as Internet services develop. The technology allows the banks to offer a whole host of accounts and rates and the best deals will be offered to the best customers. The more you spend, and the more services you use from the same bank, the more likely you are to be rewarded; however, this could mean, for instance, that you get a good savings rate at the expense of a poor mortgage rate.

There are also concerns about security. In practice, details of your account or credit card are heavily encoded and there is probably less risk than there is in normal use of credit cards and bank cards. However, not all banks have been clear about who will pick up the bill if any fraud does occur, so it is a good idea to try to clarify this before signing up to a service. You should also check that your Internet access system is compatible with the security system used by the bank.

Finally, remember to keep a note of any accompanying phone service, in case you have problems accessing the Web site. In its early days, Egg was a victim of its own success when it became clear that demand was higher than the service could support.

Some people have suggested that Internet banking may be something of a flash in the pan. In the USA, the rate of growth has slowed from 36 per cent a year to just 8 per cent in only three years. But others envisage it taking off as technology develops. Wireless application protocol, or WAP, enables you to access the Net from a mobile phone and is likely to be available for the vast majority of mobiles in the next few years. At the time of writing, Woolwich had already launched a WAP banking service and others such as Egg and Halifax are expected to follow before the end of the year.

Higher interest accounts

Just as current accounts have burgeoned, so have deposit-style accounts. These offer better rates of interest but do not normally provide cheque-book or money transmission facilities, though they may have a link to a current account and some offer a cash card.

For instant access accounts there is usually no minimum deposit. Notice accounts, where withdrawals require between one

Table 2.1   *Bank account rates*

Amount deposited (£)	No notice (%)	30 days' notice (%)	60 days' notice (%)
500–999	5.45	2.72	5.04
1000–2499	5.45	2.72	5.04
2500–4999	5.45	2.88	5.04
5000–9999	5.45	3.04	5.04
10,000–24,000	5.45	3.36	5.16
25,000- 49,999	5.45	3.64	5.24
50,000+	5.45	4.01	5.32

Note: Rates net of basic rate tax, applicable as at March 2000. Bank base rate: 6%.

Source: MoneyFacts, March 2000

and three months' notice, may require a minimum of £1000 or £2500. Generally, these will allow immediate access with loss of interest equivalent to the notice period, but the penalty may be waived if there is a balance remaining in the account of £5000 or £10,000.

Interest rates generally rise with the amount deposited and the length of notice although there can be anomalies, as the examples in Table 2.1 show.

Money market and high-interest cheque accounts

These were once the preserve of merchant banks and licensed deposit-takers, and there are still some that are essentially deposit accounts for large sums of money, with no money transmission facilities. However, most of the major banks now offer some form of high-interest cheque account. The services provided are usually more limited than the standard current account; there may be a minimum withdrawal or cheque amount of anything up to £250, or only a limited number of withdrawals free of charge, so for daily purposes you would probably need an ordinary account as well.

But, as in other spheres, competition is leading to improved options and there are a growing number of accounts which have no minimum withdrawal and offer a full range of facilities such as overdrafts, cash card, cheque card, standing orders and direct debits, with free banking as long as you remain in credit. On top of this, the interest rates can be substantially more than the token offerings on basic current accounts.

The one drawback is that they do require a relatively high initial deposit, generally of £1000. There are one or two that offer respectable rates of interest on sums from £1 upwards, but these do not provide the full range of services.

Term deposits

Fixed-term deposits pay a fixed rate of interest for a specified period of time, which may be anything from one month to five years. Some of the smaller banks offer these for as little as £500 but the minimum is usually £2500 or £5000. As a rule, no withdrawals are allowed during the term and the interest rate is fixed at the outset, but rates can vary on a daily basis, so check before you invest.

Very large sums of money, upwards of £50,000, can be placed in money market time deposits through banks. While these may be for a period of some months, it is also possible to place money on overnight deposit with automatic renewal on a daily basis, so that you can leave the money for as long as you like while having instant access to it. Interest rates are set daily or sometimes more frequently and, provided the deposit is at least £50,000, interest can be paid gross.

BUILDING SOCIETIES

Like the banks, building societies have vastly expanded their range of products in recent years. In terms of the banks versus building societies 'savings war' the societies have largely been the aggressors, moving in on the banks' traditional territory of cheque accounts. They were also granted wider powers by the government, allowing them, for example, to own a domestic bank and to raise more money from wholesale markets. But at the same time, they have faced considerable competitive pressure from each other, with the result that there have been a number of mergers, not only among smaller societies but also between the large ones. Several societies, such as Abbey National and Halifax, have changed status to become banks.

Banking accounts

Banking accounts come in two types: those that are more or less deposit-style accounts but provide cash card facilities; and those that offer a cheque-book and other banking facilities such as standing orders, direct debits and even overdrafts, though this last is rather less common. The services are generally free as long as the account is in credit, but there may be a minimum opening balance – normally not more than £200.

Interest is paid on these accounts and, while it can be rather more generous than bank current accounts, the same caveat applies, that rates are too low for these accounts to be considered as investments proper. For larger deposits, however, the rates offered are comparable to banks' high-interest cheque accounts, or similar facilities may be offered through a separate account. The minimum deposit in this case is generally upwards of £2500. Some societies offer postal accounts, which may still provide instant access but carry higher interest rates than the basic cheque account.

Instant access and notice accounts

Despite the vast array of different accounts that come under this heading, there are just three main points to consider in making a choice: the minimum investment, the period of notice required for withdrawals and the interest offered. Table 2.2 shows examples of the better offerings currently around. As can be seen, the general rule is that interest rates increase with the amount deposited and the length of notice period, though there can occasionally be anomalies where one society's instant access account offers more than another's notice account.

Notice accounts usually allow withdrawals within the notice period subject to an equivalent loss of interest, but the penalty may be waived if, say, £5000 or £10,000 remains in the account. There are also some that offer a bonus if no withdrawals are made during the year. This can be attractive if you do not expect to need access to your money but are not quite prepared to tie it up in a longer-term bond.

Deposit accounts are not shown in the table as they are scarcely heard of these days. Although some instant access accounts require a minimum of £500, a number are available for smaller sums, right

Table 2.2 *Building society variable interest account rates*

Amount deposited (£)	No notice (%)	30 days' notice (%)	60 days' notice (%)
500–999	5.6	3.2	4.8
1000–2499	5.6	4.2	4.8
2500–4999	5.6	4.28	4.8
5000–9999	5.8	4.68	5.36
10,000–24,000	5.8	4.88	5.36
25,000–49,999	5.8	4.96	5.36
50,000+	5.8	5.12	5.36

Note: Rates net of basic rate tax, applicable as at March 2000.

Source: MoneyFacts, March 2000

down to £1, so they have largely superseded the older deposit and paid-up share accounts.

When comparing interest rates, you should look at the 'annual equivalent rate' or AER, which advertisements for almost all savings accounts must now quote. The exceptions are those that pay a set amount above base rate. The AER shows what the rate of interest would be if it were paid once a year, before tax and excluding the effect of any potential bonuses. It has been introduced with the aim of making it easier to compare returns from different types of account on a like for like basis.

One other point to watch for is when an account is closed to new business in favour of a new version. Often the old account will carry a lower rate of interest than the new one, although the terms and conditions may be identical. Not all societies inform their investors in this case – the argument being that the postage would prove prohibitive – so you need to keep an eye on developments and be prepared to switch if necessary. Local society branches will have up-to-date information on closed and new accounts.

Fixed-term accounts

Fixed-term accounts fall into two types: those that offer a fixed rate of interest during the term and those on which the interest is variable but guaranteed to be a fixed percentage above the ordinary share account rate. The minimum investment is generally

Table 2.3   *Building society fixed-term account rates*

Term	Minimum investment (£)	Net rate (%)
6 months	5000	4.92
1 year	1000	5.6
2 years	1	5.6
3 years	5000	5.52
5 years	100	5.6

Note: Rates net of basic rate tax, applicable as at March 2000.

Source: MoneyFacts, March 2000

£1000 and terms may run from six months to five years. Withdrawals during the term may be disallowed altogether, or may be subject to a penalty (commonly of 90 days' interest). Examples of fixed rates are shown in Table 2.3.

Like banks, the larger building societies offer money market time deposits for sums from £50,000 upwards. Rates change frequently but, once you invest, are fixed for the full term.

TAX EXEMPT SPECIAL SAVINGS ACCOUNTS AND INDIVIDUAL SAVINGS ACCOUNTS

Tax exempt special savings accounts (TESSAs) first appeared in January 1991, having been announced in the previous year's Budget. In a way, they are like a little sister to personal equity plans (PEPs, detailed in Chapter 9). PEPs offer tax-free returns from equity-linked investments, while TESSAs offer tax-free returns from bank and building society deposit accounts.

The first TESSAs matured in January 1996 but the 1994 Budget introduced a follow-on opportunity. Once a TESSA had been held for its full five-year term, the capital, but not the accumulated interest, could be used to open a 'TESSA 2'. If the maximum had been invested in the first plan, this would mean £9000 could be transferred into the second and again all interest would be tax-free, providing the capital was left intact for the full five years.

However, since April 1999, it has not been possible to open a new TESSA, as they have been phased out in favour of the new Individual Savings Accounts (ISAs). Existing TESSAs can be continued for the remainder of their five-year term, subject to the same terms, and contributions will not affect ISA investment allowances.

Like TESSAs, ISAs offer tax-free interest. They have the advantage that there is no 'lock-in' period: whereas TESSA capital had to remain untouched for five years to secure the tax benefits, you can access ISA money at any time. They also offer a wider choice of investments: as well as all types of savings account, they can include taxable National Savings products. The drawback is that the investment limit is lower: for the cash element, it is currently £3000 and is due to fall to £1000 from 6 April 2001.

ISAs are also more complicated, because there are two kinds of plan: 'mini' and 'maxi'. Mini ISAs have just one component, which may be cash, stocks and shares or a life insurance policy, while maxi ISAs must offer a stocks and shares component and may also include either or both of the others. In any tax year, you may take out one of each type of mini, with different providers if you wish, or just one maxi plan.

You need to think quite carefully about your choice, because of the way the rules work.

Say you want to invest cash: you can do so through either a cash mini or the cash element within a maxi. If you choose a maxi, you are then committed to that provider if you later want to invest in stocks and shares or insurance. Some savings institutions may have less expertise in these areas or offer less choice than a specialist – the insurance element may not be offered at all, for instance.

On the other hand, if you choose a mini plan, the investment limits are more rigid. With a maxi plan, you may currently invest £7000, of which up to £1000 can be in insurance and up to £3000 in cash. For mini plans, the limits are £3000 for equities, £3000 for cash and £1000 for insurance. So if you put even the smallest amount of cash into a mini, your allowance for equities will be restricted to £3000, whereas in a maxi you could have topped up to the full £7000.

Ideally, then, you need to consider your full year's savings before you commit yourself. If the equity investment limit is not a problem or you want to invest only cash, you may do better to go for a mini and choose a provider who is a specialist. But if your circumstances change, you will effectively be stuck with your choice for the rest of the tax year because, while you can switch providers, you may only switch to another plan of the same type.

One other thing to look out for is the Cat mark, which stands for cost, access and terms. This has been introduced by the government with the intention of helping investors to recognise plans with low costs, easy access and fair terms. It is not any guarantee of performance, and is therefore not necessarily useful when choosing a plan for stocks and shares, but for cash accounts it is worth noting. The criteria for Cat-marked cash plans are: no charges for withdrawals or transfers; withdrawals available within seven working days or less and with no limit on frequency; and an interest rate of at least 2 per cent below base rate.

Further information about ISAs can be found in Chapter 9.

NATIONAL SAVINGS

National Savings products can be divided into three categories: those that pay a return completely free of tax, those that are taxable but pay interest gross, and a couple of one-offs, the First Option Bond and Premium Bonds, which do neither of these things.

Tax-free investments

National Savings Fixed Interest Certificates

National Savings Fixed Interest Certificates can currently be bought for a minimum of £100, with units of £25 thereafter. In the past, issues always ran for five years, with a fixed rate of return in each year, and some still do. The return increases over the five years, so although you can cash units in at any time, you lose out by doing so. Table 2.4 shows the interest build-up on the current 54th issue. There are now also certificates with a two-year term, currently offering a fixed return of 4.75 per cent for the 3rd issue.

As Table 2.5 shows, issues are available for varying lengths of time and give different rates of return, depending on the market

Table 2.4   *National Savings Certificates, 54th issue (five years)*

Years after purchase	Value at end of year (£)	% yield for year	Compound yield % pa
1	104.10	4.10	4.10
2	108.47	4.20	4.15
3	113.24	4.40	4.23
4	118.45	4.60	4.33
5	124.63	5.21	4.50

Note: Value for a £100 certificate; tax-free return.

Table 2.5   *National Savings Certificates, past issues*

Issue number	Dates of issue	Value of £100 certificate after 5 years (£)	Compound annual return over 5 years (%)
33rd	1.5.87–21.7.88	140.26	7.0
34th	22.7.88–16.6.90	143.56	7.5
35th	18.6.90–14.3.91	157.42	9.5
36th	2.4.91–2.5.92	150.37	8.5
37th	13.5.92–5.8.92	146.94	8.0
38th	6.8.92–4.10.92	143.57	7.5
39th	5.10.92–12.11.92	138.63	6.75
40th	13.11.92–16.12.93	132.25	5.75
41st	17.12.93–19.9.94	130.08	5.4
42nd	20.9.94–25.1.96	132.88	5.85
43rd	26.1.96–31.3.97	129.77	5.35
44th	1.4.97–9.1.98	129.77	5.35
45th	9.1.98–26.3.98	127.63	5.0
46th	27.3.98–15.10.98	126.42	4.8
47th	16.12.98–30.12.98	121.67	4.0
48th	31.12.98–2.2.99	118.78	3.5
49th	3.2.99–18.3.99	117.35	3.25
50th	19.3.99–19.5.99	118.78	3.5
51st	20.5.99–13.7.99	119.64	3.65
52nd	14.7.99–7.10.99	120.80	3.85
53rd	8.10.99–26.1.00	123.43	4.3

rates at the time and how anxious the government is to get a slice of the savings market. In 1993, it took a more aggressive stance by doubling the maximum holding in current-issue certificates to £10,000 and also doubling the reinvestment limit to £20,000.

Reinvestment is an option at the end of the fixed period, when certificates mature. Instead of taking out your money, you can either continue to hold the certificates or reinvest in the latest issue, for which there is a £20,000 maximum holding on top of the £10,000 for new investment.

Once an issue has reached the end of its fixed period, the interest rate moves to the general extension rate, which is variable and currently 3.09 per cent for the 7th to 42nd issues. The 1st to 6th issues come under different rules and are subject to a lower rate of interest. So you will do better to cash in any of these and reinvest in the current issue, rather than retaining them. More recent issues that are still within their fixed period are worth holding on to up to maturity because the guaranteed return is higher than anything you could currently get from a comparable investment.

Index-linked certificates

Like the ordinary savings certificates, the current 17th issue of five-year index-linked certificates has a minimum investment of £100 and a maximum of £10,000, with a further £20,000 allowed for rein-vestment from mature certificates. The difference is that here the return is linked to movements in the Retail Price Index over the five-year period. In addition, extra interest is added at a guar-anteed rate, which increases for each of the five years. Currently the compound return above inflation is equal to 2 per cent a year and is free of tax. All the interest earned is added to the capital value – so that after year 1 you are earning interest on the interest – and repaid in total when you cash in. Again, there is now a two-year version, currently in its 3rd issue, which is offering 3.15 per cent above inflation.

As mentioned at the start of this chapter, inflation can be a serious threat to fixed capital investments and the real returns above inflation offered by interest rates can be very small. So in principle, index-linking should be very attractive. In practice, though, it is like any fixed rate: in return for protection against doing worse, you may give up the chance to do better. For example, if inflation remains at the current rate of around 2.6 per cent, the total return on five-year index-linked certificates, including the extra interest, would be 4.6 per cent, fractionally above that offered on fixed interest certificates. But if inflation falls again, the cost of the protection may prove too high.

Individual Savings Accounts

National Savings is now offering one of the new Individual Savings Accounts (ISAs), in the form of a cash mini plan. Accounts are open to anyone over 18 who is resident in the UK for tax purposes and you can invest from as little as £10, up to a maximum of £3000 in the first year and £1000 a year thereafter.

Currently, the interest rate is 6.25 per cent, tax free. The plan is designed to meet the government's Cat standard, which means that the interest rate cannot drop to more than 2 per cent below base rate. It also means that there are no penalties or notice periods for withdrawals and the money will be sent to you within seven days of receipt of your instructions, by warrant, to your home address or nominated bank or building society account. You may also arrange for a warrant that can be cashed at a post office, for up to £250.

You can open a plan by post or, if you have a debit card, by telephone. Thereafter you can add to your account by post, phone, standing order, electronic funds transfer or by bank giro credit at a bank or building society. Interest accrues from the day your cheque or money is received and will be credited to your account annually on 5 April.

One point to bear in mind is that if you open a cash mini ISA you will not be able to have a maxi ISA in the same tax year. If you wish to invest in stocks and shares or life insurance as well as cash, you can still do so by opening further mini plans, but the investment limit for the stocks and shares will then be a fixed £3000, whereas with a maxi ISA you can invest up to £7000 in total, with no set limit on the equity component.

Taxable investments

Income bonds

Income bonds are available from a minimum of £2000 up to a maximum of £250,000 and offer a monthly income, paid on the 5th of each month. The interest rate is variable, but six weeks' notice is given of any change, which will be advertised in newspapers. The current rates are 6 per cent gross for sums up to £25,000 and 6.25 per cent gross for larger amounts, which compares reasonably well with banks and building societies. Income is paid (gross, but liable to tax) direct to a bank, building society or National Savings investment account.

Capital bonds

Capital bonds run for five years and offer a guaranteed rate of return if they are held for the full term. For the current Series U bonds this is 6.15 per cent gross. You can cash in a bond early, but this would mean you lose out, as the interest rate increases each year, and the amount you get on cashing in is the value at the last anniversary plus a special interest rate since then. No interest is paid on bonds encashed before the first anniversary.

The minimum holding is £100, with a maximum of £250,000. This maximum applies to total holdings of all capital bonds, with the exception of Series A. At the end of the five years bonds are repaid in full, together with all the interest accumulated; no further interest is earned after the fifth anniversary.

Fixed rate savings bonds

Fixed rate savings bonds are a recent introduction and are available for terms from six months to three years, for investments from £500 up to £1 million. The interest rate is fixed for the term and may be paid annually, with a final payment at the end of the term, or monthly. Interest can also be 'rolled up' within the bond if you do not want to take it. Rates vary with the frequency of payment and the size of investment, as shown in Table 2.6.

At the end of the fixed term, you can simply take the money without penalty. Alternatively, you can leave it for a further term of the same length, at whatever interest rate applies at that time, or take up any other option that is then available. All the choices will be set out in a letter sent out shortly before the bond is due to mature. Should you need to cash in early, you can do so at a cost of 90 days' lost interest and for partial withdrawals at least £500 must be left in the bond.

Table 2.6 _Fixed rate savings bonds_

	6 months (%)		1 year (%)		18 months (%)		3 years (%)	
	Monthly	Annual	Monthly	Annual	Monthly	Annual	Monthly	Annual
£500	4.56	4.68	4.64	4.76	4.72	4.84	4.76	4.92
£20,000	4.72	4.84	4.80	4.96	4.88	5.04	4.96	5.12
£50,000	4.84	5.00	5.00	5.16	5.08	5.24	5.16	5.32

Note: Rates net of basic rate tax, as at April 2000.

National Savings Bank ordinary account

With a basic interest rate of 1.75 per cent gross, the ordinary account is slightly more lucrative than a bank current account, although the facilities are more limited. Withdrawals are generally restricted to £100 on demand, with written notice required for larger sums, although if you have used the account for at least six months at one particular post office you can apply for a regular customer account, which entitles you to take out up to £250 on demand.

If you keep an account open for a full calendar year, you are then eligible for a higher interest rate for each month that the balance is £500 or more. Even so, this higher rate is only 2.5 per cent gross. The one feature that does add some attraction for higher rate taxpayers is that the first £70 of interest, or £140 for a joint holding, is free of tax. Otherwise, this is more a home for ready cash than an investment.

National Savings Bank investment account

For smaller sums in particular, this can be an attractive alternative to bank and building society deposits, as the minimum is just £20. There are seven tiers of interest rates which currently start at 3.95 per cent for sums under £500, rising to 5.1 per cent for sums from £50,000 to £100,000, the maximum holding. These are the gross rates; interest is credited gross, so you can enjoy the money for a short while before settling the tax bill. Withdrawals are at one month's notice.

Pensioners Bond

The Pensioners Bond was announced in the 1993 Autumn Budget and introduced in January 1994. It is available only for people aged 60 or over, although it can be bought by trustees, as long as the beneficiary is over 60. The minimum investment is £500 and the maximum is £50,000 per series, or £100,000 for a joint holding, for which both savers must meet the age requirement.

As with the fixed interest and index-linked certificates, there are now two types: one with a two-year term and one that runs for five years. The former has a gross interest rate of 6.3 per cent (Series 5), while the later (currently Series 14) is paying 6 per cent. The interest is taxable but paid gross and will be credited on the 19th of each month direct to a bank or building society account or a National Savings investment account.

At the end of the term, National Savings will write to tell you the guaranteed interest rate for the next five years. The money can then be reinvested or withdrawn without penalty. If you want to cash in at any other time, you must give 60 days' notice and no interest will be paid during those 60 days. Partial withdrawals can be made from a minimum of £500 as long as at least £500 remains in your holding.

Currently, the Pensioners Bond does not look particularly attractive, especially as the money is more or less tied up for five years. Although you can cash in early, the penalty is quite a deterrent – the loss of interest would amount to about £70 on a £10,000 holding. So as part of the Budget it was announced that a new product for pensioners would be introduced. No details were given but National Savings suggested it would offer a choice of time-periods with different rates of interest, allowing people to lock into a fixed rate of return, but not necessarily for as long as five years.

Premium Bonds

Premium bonds are not exactly an investment, as there is no promise of a return – but then again, that could be said to apply to equities and at least with premium bonds your capital is always safe. The odds on winning a prize also improve with the size of your holding:

at the maximum of £20,000, you should on average win 13 prizes a year, while to win once a year on average you need to hold £1450-worth. Of course, averages do not always work out; although ERNIE is quite impartial, some people seem to be luckier than others.

The minimum investment is £100, with multiples of £10 thereafter. Since 1 May 1996 the monthly prize fund has been calculated as equivalent to one month's interest on each eligible bond, at a current interest rate of 4.25 per cent a year. Bonds have to be held for one complete calendar month before they are entered for the draw. There are around 620,000 prizes awarded each month, with 10 per cent of the fund allocated to prizes between £5000 and the £1 million jackpot, 10 per cent to prizes of £500 and £1000 and the remaining 80 per cent providing prizes of £50 and £100. All prizes are free of tax.

For a complete guide to all the National Savings products mentioned, see Table 2.7.

WHERE TO FIND OUT MORE

Banks and building societies

Information on the types of account offered and current interest rates can be found in local branches. The Building Societies Association (020 7437 0655) can also answer general questions, but will not advise on current rates offered by individual societies. *MoneyFacts*, a monthly subscription magazine aimed chiefly at professional advisers, gives comprehensive listings of bank and building society accounts, TESSAs, offshore accounts and National Savings products. It is available from Moneyfacts Publications, Moneyfacts House, 66–70 Thorpe Road, Norwich NR1 1BJ, telephone 01603 476100.

Money market accounts

Information can be found in newspapers.

National Savings

Booklets on the various products are available at post offices. General information can be obtained by phoning the information helpline on 0645 645000 during normal office hours.

Table 2.6 *National Savings guide*

Product	Minimum and maximum holdings	Who may buy or invest	Income fixed or variable
National Savings Certificates 54th issue (five-year) 3rd issue (two-year)	Minimum £100, maximum £10,000 in addition to previous issues; may reinvest a further £20,000 from mature Savings Certificates	Individuals (also jointly), trustees	Increasing at fixed rate for initial term; variable extension rate thereafter
National Savings Certificates 17th index-linked issue (five-year) 3rd issue (two-year)	Minimum £100, maximum £10,000 in addition to previous issues; may reinvest a further £20,000 from mature Savings Certificates	Individuals (also jointly), trustees	Repayment value linked to changes in the RPI plus fixed annual supplement; variable after five years
Individual Savings Account	Minimum £10, maximum £3000 in first year	UK residents over 18	Variable
National Savings income bond	Minimum £2000, maximum £250,000	Individuals (also jointly), trustees	Variable; paid monthly
National Savings capital bond Series P	Minimum £100, maximum £250,000 for holdings in all series, excluding Series A	Individuals (also jointly), trustees	Fixed if held for full five years; no interest paid after five years
Fixed rate savings bonds	Minimum £500, maximum £1m	Individuals, (also jointly), trustees	Fixed for the term
Pensioners Bond 14th Series (five-year) 5th Series (two-year)	Minimum £500, maximum £50,000 in addition to Series 1 and 2	Individuals over 60 (also jointly), trustees	Fixed for five years at a time; paid monthly
National Savings Bank ordinary account	Minimum £10, maximum £10,000	Individuals (also jointly), children, trustees	Variable; credited annually
National Savings Bank investment account	Minimum £20, maximum £100,000	Individuals (also jointly), children, trustees	Variable; credited annually
Premium bonds	Minimum £100, maximum £20,000	Individuals over 16; bonds can be bought for children by parents, guardians or (great) grandparents	No interest

Tax position	Notice of withdrawal	How to buy/sell
Free of income tax and CGT	At least eight working days	Buy: through post offices Sell: repayment form from post offices
Free of income tax and CGT	At least eight working days	Buy: through post offices Sell: repayment form from post offices
Free of income tax and CGT	No notice; money is paid within seven working days	Application forms by post, or by phone
Interest is taxable, but paid gross	Three months; in the first year, interest paid at half rate from date of purchase to date of repayment	Buy: application form at post offices, send with cheque to Blackpool Sell: repayment form from post offices
Interest is taxable, but paid gross	At least two weeks; no interest paid if cashed in in first year	Buy: through post offices Sell: repayment form from post offices
Taxable, paid net	None, penalty of 90 days' interest on withdrawals during term	Buy: by phone, post or at post office Sell: repayment form on bond
Interest is taxable, but paid gross	60 days; no interest paid during notice period	Buy: application form at post offices, send with cheque to Blackpool Sell: repayment form on bond
First £70 (£140 joint) of annual interest is free of income tax	Up to £100 on demand; larger amounts require a few days' written notice	Opening and withdrawals at post offices
Interest is taxable, but paid gross	One month	Opening: through post offices Withdrawals: form from post offices to be sent to Glasgow
Prizes free of income tax and CGT	At least eight working days	Buy: through post offices Sell: repayment form from post offices

3 Fixed Capital Investments (2)

The last chapter covered the major institutions that offer fixed capital investments, most of which can be bought through high street outlets. Going a little further afield, there are a number of other products which also offer capital security, but may offer a more attractive rate of income than the standard bank and building society accounts, particularly for smaller investments.

LOCAL AUTHORITY BONDS

Local authority bonds are issued for a fixed term of between one and ten years, over which the capital value remains constant. The minimum investment starts at £500 and the interest rate is fixed throughout the term. The bonds used to be a popular way for local authorities to raise funds, but in the 1980s the administration involved and the availability of cheaper loans from other sources led to a decline in the number of issues. However, there are still bonds available and they are open to any investor – it need not be your own local authority that you buy from.

One drawback is that there is no facility to make withdrawals during the term of the bond, so your money is effectively locked in until the maturity date, although it may be possible to transfer it to a third party on written request. When the fixed term expires, there may be an opportunity to continue the investment for a further period at whatever the going rate of interest is at that time; otherwise you can simply have your original capital returned.

Table 3.1 *Local authority bonds*

Years	1	2–3	4–5	6
Typical gross rates (%)	5.75	5.75	5.5	4.875

Source: MoneyFacts, March 2000

As for the safety aspect, the bonds are backed by the local authority itself, not by central government. Hence they are marginally more risky than a government-issued security such as a gilt and usually offer slightly higher rates of return to reflect this. However, while there is no obligation for the government to help out or provide any compensation in the event of a default, there is a certain presumption that it would act if there was a danger of widespread losses, if only for the sake of political expediency.

Interest is paid out twice a year and will normally be paid net of lower rate tax. If you are a non-taxpayer, you can register to receive interest payments gross by completing Inland Revenue Form R85, in the same way as for bank and building society deposits. Once the bond has been issued, the interest rate will remain fixed for the full term. Hence the longer term bonds are most suitable for investors for whom security of income is a priority – others may find they lose out if interest rates rise in the future. The rates will vary between different authorities and across the different lifespans, and are reset on a regular basis – sometimes daily – so you should check the up-to-date position before investing. Examples of current rates are shown in Table 3.1.

GUARANTEED INCOME AND GROWTH BONDS

Guaranteed income bonds are issued by life assurance companies and are available for terms of between one and ten years, although the widest choice is for periods of four or five years. The minimum investment is generally around £5000 and the interest rate is fixed for the whole term, so these bonds are attractive to investors seeking a regular income, perhaps in retirement, to supplement a pension.

Not all life offices operate in this market and some that do issue bonds only occasionally. In any case, specific offers will only be available for a limited period, as interest rates will be reviewed at regular intervals. The rates are generally based on the return available on gilts and should give a better deal than a building society deposit, but then again, you may be committing your capital for a longer period.

Interest payments are usually made once a year, though some bonds pay out half-yearly and there may also be a monthly income option on larger investments. Some examples of the rates available at the time of going to press are shown in Table 3.2. These are net rates and apply for investments of £10,000; in some cases higher rates may be available for larger sums.

You might expect that the longer you are prepared to tie up your capital, the higher the return should be, but, as the table shows, this is not always so. The companies have to match the rates that they offer to those they can obtain on their investments, so it depends on the pattern of market interest rates. Remember, too, that the rate is guaranteed throughout the term, so at the longer end you may be sacrificing a small measure of return in exchange for the security of a fixed income.

Once you buy a bond, you are effectively locked into it for the full term. Companies vary in their willingness to provide a surrender value on early encashment, but generally any amount offered will be small. Should the bond holder die, the original capital will be returned, but again, companies have different policies on whether they will add in any income accrued since the last payment. Where payments are annual, this could be a significant amount if the bond holder dies just before a payment is due. For married couples, one way around this problem is to take out a bond on a 'joint life, second death' basis, which means payments would continue to be paid to the surviving spouse for the rest of the term. Should both partners die, the capital sum would be repaid to the estate on the second death. As with annuities, however, this kind of 'extra' may mean the income level is slightly lower.

Another version is the guaranteed growth bond. This operates on a similar principle to the income bond, but the interest earned is accumulated within the bond rather than paid out, so at the end of the term you receive back your capital plus a guaranteed profit.

Table 3.2 *Examples of guaranteed income bond rates*

Term	Income net of basic rate tax (%)	Term	Income net of basic rate tax (%)
1 year	5.35	6 years	5.2
2 years	5.6	7 years	5.2
3 years	5.65	8 years	5.2
4 years	5.55	9 years	5.2
5 years	5.45	10 years	5.2

Applicable for investments of £10,000

For comparison, these bonds were available when sample interest rates on competing products were as follows.

Product	Term or notice required	Rate net of basic rate tax (%)	Fixed/variable interest
NS certificates 54th issue	5 years	4.5*	Fixed
Building society instant access (min £5000)	None	5.8	Variable
Building society 30-day account (min £5000)	30 days	4.68	Variable
Mini cash ISA	None	7.25*	Variable

Note: *Tax-free to all investors.

Source: MoneyFacts, March 2000

Tax treatment of guaranteed bonds

The tax position of guaranteed bonds can be complex, partly because they are not all of the same structure. Longer term bonds are sometimes based on a combination of annuities: a temporary annuity, which provides the income payments, and a deferred annuity, which provides the return of capital at maturity. However, a change in the tax treatment of annuities at the beginning of 1992 made this route less attractive and the majority of bonds now issued are based on a single premium endowment policy with guaranteed bonuses.

For a basic rate taxpayer, the composition of the bond is of no concern. Income is paid net of basic rate tax, so you have no further liability. Non-taxpayers, however, cannot reclaim the tax paid from an endowment, so as a rule these bonds are not suitable to those investors.

Higher rate taxpayers are in a different position again. With an endowment, up to 5 per cent of the original sum invested may be withdrawn each year free of tax – it is counted as a return of capital – and any unused part of this allowance can be carried forward to subsequent years. Where a bond pays income annually, the mechanics are such that you will usually be 'in credit' with this allowance for most or all of the term. At maturity, however, tax may be charged on the 'profit', taking into account the money paid out and the amount originally invested. Further details of the taxation of single premium policies are given in Chapter 10.

Older investors who qualify for age allowance may also be affected by the tax rules. For these and higher rate taxpayers, an insurance broker or other professional adviser should be able to offer guidance on the best buy.

CASH UNIT TRUSTS

Unit trusts are usually associated with equity investments, which are far from capital secure, but cash trusts are a fairly new breed. They invest chiefly in money market instruments and, by virtue of the size of the fund, they can secure top rates of interest. The minimum investment varies between £250 and £5000.

Cash trusts offer complete capital security and in most cases there is no initial charge. There is an annual management charge, which has to be met from the income the trust generates, but it is generally no more than 0.5 per cent. The return varies according to the interest rates available in the market; at the time of writing, gross yields go up to 5.6 per cent.

Income can be paid out or reinvested in the fund. Interest is credited net of lower rate tax, which can be reclaimed by non-taxpayers, while higher rate taxpayers will be liable for the extra amount due. A few trusts provide a cheque-book facility; otherwise, if you want to get your money out, the manager is obliged to issue a cheque within 24 hours of receiving the redemption form.

Further information on cash unit trusts can be found in Chapters 6 and 7.

OFFSHORE DEPOSIT ACCOUNTS

All the major banks and building societies now have offshore branches or subsidiary companies, situated in either the Isle of Man or the Channel Islands. Like their onshore parents, they offer a variety of accounts, depending on how much you want to invest and how quickly you want to be able to access your money. The choices include instant access, 90-day notice accounts, fixed interest term deposits with periods from a number of months to a number of years, money market accounts and high-interest cheque accounts. All of these operate in very much the same way as their onshore equivalents.

As a rule, interest rates are tiered with the size of the deposit and the notice period (see Table 3.3). At the bottom end of the scale, minimum deposits start around £1000, while money market accounts start at around £10,000 and can go up to more than £100,000.

Offshore deposit accounts enjoyed particular popularity when onshore accounts were subject to composite rate tax, which was deducted at source and could not be reclaimed by a non-taxpayer. Nowadays that advantage no longer exists and for UK residents who are basic rate taxpayers, there is a slight advantage in onshore accounts, which deduct only lower rate tax. However, offshore accounts do have the slight advantage that interest is paid gross, so the tax bill is deferred for a while.

The other important consideration is how safe your investment is. 'Offshore' used to be synonymous with shady, or at least

Table 3.3 *Examples of offshore deposit rates*

Type of account	Gross annual interest rate (%)
Instant access, min £1000	4.6
Instant access, min £5000	5.0
Instant access, min £50,000	5.75
30-day notice, min £10,000	6.0
60-day notice, min £10,000	6.1
90-day notice, min £10,000	6.0
Money market account, min £50,000	4.25

Source: MoneyFacts, March 2000

dubious, dealing, but the image has been considerably cleaned up in recent years. The Isle of Man, which had a salutary experience with the collapse of the Savings and Investment Bank in 1982, now has a compensation scheme for bank and building society deposits. In addition, building society subsidiaries are covered by their parents for the full amount of their liabilities. The Channel Islands keep a tight rein on financial businesses by having a strict vetting procedure for any institutions applying to set up in the islands.

OFFSHORE MONEY FUNDS

Sterling offshore money funds are similar to the money market funds mentioned in the last chapter, investing in much the same kind of holdings, such as bank deposits and certificates of deposit. In addition, however, there are offshore money funds denominated in a variety of different currencies – such as US dollars, Japanese yen, Swiss francs and now also the euro. At present, interest rates on euro funds look low, but UK rates are expected to fall towards those in Europe, even though the UK is not yet a member of the European Monetary Union. Also, the euro is expected to appreciate against the pound, which would add to the overall return.

Of course, currency movements can be negative as well as positive, which makes foreign currency funds more risky than sterling funds. You can reduce the risk by investing in a managed currency fund, where the manager will switch between various currencies according to their perceived prospects. There is still the potential to lose on exchange rates, but it is rather like investing in a unit trust instead of a single share: if one currency falls, another may rise, so the risk is spread.

Some money funds have no set minimum investment, while others may require £1000 upwards. One point to watch for is that these funds carry an annual management fee. The usual figure is around 1 per cent and anything higher than this should be treated with caution, as it will cut into the returns available.

Taxation of offshore funds

The tax position of offshore funds is a little complex, as they are classified into two types: those with 'accumulator' status, also known as 'roll-up' funds, and those with 'distributor' status.

Prior to 1984, all funds were of the roll-up type, which meant that all interest earned was accumulated within the fund and added to the capital value. As a result, when investors came to sell, they were liable only to capital gains tax on the profits. Since there was the annual exemption allowance to make use of, and the top rate of capital gains tax at that time was only 30 per cent, this provided excellent tax efficiency, for higher rate taxpayers in particular.

Since 1984, however, the Inland Revenue has introduced new tax rules based on the dual classification. Roll-up funds still accumulate all the interest in the old way, but when you come to sell your holding, all the profits – whether they arise from capital gains or interest – are taxed as income.

For investors who are not in need of a regular income, there are still some advantages in roll-up funds, because the tax liability is deferred until you cash in your investment. This means that, meanwhile, you continue to earn interest on the full amount. Also, you will benefit if you wait to sell until your tax rate is lower than it is now, perhaps after retirement. Better still, if you retire or move abroad and cease to be a UK resident, you can escape UK tax altogether by cashing in the holding after you have left the country.

Distributor status was introduced as a special concession. To qualify, funds must distribute at least 85 per cent of their income and this will be taxed in the hands of the investor at normal income tax rates. They must also not engage in 'trading' primarily, procedures designed to convert income into capital gains and thereby reduce the tax liability. Distributor status is only granted in retrospect, so funds that could be borderline tend to opt for accumulator status rather than risk their investors being faced with an unexpected tax position.

Distributor funds can be useful for non-taxpayers. Even for those who do pay tax, there is a small benefit compared with onshore funds as interest is paid gross, so there will be a short period of grace before you have to give the taxman what is due.

WHERE TO FIND OUT MORE

Information on all the products mentioned in this chapter, with details of current offers and interest rates, can be found in the financial pages of newspapers (advertising and editorial) and in specialist magazines. *MoneyFacts*, a monthly publication, gives a guide to investment rates, including local authority bonds and offshore deposit accounts. It can be contacted on 01603 476100. Alternatively, you should consult an insurance broker or other professional adviser.

4 The Gilts Market

In recent years, the government has done a fair amount to encourage saving – with the introduction of personal equity plans and tax exempt special savings accounts. Yet the government itself frequently lives beyond its means by spending more than its revenues, hence the National Debt, which grows rather more often than it is reduced.

National Savings products, outlined in Chapter 2, are one form of borrowing by the government, but by far the biggest chunk is through gilt-edged securities, or gilts for short. These are issued regularly and come in a variety of types. Most have a lifespan of up to 20 years, though some last indefinitely, but although they cannot be cashed in before their maturity date, they can meanwhile be traded on the Stock Exchange.

Gilts are regarded as being one of the safest of all investments. This is not to say that you cannot make a loss on them – the prices fluctuate, so your capital is not guaranteed. But the promises made by the gilt itself – the interest payments and the redemption value – are as secure as you can get; the government has never yet been known to default.

TERMINOLOGY

One of the off-putting things about gilts is the jargon. If you go along to a building society, the accounts may have fancy names, but the descriptions of 'instant access' or '90 days' notice' are usually pretty clear. In fact, the title of a gilt is descriptive of what it offers, but you need to be able to decipher the code. As an example, let us suppose you are offered £100 nominal of Treasury 9.5 per cent 2000.

To start with, 'nominal' refers to the face value of the gilt, which is the amount the government will repay at the date of redemption. This is also called the 'par value'. But between now and the redemption date, the price of the gilt will vary and may be above or below par. So your £100 nominal may cost you more or less than £100, but if you hold it for the rest of its life-span, that is what you will get back. It follows that at the time you buy, there is an inbuilt capital gain or loss if the gilt is held to redemption.

The name 'Treasury' can effectively be ignored. Some gilts, like 'War Loan', have names that reflect the original purpose of the borrowing, while most that are around today are called Treasury or Exchequer. Either way, the name has no relevance to the investment characteristics.

The percentage, 9.5 per cent in this case, refers to the 'coupon', or the interest rate that will be paid on the gilt. The rate applies to the nominal value of the gilt, so £100 nominal at 9.5 per cent will earn £9.50 interest a year. In practice, the true rate of return on your money will depend on the price you pay for the gilt. If you buy below the par value, you will be getting a higher rate than the one quoted. For example, if your £100 nominal costs you £98, the £9.50 interest works out at just under 9.7 per cent. This is known as the 'flat' or 'running' yield of the stock.

Finally, 2000 is the redemption date, when the nominal value will be repaid to whoever holds the gilt at that time. Some stocks are 'double-dated': they carry two redemption dates, for example, 2001–2004. This means that the government can choose to redeem the stock at any time between those dates, but no later than the second one. As a rule, if a stock is standing above its par value as redemption approaches, the earlier date is more likely; if it is below par, the later date.

TYPES OF GILTS

Conventional gilts are classified into four types, which are generally shown separately in newspaper price listings. Those with up to seven years left to run before redemption are called 'short-dated' or 'shorts'; those with remaining lives of 7 to 15 years are called 'mediums'; 'longs' are those with more than 15 years to run; and half a dozen or so stocks are undated, which means there is no fixed redemption date.

The nearer a gilt is to its redemption date, the closer its price will get to the nominal value, in anticipation of the repayment due. So short-dated stocks should have the least volatile prices. Mediums and longs, on the other hand, may fluctuate substantially in either direction. Because of the difference in coupon, two stocks with the same nominal value and the same redemption date may have quite different prices on the market.

Undated stocks could in theory be redeemed at some point, but it seems very unlikely. The coupons are low, between 2.5 and 4 per cent, so there is no incentive for the government to redeem them, only to have to borrow new money at higher cost.

In addition to these various conventional gilts there is another category, index-linked stocks. With these, both the interest and the capital repayment value are adjusted in line with the Retail Price Index (RPI). In practice, the figure used is the level of the index eight months before payment is due, to ensure that the amount of payment is always known in advance. This is compared with the base index for the stock, which is the level of the RPI eight months before the stock was issued; the base index for each stock is shown in newspaper price listings.

The coupons on these stocks look lower than those for conventional gilts because the figure quoted is the unindexed amount, which is then multiplied up by the inflation factor. Like conventional stock, prices will vary and as the redemption date approaches will move towards the repayment value, but this will be the indexed value, not the £100 nominal.

GILT PRICES

The prices of gilt stocks are listed in newspapers alongside other share prices, generally under the heading of 'British Funds'.

The prices listed are normally the mid-market prices that applied at the close of trading on the previous day. This will give a reasonable guide, but prices are changing all the time; for an up-to-date figure you would need to consult a broker. You also need to remember that the actual buying and selling prices involve a spread – the buying price will be slightly above the mid-market figure quoted and the selling price slightly below it.

One other factor affecting the quoted price is the accumulated interest. Inevitably there is a time-lag involved in preparing and sending out interest payments and meanwhile stocks could change hands, so the rule is that payments are made to whoever was the registered holder seven working days before the interest payment falls due (10 working days for 3.5 per cent War Loan). At this point the stock becomes 'ex dividend', indicated in price quotations by the letters 'xd'. If you sell a stock that is ex dividend you will still receive the interest payment, but the part of it that relates to the period after you sold will be subtracted from the sale proceeds. Similarly, if you buy a stock ex dividend, this portion of interest will be deducted from the cost, to compensate for you not actually receiving it.

If you buy at other times, you will have to pay for the interest that has accumulated since the last payment date. For example, if you buy two months after the previous payment, your purchase includes two months' worth of interest and the value of this will be added to the price.

Aside from these factors, there are a number of influences on the general level of gilt prices, chief of which is interest rates. In simple terms, if bank interest rates are at 12 per cent, then a gilt with a coupon of 12 per cent should trade around its par value. If bank rates fall to 8 per cent, the gilt looks more attractive and this will drive the price up until the effective yield, based on the purchase price, comes into line with bank rates.

In practice, though, prices will reflect not only current interest rates but the market's expectations of future rates. Once you have bought a gilt, you have locked into a particular rate of return, so if general interest rates fall, you will be doing well. On top of this, a fall in interest rates will tend to mean a rise in gilt prices, so there will be a capital gain if you sell. Conversely, if interest rates are forecast to rise, the prospects are less attractive. Inflation will also affect the true value of both future income and capital value, so, again, prices will be influenced by the market's expectations.

THE YIELD

As mentioned above, the flat yield on a gilt depends on the purchase price as well as the quoted coupon. It can be calculated by dividing the coupon by the price and multiplying by 100. This then represents the interest rate you will get on your investment. But the flat yield is not the whole story. The total return to be made from a gilt also depends on the change in the capital value between when you buy and when you sell or when the stock is redeemed.

If you hold the stock to redemption, you will make a known capital gain or loss depending on the price at which you bought it. Even if you stand to make a loss, this need not mean that the stock is not worth buying. For one thing, if the maturity date is still some way off, the price may rise before then, allowing you to sell at a profit. Alternatively, if you hold on to the stock, the interest payments may be enough to outweigh the capital loss and still represent an attractive return.

This return can be judged from the redemption yield, which takes into account the capital gain or loss as well as the flat yield. The calculation is complicated, but figures are included in newspaper listings and can also be obtained from stockbrokers, who have computer programs designed for the purpose. The figures assume that all interest payments are reinvested in the same stock at the same redemption yield.

A comparison between flat yields and redemption yields is shown in Table 4.1. Here, the high-coupon short-dated stocks are standing above their par value and the redemption yield is therefore a lot lower than the flat yield, though still competitive with, say, bank and

Table 4.1 *Gross flat and redemption yields on gilts*

Stock	Price (£)	Flat yield (%)	Redemption yield (%)
Treasury 10% 2001	103.41	9.67	6.386
Treasury 7% 2001	100.98	6.932	6.368
Funding 3.5% 2004	91.53	3.824	5.716
Conversion 9.5% 2005	115.08	8.255	6.036
Treasury 9% 2008	122.37	7.355	5.680
Treasury 8% 2015	133.44	5.995	4.924

Source: MoneyFacts, March 2000

building society accounts. The low-coupon Funding 3.5 per cent stock, on the other hand, offers only a modest running income but a higher redemption yield, as there is a capital gain to be made.

These figures are for gross yields. When tax is taken into account, the picture can change again, as explained on pages 54–55.

BUYING AND SELLING

There are three ways of buying gilts: direct, when there is a new issue; through a stockbroker; or through the Bank of England's brokerage service.

When a new stock is issued, prospectuses are published in newspapers and are also available from the Bank of England Registrar's Department and the UK Debt Management Office. If you are interested in buying gilts regularly, you can contact the Bank of England Registrar's Department to go on a mailing list for details of new issues.

Stocks are auctioned, which means institutions register the price they are prepared to bid and only the highest bidders will receive stock if the issue is oversubscribed. Private investors may bid competitively if they wish, but can also make a non-competitive bid, for a minimum of £1000-worth of stock. They will then pay the average of the successful bid prices. Usually they are asked to pay the nominal value up-front and the Bank of England then makes a refund or asks for more money, depending on the average price set. The advantage of buying new stock in this way is that there is no commission on the purchase.

For existing stocks, you can deal through a stockbroker or bank. Commissions on gilt dealing are usually lower than for equities but will still be subject to the broker's minimum, which may be £30 or more in London. Hence this is likely to prove an expensive route for small investments, especially as further commission will be payable when you come to sell.

A cheaper alternative is the Bank of England's brokerage service, which has replaced the National Savings Stock Register. Forms are available from post offices or from the Bank of England (see 'Where to find out more' on pages 59–60 for a contact number). The costs of buying and selling are shown in Table 4.2.

Table 4.2 *The cost of dealing in gilts through the Bank of England*

Up to £5000	0.7% subject to a minimum charge of £12.50 for purchases
Over £5000	£35 plus 0.375% of the amount in excess of £5000

Examples

Purchases		Sales	
Cost of transaction	Commission	Proceeds of sale	Commission
£250	£12.50	£250	£1.75
£1000	£12.50	£1000	£7.00
£5000	£35.00	£2500	£17.50
£10,000	£53.75	£7500	£44.38
£20,000	£91.25	£15,000	£72.50

The drawback to this method is that it has to be done by post. Dealing will normally be carried out on the day that instructions are received, but you will not know what price applied until later, when you receive a contract note for the transaction. The Bank cannot deal for you at a specified price or 'at best', as a stockbroker could.

One other route into the gilt market is through a collective investment such as an insurance company product or a unit trust. This gives you a stake in a portfolio of gilts for a much smaller outlay than buying your own collection and with professional management as well, but of course there is none of the certainty you can get by buying stocks to hold to redemption.

GILTS AND TAX

Interest payments on gilts are usually made twice a year. The interest on gilts registered with the Bank of England is normally paid gross, although taxpayers will be liable via their tax return. If you wish, you can opt to have payments made net by applying to the Bank of England Registrar's Department.

Special rules apply to interest that has accrued shortly before you buy or sell. Where accrued interest has been allowed for in the purchase price, that part of the subsequent interest payment will not normally be liable for tax. Conversely, when you sell, you will be charged tax on the amount of interest earned before the sale, calculated on a daily basis. However, these rules do not apply when your holdings of gilts have not recently been worth more than £5000. In this case, tax applies only to interest that has actually been paid; so if the sale price includes an allowance for, say, three months' accrued interest, the profit is treated as a capital gain.

This is an advantage, as all capital gains made on gilts are tax free for private investors. The government caused a scare in 1995 by announcing that in future all gains would be subject to income tax, but eventually decided to exclude private investors from the ruling, although it does apply to companies.

As a result, higher rate taxpayers can continue to use gilts in a tax-planning strategy. By opting for a low-coupon stock and holding it to maturity, they can ensure that most of the return will come in the form of a tax-free capital gain.

With index-linked stocks, the inflation component of the capital return is also tax free, although the full amount of interest paid is taxable in the normal way.

GILT STRIPS

The tax change was a prelude to the introduction of a gilt 'strips' market, which was set up in December 1997. This divides a gilt into its component parts of interest and capital, which can then be traded separately. For example, a gilt maturing in five years' time could be divided into 11 strips: one for each of the 10 half-yearly interest payments due and one for the final capital repayment. In each case, the nominal value of the strip will be paid out at maturity, with no interest meanwhile. Hence the strips are referred to as 'zero coupon'.

However, although there is no ongoing income, there may be an ongoing tax charge. If you hold strips at 5 April in any tax year, they will be treated as if you sold them that day and reacquired them on 6 April, with a tax charge on any increase in value since the previous year. In other words, you can find yourself paying tax on an asset that produces no return until you sell it or it matures.

For this reason, strips are likely to appeal primarily to institutions rather than private investors, although they could be useful if you have a set liability to meet in the future, such as school fees, or for saving for retirement. Not all gilts are strippable; if you hold one that is, it can be stripped by one of the Gilt-Edged Market Makers. These are broking firms that buy and sell gilts, mainly on behalf of institutions such as insurance companies and pension funds. You can also buy and sell strips through a stockbroker.

WHY BUY GILTS?

The Bank of England has made dealing in gilts simpler for private investors, but should you be tempted? When interest rates are low – and currently they are expected to fall further, towards European levels – high-coupon gilts compare very favourably to bank and building society accounts as regards the running yield they offer. If income is your priority, gilts certainly have an appeal, but remember that if high-coupon stocks are at a premium – the price is above the par value – and you hold the stocks to redemption, the high income will be achieved at the expense of a guaranteed capital loss.

This should be viewed in the context of future prospects from alternative investments. Any investment has an opportunity cost – by choosing one, you are giving up the chance of another. Of course, you can never be certain of getting the best, but you can consider probabilities. The lower the rates of interest and inflation, the more likely it is that they will rise in future. This will work against gilts in that the yield will become relatively less attractive, prices will fall, and the ultimate redemption value will be worth less in real terms.

Timing makes all the difference to a gilt investment. Ideally, they should be bought just as interest rates start to fall and sold just as they are about to rise – even though they may appear most attractive when interest rates are at their lowest. But much depends on your investment criteria. On a long-term comparison, gilts have consistently performed less well than equities, but for some investors the fixed income and capital return may carry more weight.

CONVENTIONAL VERSUS INDEX-LINKED

If inflation is the enemy of investors, index-linking should be the saviour. The return offered is guaranteed to stay in line with inflation, while the capital value at maturity is also protected from erosion. The redemption value of a conventional gilt, on the other hand, may be worth a lot less by the time it matures.

While current interest rates are influenced by current inflation, index-linked gilts look to the future in that prices will be influenced by expectations about the trend of inflation. Lately, index-linked stocks have tended to outperform conventional gilts; with the economy out of recession, and in the early days of a new government, inflation could start to pick up again. In this scenario, index-linked gilts look more attractive, as the inflation protection will prove rewarding, while if interest rates rise alongside inflation, the prices of conventional gilts are likely to fall, so they have less appeal.

One way of judging the relative merits of index-linked and conventional gilts is shown in Table 4.3. This matches index-linked stock with conventional issues of the same or similar maturity date and then shows what the real returns would be for the conventional stock at sample rates of inflation. The real return for the index-linked stock is, of course, the quoted coupon. So, for example, the first stock in the table offers a real return of 2.5 per cent. The matching conventional issue will offer more than this for all the inflation rates shown. In all the other cases, the index-linked

Table 4.3 *Index-linked versus conventional stocks*

Stock	Price (£)	Comparison stock	Real returns at inflation of:		
			5%	3%	2.5%
2.5% 2001	205.15	Treasury 7% 2001	3.097	3.819	4.002
4.375% 2004	128.28	Treasury 6.75% 2004	2.687	2.945	3.010
2.5% 2009	214.80	Treasury 8% 2009	1.983	2.113	2.146
2.5% 2013	192.15	Treasury 8% 2013	2.018	2.110	2.133
2.5% 2020	216.50	Treasury 8% 2020	1.859	1.924	1.941
4.125% 2030	190.80	Treasury 6% 2030	1.648	1.702	1.715

Source: MoneyFacts, March 2000

stock currently offers a better return for inflation rates down to 2.5 per cent.

Of course, it is still a matter of judgement when deciding how high or low inflation might be over the period in question. The further away the redemption date, the harder this is, as inflation is likely to go both up and down more than once meanwhile. At the current rate of around 2.6 per cent, all but the shortest-dated index-linked stock look attractive, but in June 1993 inflation hit a low of just 1.2 per cent, so the medium-term conventional stocks cannot be written off.

PERMANENT INTEREST BEARING SHARES

Permanent interest bearing shares (PIBS) are issued by building societies as a means of raising permanent share capital. They are similar to gilts, in that they pay a fixed income, but the majority are irredeemable unless the issuing society is wound up. They can, however, be sold to a third party and are traded on the Stock Exchange.

Interest is paid twice a year and is paid net of basic rate tax, although non-taxpayers can reclaim it. Higher rate taxpayers will be liable for the extra amount. Any profits made on the sale of shares are not liable to tax for private investors, but are taxable for companies under the same rules as for gilts described on page 54.

The interest rates are more attractive than those offered on the standard range of building society accounts, but there is, of course, a capital risk. Share prices move inversely to interest rates and are particularly sensitive to long-term rates. So, for example, if market rates move downwards, prices will rise, which reduces the effective yield as a percentage of the purchase price. This is illustrated in Table 4.4, which shows the current prices on a selection of shares and the corresponding yields. All the shares were issued at an original price of around 100p, but falling market interest rates since issue have generally driven up the price. Equally, if rates rise again in future, the share prices will fall, so, unlike building society accounts, these are investments you should review regularly.

Table 4.4   *Examples of PIBS prices, coupons and yields*

Current price (pence)	Fixed coupon (% gross)	Gross yield (%)
105	8.00	7.62
143	10.75	7.52
155	11.62	7.50
168	12.62	7.51
172	13.00	7.55

Source: Financial Times, April 2000

At one time there were 18 PIBS available but currently there are just nine. As the table shows, the yields vary, reflecting the market's view of the issuing society. Shares can be bought and sold through stockbrokers, who may advise on which appear most attractive. The minimum investment is generally £1000, but most stockbrokers have a minimum commission, which can be around £25, making dealing expensive for small sums. PIBS are not normally liable to stamp duty.

Aside from the capital risk, there are other safety aspects. Interest payments are not guaranteed to be made if the board of the society decides payment would damage business interests or if interest has not been paid on shares and deposits. Also, PIBS are not covered by the building societies' investor compensation scheme, and if the issuing society were to go into liquidation, holders would be last in line for repayment, behind all depositors and ordinary shareholders. On the other hand, if the society is taken over by another, the PIBS will continue as the liability of the society making the take-over.

In 1997, an investment trust was launched that invests in PIBS in the hope of benefiting from the spate of mergers in the building society world. Currently, the trust has a gross yield of 6.3 per cent a year, with the prospect of additional cash or shares from bonuses payable if any of the societies whose shares are held undergo a merger or conversion.

WHERE TO FIND OUT MORE

Newspapers such as *The Daily Telegraph* and the *Financial Times* publish the prices of gilts on a daily basis, along with gross interest and redemption yields. Net redemption yields, break-even inflation figures and general advice on buying and selling can be obtained from a stockbroker. Stockbrokers can also provide information and advice on permanent interest bearing shares.

For a booklet on investing in gilts and application forms to buy or sell through the Bank of England's brokerage service, phone 0800 818614. Further information is available on 01452 398333. To be put on the new issues mailing list or for information on individual holdings and stockholder services, phone 01452 398080. Finally, for general enquiries on gilts, you can contact the UK Debt Management Office on 020 7862 6501.

5 | Equities

Equities could be said to come somewhere near the top of the investment tree. This is not because they necessarily demand a lot of money – privatisation issues have allowed people to own shares for a down-payment of just £100. But if you had only £100 to invest, the stock market would not normally be considered the ideal place to put it. Most investors come into equities only after they have built up more cautious funds elsewhere.

This chapter focuses mainly on the UK Stock Exchange. In fact, many of the points would apply in a similar way to overseas markets but, despite sophisticated communications technology, dealing in foreign shares tends to be both more expensive and more difficult. Unless you have a very large portfolio, it is more practical to invest abroad through pooled funds such as unit and investment trusts.

THE STOCK EXCHANGE

The London Stock Exchange has its origins back in the 18th century, when people used to meet in coffee houses to exchange shares and arrange deals. It was formally constituted in 1802, in purpose-built premises on the same site as the current building, which was opened in 1973.

The Exchange has two purposes: to act as a market for people wanting to buy and sell existing shares, and to raise money for companies by issuing new share capital. There are also two separate operations involved, jobbing and broking, corresponding to wholesale and retail functions. Jobbers used to be known by the more descriptive name of market-makers – they make a market in shares by acting as primary buyers and sellers and holding stocks on their books – but have now been renamed again, as 'Retail Service Providers' (RSPs). Brokers act as intermediaries between the market-makers and the end-clients, investors; they take orders from their clients and look for the best prices among the market-makers.

Trading used to take place physically on the Stock Exchange floor, but that came to an end with Big Bang, which reorganised the workings of the Exchange. Broking and jobbing firms were allowed to be taken over by companies, where previously they were partnerships, and both functions may now be carried out within a single company. They must, however, be kept separate, by means of a 'Chinese Wall'; this is to guard against any unscrupulous manoeuvring between them at the expense of the investor. If, for example, the broker knew that the market-maker wanted to get rid of some undesirable shares, he could connive at it by advising his clients to buy them.

Another effect of Big Bang was to remove the standard commission levels for buying and selling shares which were previously set by the Stock Exchange. Although some firms still roughly follow the old scales, there can now be wide differences. Much of the competition, though, is at the upper end and, for smaller investors, the general effect has been to increase costs. This is chiefly because brokers set a minimum commission, which can be as high as £40 for a London firm, making small transactions disproportionately expensive. Provincial brokers are generally cheaper, as they have lower overheads, and commission levels also vary according to the type of service provided.

ROLLING SETTLEMENT

The volume of shares traded has increased enormously since Big Bang. While prices have been posted on screens for several years, dealing used to involve a mass of paperwork and administrative logjams were uncommon, delaying the issue of certificates for shares bought and settlement for shares sold. The Stock Exchange originally planned to deal with this problem with the introduction of Taurus, a paperless dealing system that would have replaced certificates with electronic accounts, but after years of problems and delays it finally collapsed in March 1993.

Instead, it introduced a system called Crest. The first step was taken in July 1994 with the introduction of a 10-day 'rolling settlement' period.

Previously, the settlement system was based on two- to three-week periods known as 'accounts'. Settlement of transactions undertaken during any one account would normally take place on a fixed account day, some 10 days after the end of the period. Meanwhile, investors could enjoy credit for shares bought, but would be waiting for the proceeds of sales.

Under the new system, settlement for both sales and purchases has to take place within a set period from the transaction date, either 5 or 10 days. Electronic dealing – where shares are registered electronically and there are no certificates – is usually done in 5 days, known as T+5. But many private investors still hold paper certificates and in this case deals can be done in 10 days – T+10.

However, there is a risk in this. If you are selling shares, you must get the certificate to your broker in time for it to be handed on to the new buyer within 10 working days of the deal being struck. This will generally mean that it should be in the broker's hands no more than eight days after dealing. Since 1 March 1999, there has been a system of fines if certificates are delivered late and, although these will be levied against the broker or share dealer in the first instance, they are likely to be passed on where it is the investor's fault.

If you are more than five days late returning the certificate, the dealer may simply buy the shares in the market, to cut the cost of the fine, and will then charge you the commission and perhaps a fee for administration on this second transaction. You could also find yourself further out of pocket if the price of the shares has moved adversely.

The problem can be avoided if you use a nominee account, which allows the broker to deal electronically for you. Nominee accounts are accounts in the name of a nominee company, which holds the shares on your behalf while you remain the beneficial owner. They are already used in a number of situations, such as for discretionary broking services and personal equity plans.

Nominee accounts are certainly convenient, but do have some drawbacks. You may lose out on share perks, since the shares are not registered in your own name, and you will have to make arrangements with your broker if you want to receive copies of annual reports or go to shareholders' meetings. This may involve a cost, on top of any fee charged for running the nominee account.

Another effect is that margin trading may become more popular. This is a facility whereby the stockbroker gives credit to settle share purchases, using existing shares held in a nominee account as security. This is not just a convenient way of making settlements but also allows you to 'gear' your portfolio, by borrowing against it to buy more shares. The disadvantage is that if the market crashes, the value of shares held as security could end up being worth less than the credit given.

For this reason, stockbrokers are likely to lend only against blue chip shares and will need to monitor portfolios closely. Currently there are no regulations on margin trading but, given the potential risks, rules may be introduced if it becomes widespread.

THE STOCK EXCHANGE ELECTRONIC TRADING SYSTEM

In October 1977, the Stock Exchange introduced a new dealing system known as SETS – the Stock Exchange Electronic Trading System. Covering deals in FTSE 100 stocks worth a minimum of £4000, this matches buyers and sellers electronically, by computer. A broker, for example, can post a sale order and the system will then come up with the best buy offer currently available.

The expectation, when the system was introduced, was that it would reduce the cost of dealing in shares – the bid/offer spread. This is because it cuts out the market-maker, who usually acts as the middleman between buyer and seller and makes a 'turn' on the transaction. The experience of European stock markets that have moved to similar order-driven trading systems is that spreads have fallen by up to two-thirds.

The early experience here, however, was that spreads tended to widen, particularly during the first and last hours of a day's trading. The small number of deals done during these times means prices can be erratic and this can be compounded by dealers 'testing the water' or just chancing their arm. As a result, private investors who instruct their brokers to deal 'at best' may get caught out by unrealistic prices at these times. It may be better to specify a price range and also to deal in the middle of the day, when the system is busier and experience shows that spreads have tended to narrow.

Of course, many private investors will be involved in smaller deals that are outside the SETS limit. These will go through retail service providers (RSPs), as the old market-makers are now known. However, they are still likely to be influenced by SETS prices, for better or worse.

THE ALTERNATIVE INVESTMENT MARKET

The Alternative Investment Market (AIM) was launched in June 1995 as a replacement for the Unlisted Securities Market. As the name implies, it offers an alternative market-place for companies that are too small or not yet ready to seek a main stock market listing.

To join, companies have to supply a prospectus, background details on all directors, details of promoters, names and holdings of major shareholders, a working capital statement and a risk warning.

They also need to have a 'nominated adviser' and a 'nominated broker'. The former must be chosen from a Stock Exchange register and is, in effect, the company's mentor for the market, ensuring it meets the AIM rules. The broker is responsible for providing information to the market and for matching prospective buyers and sellers of the company's shares if there is no market-maker.

For investors, AIM shares generally carry more risks than the main market. This is partly because the companies are mostly smaller and have less of a business track record on which their prospects can be judged, but also because the market itself tends to attract far fewer buyers and sellers – the institutions, which dominate trading, naturally prefer the main market where deals can be much larger. Where there is no market-maker, deals are on a matched basis, which means you could find yourself stuck with shares for which there is no buyer available.

There are, however, tax benefits. Capital gains tax can be deferred on the profit from selling an asset if the proceeds are rein-vested in qualifying AIM shares, while any transfer of AIM shares will avoid capital gains tax if it is at cost value rather than market value. Some shares also qualify under the Enterprise Investment Scheme (see Chapter 12), which offers upfront income tax relief and capital gains tax relief on sales. Finally, AIM companies may be eligible investments for venture capital trusts, which offer their investors benefits similar to those of the Enterprise Investment Scheme, plus tax-free dividends.

MARKET INDICES

Movements in the stock market are generally measured with reference to an index. For the UK market, there are two that are principally used: the FTSE All-Share Index and the FTSE 100 Index – known colloquially as 'Footsie'.

The All-Share Index does not in fact cover all shares quoted on the market, but the 830 or so that it does cover account for around 96 per cent of the total market capitalisation. Consequently, it gives the most representative overall picture.

The Footsie, which began at the start of 1984, covers the top 100 companies by size. The prices are calculated every minute during the trading day, so it gives immediate feedback to dealers on what is happening. However, there has been some concern among insti-tutional investors that the FTSE 100 is no longer as meaningful as it used to be, as nearly half the value of the index is now concentrated in the 10 largest companies, thanks to a number of large-scale mergers such as BP Amoco and Glaxo Wellcome.

Although share price movements, and those of unit trusts, investment trusts and so on, are often measured in relation to the

All-Share or the Footsie, there are various other indices covering particular sectors, such as smaller companies or individual industries. These can be more relevant for judging the performance of an individual share or specialist trust. For example, smaller companies are unlikely to follow the same pattern as the large companies represented by the Footsie Index; if the smaller companies sector is booming, a share that is performing only in line with the Footsie is probably doing relatively badly.

PRIVATE INVESTORS

Until quite recently, private investors were very much in decline in terms of their representation in the stock market. Meanwhile, the institutions saw a steady and substantial increase in the funds under their control and took on a heavily dominant position.

While there is still a heavy imbalance in favour of institutions, the private investor has staged a comeback. Currently, about one in four people own shares, a substantial increase on 10 years ago. There have been several reasons for this.

First, there has been an increase in inheritances following on from the growth in home ownership. People who already have a basic portfolio of investments and are then presented with a 'windfall' of, say, £50,000 to £100,000 are quite likely to give some thought to equities. Another factor has been the growth in company share option schemes for employees.

The third, and most major, influence has been privatisations. These have been something of a mixed blessing. They have certainly brought about wider share ownership but, one could argue, of the wrong kind. Few of the new shareholders are active dealers and many simply hang on to the few shares they bought, either for the incentives attached or because they have virtually forgotten they have them.

Perhaps more dangerous was the reputation privatisation issues acquired as 'get rich quick' schemes. Priced to be enticing, the earlier issues in particular gave opportunities to make immediate attractive profits – and many buyers made the most of it, selling the shares as soon as they had the letters of allocation. While there is nothing wrong in making a quick profit, anyone who thought the principle could be extended to other shares, with the same degree – or lack – of risk, is likely to have been severely disappointed.

Another major boost to share ownership has come from the spate of flotations of building societies and insurance companies. Halifax, Woolwich, Alliance & Leicester and Northern Rock gave away £24 billion in cash and shares and, altogether, some 20 million people received shares. A number of them no doubt sold almost immediately, but the societies encouraged people to keep them – and provide new business – by offering special personal equity plans.

On a positive note, privatisations and flotations have boosted the growth of dealing services aimed at smaller investors. The Stock Exchange has also made overtures to smaller shareholders through a national campaign and a new Private Investors' Committee, and stockbrokers have adopted a more user-friendly approach.

A new employee share scheme, the All Employee Share Ownership Plan (Aesop), comes into effect in 2000, having first been announced in the 1999 Budget. Employees may spend up to £1500 of pre-tax income on shares in their own company and will get increasing tax benefits the longer they hold them. If they sell in the first three years, they will have to pay income tax on the sale value, but if they retain the shares for three to five years, the tax will be based on the original amount of salary spent, meaning any profit made is tax-free. Between five and seven years, tax will be charged on 80 per cent of the salary spent; between 7 and 10 years, on 60 per cent; and if the shares are held for more than 10 years, on just 40 per cent. Should the shares fall in value, tax will be calculated on the sale proceeds, rather than the amount invested.

There are further tax relief ploys for the scheme. First, all dividends will be tax free if they are reinvested to buy further shares in the company. Second, employers may give away free shares in proportion to the amount spent by employees, up to a maximum ratio of two to one and a maximum value of £3000. For example, if an employee buys £1000-worth of shares, his employer may give him up to £2000-worth. Employers may also give away up to £3000-worth of shares to any employee, whether or not he buys any himself. Finally, a change to capital gains tax taper relief for business assets means that the tax rate will fall to just 10 per cent if shares are held for at least four years.

If all these various developments help to dispel some of the mystique that has traditionally surrounded the stock market, that is a step in the right direction. The next stage is to learn a little more about the rest of the market.

ORDINARY SHARES

To begin at the beginning, an ordinary share represents a stake in the ownership of a company. In theory, it also confers the right to have a say in how the company is run, at least to the extent of having a vote at the annual general meeting. In practice, of course, most private investors do not have enough shares for their vote to count for much and many do not even bother to go to the meeting; nevertheless, the right exists.

Shareholders are also entitled to a portion of the company's profits, paid out in the form of dividends. As a rule, some of the profits will be kept back to be reinvested in the company itself for future growth. The remainder are distributed at so much per share; the more shares you hold, the larger the total dividend.

In return for these rewards, you take on a risk. Should the worst happen and the company be forced into liquidation, the ordinary shareholder is last in line for getting any of his money back. As a rule, though, you can only lose as much as you put in – you will not be called upon to make good anyone else's losses. This is because companies listed on the Stock Exchange have limited liability – hence the term PLC, or public limited company.

An exception is if the shares have been issued partly paid, as several privatisation issues have. This means that at the time you buy the shares, you pay only part of their price, with subsequent calls being made for the rest of the money. In this case, if the company incurs debts it cannot meet, you could be required to pay over the outstanding balance on the shares you hold. The majority of shares, though, are dealt in on a fully paid basis, so your maximum loss is equal to your investment.

With luck, the worst case will not happen and the company will stay in business, but you still stand to lose a part of your investment if the share price falls. Equally, of course, you will make a profit if it rises. So what factors make a share price move?

The short answer is supply and demand for the shares. Quite simply, if demand outstrips supply – if there are more willing buyers than willing sellers – the price will move up; in the opposite case it will move down. So the next question is, what affects supply and demand?

In the first place, all shares are influenced by what might be termed national events: the general economy and the political situation. Increasingly, these days, they are also affected by international events; one country's exports are another's imports, so a recession in the latter country means it will buy less, restricting export growth in the former.

There are further influences at sector or industry level; again, there are trade factors, and also strikes, which can have a knock-on effect if the striking company or industry is a major supplier to another.

Then you come down to the particular company, and what drives demand here is quite simply the expectation of profit. For individual investors, the anticipated profit may be in the form of capital growth – the expectation that the share price will increase. But what lies behind such an increase is the profit made by the company, translated into rising dividends; it is the income potential that ultimately underpins the share price.

Anticipation also plays an important part in determining share prices. An obvious example is a general election, where the market may react in advance to what people think is the likely outcome. This is referred to as discounting an event – if it happens as expected, there will be little further movement, but if expectations are confounded, it could produce a violent swing.

But while it is perfectly in order to act on guesswork, it is illegal to engage in insider dealing, which amounts to taking advantage of unpublished information that may affect share prices.

DIVIDENDS

Dividends are generally paid twice a year, the first payment being the 'interim' dividend and the second the 'final' dividend, paid at the company's year-end. The amount is generally expressed in terms of pence per share, net of lower rate tax; this can be reclaimed by a non-taxpayer, while higher rate taxpayers must pay the difference.

As explained above, dividends underpin the share price and anticipation comes into play. Hence the price will often move ahead of the declaration and, if it fails to live up to expectations, the price can fall back, even though the dividend itself may have increased since the last declaration.

The yield on a share is the gross dividend divided by the share price. The average yield on UK shares is generally around 3 to 4 per cent; if interest rates creep up, this does not look particularly enticing. But what shares also offer is the prospect of growing income and, given inflation, this is a valuable asset.

Yields do, of course, vary, both between companies and between sectors. Broadly speaking, sectors with lower growth prospects will tend to have higher yields. For individual shares, the yield will obviously rise if the share price falls, while the dividend is maintained; the key question then is why the share price has fallen. It may be owing to 'technical' or short-term factors and, indeed, unit trusts in both the Income and Recovery sectors tend to look for just this type of share, which offers capital growth prospects and good income in the meantime. But it may be that profits, and dividends, are expected to fall in the future, so a share cannot be judged by its yield alone.

As mentioned, companies do not usually pay out all their profits as dividends, but retain some for future use. In this case, the dividend is said to be fully 'covered'. Equally, though, they could call upon these reserves to boost dividends in a year when earnings have been low, in which case the payment would be uncovered. Some degree of smoothing from year to year is perfectly acceptable, but a fully covered dividend is always more reassuring.

Since April 1999, new rules have applied to tax on dividends. The tax credit has been reduced from 20 per cent to 10 per cent, while the additional tax payable has changed to 10 per cent for basic rate taxpayers and 32.5 per cent for higher rate taxpayers. The overall effect is to leave these two groups paying just the same tax as before: 20 per cent and 40 per cent respectively. However, non-taxpayers will no longer be able to reclaim the tax deducted at source.

Tax reclaims will be allowed on dividends from stocks and shares held within a personal equity plan (PEP) or Individual Savings Account (ISA), at a rate of 10 per cent. This means that non-taxpayers will have a reason to consider investing in an ISA, whereas PEPs formerly offered them no benefit. However, both they and basic rate taxpayers will have to decide if the tax gain is worth while when set against plan charges. For higher rate taxpayers, on the other hand, there will still be a significant tax benefit, although slightly less than PEPs have offered in the past.

An alternative to cash dividends is a 'scrip' dividend, where the company offers the option of additional shares instead of money. In some cases, the value can be much higher, and if you are looking for cash, you can simply sell the extra shares. Of course, there will be dealing costs, but you may still come out ahead and companies may also offer a buy-back scheme, which will cut the costs for small investors.

In principle, you cannot lose on this type of offer, but you do need to take care over the capital gains tax implications; if you have already used up the annual exempt allowance, you will be faced with a tax bill, although in the longer term it could reduce the liability on your remaining holdings in the shares. Scrip dividends are also treated by the Inland Revenue as having paid 20 per cent income tax which cannot be reclaimed. If you are in any doubt, you should seek independent advice.

PRICE/EARNINGS RATIO

Besides the dividend, another means of judging shares is by the price/earnings ratio, or p/e for short. This is calculated as the share price divided by earnings per share and the result shows how many years it would take the company to earn enough to match the share price, if both remained unchanged.

In practice, the p/e ratio is used as a measure of the 'cheapness' of shares – the lower the ratio, the cheaper the share, relative to the company's earnings potential. But it has to be viewed in context. Average ratios vary between sectors and are also affected by the economy in general – high inflation should lead to lower p/e ratios, since future dividends will be worth much less in real terms than the share price you have to pay now.

Also, while a high ratio means a share is relatively expensive and should be viewed with caution, a low ratio is not always a reason to rush in and buy. It could be that the share price is low for good reason, because the market does not rate its prospects.

If you plan to invest overseas, you should bear in mind that p/e ratios may be on a quite different level to those in the UK. In fact, the UK has a relatively low average compared to markets worldwide, while Japan's is notoriously high.

HOW TO BUY AND SELL

It is no longer necessary to have a family stockbroker to gain access to the stock market. As mentioned above, the combination of Big Bang and privatisation issues has boosted the growth of new dealing services, often with low or no minimum investment requirement, while stockbrokers have been opening their doors to newcomers with a more obvious welcome than was once the case. Some larger companies have also become involved in share-dealing services, particularly where they offer corporate personal equity plans that may include the shares of other companies.

Banks have also expanded the range of dealing services they offer. National Westminster, for example, has a computer-based 'Touchscreen' service that offers instant dealing. It was initially developed in response to privatisation issues but, at the time of writing, it can now be used to deal in 500 different shares and is available in around 300 branches across the country, for both customers and non-customers.

Several banks also provide postal and telephone dealing services, the latter generally confined to existing customers, while the former are open to anyone. For the most part, these are purely dealing services, though occasional advice may be given.

If you want more comprehensive advice, a bank may have its own associated stockbroker service, but you may be just as well off choosing a broker for yourself. The Association of Private Client Investment Managers and Stockbrokers (Apcims) produces a brochure that includes a directory of its members, outlining in brief the services they offer.

But there was a setback for private investors on 1 January 1996 when the Stock Exchange decided to abolish the rule that at least 25 per cent of new share issues had to be set aside for retail investors. Floating companies can now decide the proportion for themselves – or place all shares with institutions.

However, a couple of brokers have responded by setting up new services that provide information on forthcoming new issues and a way of participating.

Another way for smaller investors to play a more active role in the stock market is through an investment club, of which there are now more than 1000 in the UK. ProShare, an organisation dedicated to promoting wider share ownership, offers a matching service to put people in touch with existing clubs or with each other if they want to start a new club. It also publishes a manual on setting up and running a club.

FINDING A BROKER

When it comes to choosing a broker, the first step is to make sure what type of service you want. As regards share dealing, there are three options, as follows:

1. *Execution-only*. This is essentially for dealing only, with no advice given, although company reports or recommendations may be available. Some brokers may be prepared to accept 'limit' orders, under which you specify a maximum buying or minimum selling price; others may only be prepared to deal 'at best' – the best price that can be readily obtained on the market.

2. *Advisory*. This is offered by the majority of brokers and may cover individual share purchases and sales or provide a

Now's the moment to trade
Knockout Stamp Duty for one month

- All new customers get one month's trading free of Stamp Duty

- Highly competitive commission – 0.75%
  minimum £14.95, maximum £37.50

- No account management fees

- Competitive interest paid on cash balances

- Apply online and use your debit card to fund your account

online share dealing, realtime prices, free research
www.DLJdirect.co.uk or call 0800 358 4477

Lines open Mon-Fri 7.30am – 5.30pm Sat 8am – 4pm & Sun 10am – 4pm

Know the moment to deal

ONLINE HAS OPENED UP SHARE DEALING TO EVERYONE

Paul Lubbock, head of marketing at online share-dealing specialists, DLJdirect, highlights the advantages of using the Internet to invest in the stockmarket

Although once perceived as a highbrow activity reserved for a wealthy minority, share dealing is now fast becoming one of the nation's favourite hobbies. Investing in the stockmarket is sweeping the UK at a rate of over 5,000 new shareowners a week. And it shows no sign of let up as people from all walks of life start investing in stocks for the first time.

What has made the difference is the e-revolution. Buying and selling shares has never been easier, cheaper or more accessible. The advancement of communications technology – the Internet, mobile phones and interactive TV – now means that anyone, anywhere, can tap into the stock market at any time.

The significant time and cost advantages that investing online affords are clear drivers in this surge towards the dot.com world of financial planning. In particular, increasing competition in the online share dealing sector has caused the better brokerages to innovate and use the Internet to reduce commission charges and offer improved services, in the battle to attract prospective customers.

Price is undoubtedly a motivating factor. Investors new to share dealing can currently choose from a range of different pricing structures – from flat trading fees, fixed and capped commission rates to totally free dealing for limited periods.

But while many of these price deals will look attractive on the surface, investors will need to watch out for hidden charges. For example, many brokers levy account administration fees and quarterly handling fees, some apply charges for news and information, and others charge extra for research forecasts. As a rule, simplest is best – and it is worth seeking out brokers who have just one straightforward charge.

Some brokers require a minimum account deposit before dealing can begin and many offer discounted 'frequent trader' commission rates for those who intend to buy and sell shares on a regular basis.

Of particular importance, perhaps for first timers in search of both guidance and reassurance, are the back up services – such as telephone helplines and postal confirmation of transactions – that some brokers offer. Those not wholly comfortable with e-communications may feel safer in the knowledge that they can phone a broker at any time.

Investors would do well to also visit and explore several online sites, and decide upon the level of service they require, before they commit themselves to opening an account with one specific broker. With some sites, investors can test the system and 'play' the stock market through a simulated portfolio demo programme – which is always a good way to 'try before you buy'.

As well as reducing the actual cost of share dealing, the online medium enables investors to deal on a real-time basis. This means that investors can access the exact price of any stocks or shares at any given moment. Share prices are sensitive to a whole host of market conditions and can move up or down from one minute to the next – so by choosing a broker who offers firm, guaranteed prices you'll always know exactly where you stand.

While the Internet has certainly brought the stock market closer to home for the majority of current share dealers, it has also been instrumental in changing attitudes to investing. Trust in the security of the Internet and confidence in personal financial planning is growing in this country. As a result, the traditionally cautious UK investor is now not a million miles behind his more adventurous and investment-ready US counterpart.

This is particularly true where private investors can access high quality research and information, previously the exclusive province of fund managers and institutional investors, from their broker. Many brokers are also offering a wide range of independent news and investment analysis free of charge to investors.

This means that customers can research share price history, read up-to-the-minute news and make comparisons against other shares and markets. They can also receive e-mail alerts, check company accounts and information, exchange ideas with other investors and get the latest analysis from experts and commentators.

First of all, investors may wish to visit *Find*, the independent UK Internet directory of financial services at http: //www.find.co.uk for a list of online brokers. It is a good starting point to finding out about investing.

The advent of Investment Clubs has also helped to open up investment opportunities for those who like to make their investment decisions within a group environment. Joining an Investment Club is a great way to get to grips with the workings of the stock market and, with safety in numbers, it is a good way of spreading risk. And, of course, there is also a social side to Investment Clubs.

Most online brokers offer a special service for Investment Clubs, which are worth checking out whether you are already a Club member or whether you are thinking of starting up your own Club.

The accessibility and the ease of online investing shouldn't blind investors to the risks that are inherent in share dealing. Share dealing can be lucrative – but don't forget to put money aside also for your pension and into your bank or building society account for your week-to-week spending.

That said, the Internet is really a fantastic vehicle for online share dealing it will be employed more and more as investors become increasingly experienced in using the Internet for financial transactions, as more brokers and product providers commit to going online – and as the cost of using the web comes down.

Five Easy Steps To Getting Started

1 Work out your investment strategy, including how much you want to invest and how frequently you are likely to deal.

2 Thoroughly research several online brokers, visit their sites, evaluate their service and make a note of their pricing structure. Look out for account fees, minimum deposits, charges for news and information, interest paid on cash balances – never settle for low interest – and discounts for frequent trading and free trial offers.

3 Decide which broker can offer you the best service. With most online brokers, you can open an account online or you can print out, complete and post a registration form – usually you will need to include two forms of identification, bank account details plus an initial deposit to open your account.

4 Once your application has been accepted, you will receive a unique customer ID and security password to gain access to your account and the real-time trading service. Use this to key into additional services offered by your broker.

5 Research and consider carefully which shares you would like to invest your money in. Double-check and then confirm your trade online. Congratulations you're now an online investor.

Source: DLJ*direct*

DLJ*direct* offers a wide range of company and market information and the ability for UK residents to deal in both UK and US (including Nasdaq) shares. It also provides demonstrations and education about investing online.

The DLJ*direct* website can be visited at http://www.dljdirect.co.uk or telephone one of the DLJ*direct* Investor Service representatives on 0800 358 4477.

Further information:

Paul Lubbock DLJ*direct* 020 7886 3567 or
plubbock@dljdirect.co.uk
Lisa Carruthers First Financial
020 7353 3444 or
lcarruthers@first-financial.co.uk

comprehensive portfolio service. At the outset, the broker will discuss with you your needs and desires, without obligation; thereafter you will be consulted before any transaction can take place and you can also initiate consultations or deals.

3. *Discretionary.* In this case, you hand over all responsibility to the broker, although there will be an initial discussion to sort out your aims, attitude to risk and so on. You will also be kept informed of all transactions, as well as receiving regular valuations and reviews.

In addition to these dealing services, stockbrokers may also offer a comprehensive financial planning package. This would include, for example, advice on cash management, school fees planning, retirement planning, life assurance and tax planning.

The majority of stockbrokers are regulated by the Securities and Futures Authority, through which they are authorised on an individual basis to give advice. Clients are eligible for the Investors Compensation Scheme in the event of default, and brokers generally also carry professional indemnity insurance against fraud and negligence.

COSTS

The stockbroker's charges will usually be in the form of commission on dealing, though where there are additional financial planning services there may be an annual fee. The level of commission charged will vary from firm to firm, but will generally depend on three factors:

1. *The type of service*: execution-only dealing is usually cheaper than advisory or discretionary facilities.
2. *The location of the broker*: provincial brokers are usually somewhat cheaper than their London counterparts by virtue of having lower overheads.
3. *The size of the deal*: the scale of charges reduces for larger transactions and there is usually a minimum charge at the bottom end.

On top of the commission, you will also be liable to stamp duty at 0.5 per cent. Examples of charges are shown in Table 5.1.

Table 5.1   *The costs of buying shares*

£1000-worth	
Stockbroker's commission	£22.00
Stamp duty at 0.5%	5.00
Total	£27.00

£10,000-worth	
Stockbroker's commission	£133.50
Stamp duty at 0.5%	50.00
Total	£183.50

£25,000-worth	
Stockbroker's commission	£263.50
Stamp duty at 0.5%	125.00
Total	£388.50

You may be able to deal within specified price limits, or at the best available price in the market that day. Once the order has been executed, you will receive a contract note from the broker, showing the price of the shares and the dealing costs. Settlement will follow within three working days of the transaction.

SHARES IN A PORTFOLIO

The minimum portfolio size specified by stockbrokers varies considerably, from firm to firm and depending on what type of service you want. Equally, different brokers will vary in their views on what constitutes a sensible minimum, regardless of what they might be prepared to accept – some will say around £25,000, others anything up to £100,000.

Chiefly, it depends on your circumstances and the amount of risk you are prepared to accept. The points to bear in mind are first, that small deals cost relatively more than larger ones, as Table 5.1 shows, and second, that to achieve a spread of risk you should think in terms of holding 10 to 15 shares. If you were to put £5000 into each of 10 holdings, that would mean a portfolio of

£50,000; if you then add in 'safety' money in alternative invest-ments, you can begin to see why some advisers think in terms of six figures.

If you are only investing the odd few thousand, you will be restricted to the UK and only a small number of shares at that, whereas a unit trust, for instance, could give you a stake in a worldwide spread of holdings.

That said, there is nothing to stop you going directly into equities with any amount to invest. The so-called 'Super Sid' investor would usually be in the £5000 to £20,000 bracket and stockbrokers are generally prepared to accept smaller sums than they used to, particularly as they might now see only the equity portion of a larger portfolio, whereas in the past they tended to be given charge of all a client's investments. The only 'rule' is to appreciate the risks involved and the same is true of speculation; as the saying goes, if you don't know whether you are a speculator or an investor, the stock market is an expensive place to find out.

There are, of course, a host of such sayings, many of them contradictory, and there is no guaranteed formula for investment success. If you plan to be a middle of the road, long-term investor, the best attributes are probably moderation and patience: don't expect to get rich overnight and don't hold out for even bigger profits at the risk of losing what you already have. Few people ever manage to buy at the very bottom of the market and sell at the very top; if you can come somewhere close, you should find ample rewards.

One other point on portfolio organisation is that it is worth considering an Individual Savings Account (ISA), in to which you can put up to £7000 in the 2000/01 tax year. ISAs were introduced in April 1999, as the replacement for personal equity plans. As with PEPs, the advantage is that all income and capital gains arising from the investment are tax free. Against this have to be set the plan charges; for unit trust-based plans, there are usually no charges other than those on the trusts themselves, so if you are investing in trusts as well as equities, you may do better to use the PEP allowance for the former. ISAs are discussed in detail in Chapter 9.

BUYING ON THE INTERNET

Perhaps the biggest change for private investors is the facility to buy and sell shares via the Internet. There has been massive growth in Internet share-trading lately and it is estimated that around a fifth of all execution-only deals are carried out online. Around 5000 people a week are opening new online accounts and the number of services is also growing fast. They allow anyone with access to the Net to trade in shares on most of the world's stock markets and are likely to be cheaper than traditional stockbroking services. Net traders are generally active, trading on average more than 20 times a year. They are not, however, necessarily experienced. Around a sixth have been dealing in shares for less than a year and nearly one in 10 have only dealt over the Internet.

The main benefit of using the Net is that you have, quite literally, the world at your fingertips. You do not even need to use a UK-based broker and in some cases it may be better not to. For buying overseas stocks, in particular, it may be cheaper and more efficient to use an overseas service.

So how do you set about choosing a broker? As with traditional services, you need to consider reliability, ease of use, service and price. Because services are still quite new, and the providers are still learning, reliability can be an issue. One idea is to sign up with one of the larger services to provide you with a back-up, while testing out others that may be smaller and cheaper. Similarly, ease of use is something you can only really decide by trying out the service, or getting a recommendation from a friend.

The cost of a service is mainly commission on deals, which may be a percentage, a flat rate or some combination of the two. As with traditional broking services, you should look at the cost in the light of the size of trades you are likely to make: a high minimum will penalise you if you tend to make small deals. If you expect to trade frequently, look out for special offers: Stocktrade's Star Trader package has reduced commission rates for those who trade more than 50 times a year, while Charles Schwab has a Frequent Traders Club with a flat fee for each deal, regardless of size, though it does carry an annual membership fee.

Some brokers offer an initial period of commission-free dealing, allowing you – at least in theory – to try them out before you become committed. In practice, though, it is not quite so easy. The regulations require an actual signature for applications, so you have to resort to the good old-fashioned postal service and the process may take a while. You may also need to provide a minimum cash deposit before you can start trading.

Services can vary significantly in the amount of information they provide. Barclays, for instance, is one of the largest, but provides very little by way of research. Charles Schwab is another large firm and provides share prices for free, plus access to the Reuters Investor Premium Service at a cost of £10 a month. E*Trade, which charges an annual fee of £50, offers a considerable amount of free research, including share prices, news, annual reports, company portfolios and charts. Subscribers to Stocktrade also have access to company information and share-price analysis, while DLJ*direct* offers price data, market reports and analysts' reports, plus the facility to create model portfolios.

If your broking service does not offer all the information you would like, it may be possible to find it elsewhere on the Net, either at a cost or for free. Sites run by Bloomberg, Interactive Investor, Market-Eye and the *Financial Times*, for instance, are all sources of free and useful information. Hemmington Scott is another news provider and, together with ProShare, has set up a site for investment clubs. This is specially designed to help clubs track their investment portfolio, gain access to company information and also to help members keep in touch with each other.

But a word of warning: not all information you may find on the Net is accurate. Misleading reports may arise through genuine error or deliberate share ramping. Bulletin boards and chat rooms provide easy opportunities for anonymous comment, so while the ramping is illegal, the regulators are more or less powerless to act. *Caveat emptor* is a very relevant motto for Net dealing.

Other possible problems that can arise are lack of access and failure of the broker to execute an order. If the market, or even a popular share, suddenly starts to fall, sites could be jammed with investors trying to sell and you might be unable even to place your order until too late. In other circumstances, you might place an order but find that, for some reason, it was not carried out, or not as

HOT SHARE TIP:

REAL-TIME ONLINE DEALING FOR AS LITTLE AS £11.99.

Barclays Stockbrokers

Barclays Stockbrokers feature real-time dealing where the share price quoted is the price you get. Commission is charged at a flat rate of 1%, with a minimum charge of £11.99 and a maximum charge of £39.99.

Visit www.barclays-stockbrokers.co.uk

BARCLAYS

BARCLAYS STOCKBROKERS

Stock markets have behaved in an extraordinary way during the past year - in the UK, as elsewhere, a two-tier market developed as investors sold respectable, good value company shares and sought to identify the beneficiaries of the new Internet-related technologies, primarily the TMT stocks - Telecoms, Media and Information Technology. We have since seen a significant correction and a return to 'value' stocks. But is it clear that the new technology sectors remain major growth areas for the future?

The Internet currently represents the most important development in the functioning of the economy, both in the UK and on a global scale. It is estimated that in the US, around 72 million adults are already on the Internet, and worldwide, 350 million Web users are expected by 2003. Even these estimates appear likely to be exceeded as actual figures become confirmed.

We are seeing dynamic changes in the way our businesses are run, brought about primarily by the speed of technological change. Many industries have to change fundamentally the way they operate. Of course, we will still go shopping but not necessarily in the way we have before. Financial services will be more important that ever, but not in the way they used to be. In 1996, for example, independent travel agents handled 80 per cent of US airline reservations, but today their share is down to around 50 per cent as airlines deal directly with travellers via the Internet.

So the Internet is playing an increasingly important part in our daily lives, from shopping to banking, from planning a holiday to pursuing a hobby. Economic growth and the fall in the cost of technology will mean that more people can afford to keep up with the latest developments to access the new services on offer. Investing in the stock market is no different.

The last year has seen a rising number of individuals investing in shares - attracted in part, at least, by some of the new 'high-tech' growth stories. This has coincided with the major UK financial institutions developing and implementing the latest technological advancements in an attempt to make their services more accessible and meet the needs of an increasingly sophisticated client base. A significant aspect of this process has been the increased improvement of communication and delivery channels.

At the forefront of communication delivery is the increased importance of the Internet. This channel of communication is growing in importance on a daily basis. Although much has been written about the capabilities of this new tool, how useful it is for the private investor is still a matter of contention.

Information has long been a stumbling block for private investors; the Internet has become a powerful tool in providing access to financial information. These information sites differ in terms of quality, content and sophistication; some of the most efficient and effective sites include Bloomberg, MoneyWorld, and the

Motley Fool each offering advice, commentary and up to date information. This area of the Internet is also growing at a rapid pace. For some of the sites there is a charge for the most detailed information, and you will have to make a decision as to whether this offers value for money. You may also be able to take advantage of the many bulletin boards or 'communities' as they are known in the States. These sites allow a group of personal investors from a wide geographical location to join together and pool their knowledge. This can provide useful information, although many of the sources can be described as dubious at best.

Perhaps the most exciting addition to the financial package offered by the Internet is the accessibility of the online dealing services. The online dealing services offered by companies vary quite dramatically. The first to launch a full real time dealing service was Barclays Stockbrokers. The service offers the very latest technology in a user-friendly format and registering for the service could not be simpler. In order to set up an account all you have to do is visit the web site at

www.barclays-stockbrokers.co.uk where you can register and deal.

Once you are ready to deal you can click onto the dealing screen which will allow you to obtain quotes on around 2,400 stocks, which are listed on the London Stock Exchange. The price that you are quoted will be the real-time price. This gives you the advantage of being able to see the price that you are dealing at with the knowledge that it is a live price.

When you have received the quote, Barclays Stockbrokers will guarantee that price for 15 seconds, you will then be given the option to execute the deal. When you decide to deal an electronic contract note will automatically be sent to you.

The Internet offers private investors all the trappings of a city dealing room in their own home. Although this is a relatively new phenomenon in Britain, recent data shows that around 250,000 people in the UK already have online dealing accounts. If we look at the United States, however, we see that around 12 million people, or 10 per cent of the adult population, now have online share accounts. If the usual investment pattern continues, online dealing is sure to play a big a role for private investors in Britain as it does for our American cousins.

Barclays Stockbrokers is the Group name for the businesses of:-
Barclays Stockbrokers Limited. A member of the London Stock Exchange and regulated by the Securities and Futures Authority.

Registered in England
Reg. No. 1986151.
Registered Office:
54 Lombard Street, London, EC3P 3AH.
Barclays Bank Trust Company Limited. Regulated by IMRO and the Personal Investment Authority. A member of the Barclays Marketing Group.
Registered in England.
Reg. No. 920880.
Registered Office:
54 Lombard Street, London, EC3P 3AH.

Investors should be aware that the value of investments and income derived from them can fall as well as rise, and past performance is no guide to future performance. The information contained in this article does not constitute a personal recommendation. Dealing in shares and other equity investments may not be suitable for all investors and if you're in any doubt you should contact an independent financial advisor.

fast as you would have liked. Again, the explosion in Internet dealing may affect efficiency.

Finally, beware of becoming hooked! Perhaps the greatest danger of Net trading for the ordinary investor is that it makes share-dealing very easy and 'day trading' becomes something anyone can do. This involves buying and selling in a very short space of time, taking advantage of short-term movements in the prices of volatile shares. It is less likely to feature in Britain the way it has in the USA because of the costs of stamp duty and broking commission, but it is still a matter for concern, because of the de-stabilising effect it could have on the market. US regulators have been looking at ways to curb trading volumes and those in the UK may need to follow their example.

OTHER WAYS TO PLAY THE MARKET

Warrants

Buying shares is not the only means of investing in the equity market. An alternative is to buy warrants, which may be available on the shares of trading companies and investment trusts.

A warrant conveys the right to buy a share in a company at some future time. The price is fixed at the outset and known as the 'exercise price', and the option may be taken up on specified 'exercise dates'. These may be a particular day, or a set of dates, each year up to a final date when the option lapses.

Buying the share would be worth while if the exercise price plus the original cost of the warrant added up to less than the current market price of the share, although if you planned to sell the share for a quick profit, you would also have to take your sale costs into account. If there is no opportunity for profit, the right to buy need not be taken up, but the warrant will lapse without value once the final exercise date has passed.

Like shares, warrants are traded on the Stock Exchange so can be bought as investments in their own right with no intention of taking up the exercise rights. The price of a warrant is generally much lower than the price of its related share, but will move in line with it, giving you exposure to the share's fortunes for a lower outlay.

But, by the same token, warrants are much more volatile, and therefore riskier, than the shares themselves. If, for example, the share price rises by 50p, the warrant price will rise by a similar amount, but the lower starting-point means the proportionate rise will be much greater. Equally, the effect of any fall in the share price will be enhanced. This is called the 'gearing' on the warrant, which is measured as the share price divided by the warrant price.

A high level of gearing offers high potential rewards but also greater risk. The other factors involved are the remaining life-span, up to the final exercise date, and the premium, which is the excess of the exercise price plus the cost of the warrant over the current market price of the share. The longer the life-span, the higher the premium may be, as there is more time for the share price to rise high enough for the warrant to generate a profit.

Assuming the risk is acceptable, warrants can be suitable for higher rate taxpayers as they do not pay any dividends. Hence there will be no liability to income tax; profits will be taxed as capital gains, which can be offset by the annual £7200 exempt allowance.

Options

Futures and options contracts both come under the generic heading of derivatives – a family of financial instruments that allow a number of techniques both to increase and to decrease risk. But while futures are out of the price range of the ordinary investor, options can be very useful. They are traded through the London International Financial Futures and Options Exchange (Liffe) and there are a number of stockbrokers who will deal in them on behalf of private clients. You can go to one of them for just this service alone, even if your main portfolio is handled by a different firm.

The options used by private investors are based on either individual shares or an index. In the former case, a standard contract covers 1000 shares in a particular company, while index options are based on the value of the FTSE 100 Index. In either case, there are two types of option: 'calls' and 'puts'.

Take the case of an equity option. Here, the buyer of a call option has the right to buy a quantity of shares, at a specified price, at any time between now and the expiry date, which can be up to nine months away. A put option confers a similar right to sell shares.

The buyer of the option is not obliged to take it up, but if he chooses to, the seller must honour it; either way, the seller gets to keep the cost of the option, which is known as the 'premium'.

Suppose you expect a share price to rise. Instead of buying the share itself, you can buy a call option, which will cost a lot less. If the price does then rise – above the price specified in the option, plus the premium you paid for it – you have two choices. First, you can exercise the option, then sell the shares for a profit. Alternatively, you can sell the option, for a higher premium than you paid, making a smaller profit but for a much lower outlay than if you had bought the actual shares.

Put options can be used as insurance if you believe that the price of a share you hold will go down. If it does fall, you can exercise the option and thereby limit your losses. If the price rises instead, you can simply let the option lapse and perhaps recoup its cost by selling the shares at a profit.

You can also sell, or write, options, but unless you are prepared to take on a heavy risk you should only do so if you have the shares to sell or the money to buy. Suppose, for example, that you hold shares whose price looks likely to remain rather flat. You can then write a call option against them. If your predictions are correct, the buyer of the option will probably not want to exercise it, so you have gained the premium for no outlay. If the share price rises and the option is exercised, you will lose out on the price rise, but you still keep the premium, so you will be better off than if you had sold the shares at the original market price.

As with equities, dealing services in options can be on an execution-only, discretionary or advisory basis. If you are a beginner, an advisory service is probably best, as it allows you to build up a knowledge of the market. Commission scales tend to start somewhat higher than those on equities, but again, it will vary from firm to firm, so it is worth shopping around. A list of firms that deal in options can be obtained from Liffe.

One other possibility is to bet on the index, which can be done through a couple of organisations. The effect is similar to using an option, but losses are not automatically limited – you have to decide to close the bet if the index is moving against you. Winnings are also tax free, as the betting tax will be paid by the company and included in the quoted price spreads.

OTHER TYPES OF SHARE

As well as ordinary shares there are other types that investors may consider.

Preference shares carry the entitlement to a fixed dividend each year. Most of them are 'cumulative', which means that if the dividend is missed one year, it has to be made up later if the company resumes dividends on its ordinary shares. Preference shares also take priority over ordinary shares if the company is wound up. Currently, with interest rates at low levels, the income from preference shares looks attractive but, as with any shares, the capital value is not guaranteed.

Convertible stocks are securities that carry a fixed dividend plus the option to convert them into ordinary stock, at a set price, at some fixed time in the future. They also rank ahead of ordinary shares in the event of liquidation. Again, the yields look attractive when interest rates are low, and there is also the chance of making a profit from the conversion.

Debentures are loans to a company that are secured on a specific asset, such as property. The yield is fixed and there is a stated redemption date when the loan will be repaid.

STOCK MARKET TERMS

Most readers will no doubt have come across stock market jargon, at least to some extent, but this is a reminder of the more common terms.

Bear: someone who believes the market will fall
Blue chip: companies regarded as high quality and the safest – said to be named after the highest value chip in poker
Bull: someone who believes the market will rise
Nominee account: a facility whereby shares are held on behalf of an investor in a company's name
Partly-paid: an issue of shares on which only part of the price is paid up-front
Rights issue: the offer of new shares in a company to existing shareholders at a price below the current market price

Scrip issue: a free issue of shares to existing shareholders
Stag: someone who buys a new issue in the hope of selling immediately for a quick profit

WHERE TO FIND OUT MORE

A directory of private client stockbrokers, listing their services, can be obtained from the Association of Private Client Investment Managers and Stockbrokers, 112 Middlesex Street, London E1 7HY; tel 020 7247 7080.

A free information pack and a list of brokers dealing in traded options can be obtained from Liffe, Cannon Bridge, London EC4R 3XX; tel 020 7623 0444.

Other useful telephone numbers are:

The Stock Exchange: 020 7797 1000
The Securities and Futures Authority: 020 7378 9000
ProShare: 020 7600 0984

6 Unit Trusts and Offshore Funds (1)

Unit trusts, offshore funds, investment trusts and life assurance products all have a common characteristic: they pool investors' money into a large fund, so that smaller investors can participate in a broad spread of assets that they could never achieve by their own means. The concept was set out in the prospectus of the very first investment trust to be launched, in 1868, and it is still quoted by that trust in its literature today: 'We intend to provide the investor of moderate means with the same advantages as large capitalists in diminishing the risks ... by spreading investment over a number of stocks.'

The primary advantage of collective investments, as they are known, is this reduction of risk. If you hold only one share and it crashes, you lose everything, but if you have a stake in a portfolio, one failure will be cushioned by other successes. There are also other plus points which will emerge over the next few chapters, such as professional investment management, ready access to overseas markets and certain tax benefits – particularly through personal equity plans, which are discussed in Chapter 9.

Unit trust investments can start from as little as £500 for a lump sum and there is no set maximum. As mentioned in the last chapter, many people would consider £25,000 to be the working minimum for a direct investment into the stock market, but investors with up to £100,000 available may find that the range and scope of collective investments will amply satisfy their require-ments. Larger investors may also find them useful to add an overseas content to their holdings, even where they are investing directly in UK equities.

The growth in the unit trust industry over the last decade has been substantial. In 1984 there were 102 companies, running 687 trusts, which had a total value of £11.7 billion. At the end of 1999, there were 152 companies, operating 1739 trusts, with a total value of funds under management of £183 billion. These trusts span a huge variety of geographical and industrial specialisations, from broad-based UK General funds to Asian Smaller Markets or International Technology. Investment choice is examined in the next chapter.

The size of companies, and the number of trusts they run, vary considerably: the top 10 alone account for over £100 billion of funds under management and the top 20 for almost £146 billion, as shown in Table 6.1. Most companies are members of the Association of Unit Trusts and Investment Funds, which can supply a range of information and contact details.

Table 6.1   *Top 20 unit trust groups by funds under management*

Group	Funds under management (£m)
Schroder	14,891.2
Fidelity	14,377.0
M&G	11,385.9
Threadneedle	10,236.5
Perpetual	9557.1
Gartmore	9115.6
Mercury	8592.4
Standard Life	7860.0
Lloyds TSB	7380.4
Barclays	7055.1
Friends Provident	5917.5
Save & Prosper	5431.6
Aberdeen	5078.9
Invesco	4862.7
Legal & General	4852.2
Jupiter	4395.1
Baring	4015.3
Equitable	3677.6
Hill Samuel	3630.8
Deutsche	3628.8

Source: Association of Unit Trusts and Investment Funds, January 2000

UNIT TRUST REGULATIONS

A unit trust is subject to a trust deed, which lays down the terms under which it operates; for example, where and how it will invest, the calculation of unit prices and the charges it may levy. The money in the fund is held on behalf of investors by trustees, generally a bank or insurance company, who are responsible for ensuring that the managers conform to the rules laid down in the trust deed.

The regulation and authorisation of unit trusts is in the hands of the Securities and Investments Board, which lays down rules on what investments are available to a unit trust. The bulk of the portfolio will normally be invested in quoted shares or gilts, but up to 10 per cent may be in unquoted securities, including up to 5 per cent in other unit trusts, and up to 5 per cent may be invested in warrants. Trusts may also make use of traded options and futures contracts for the purposes of efficient fund management, but these must be covered by holdings of cash or near cash, such as government securities.

To ensure that a trust preserves an adequate spread of risk – which, after all, is a prime objective – not more than 5 per cent of the portfolio can normally be held in the shares of any one company. However, provided the total of 5 per cent plus holdings does not itself exceed 40 per cent of the portfolio, an individual holding may go up to 10 per cent. This means that if one share suddenly shoots up in value, it will not have to be immediately sold. In practice, a trust would normally have upwards of 40 different holdings, depending on its size, so it is likely to be well within the limits.

The other main rule is that a trust cannot hold more than 10 per cent of any one company's issued share capital. This is to ensure that a trust does not build up a controlling stake in a company, which could undermine its basic objectives.

CHARGES

There are two types of charge levied by unit trust managers: the initial charge and the annual charge. The level of these will be specified in the trust deed and the managers cannot raise the charges above that level without getting permission from the unit holders. For this reason, the levels stipulated are sometimes higher than the charges that are actually applied; this gives the managers the flexibility to make an increase at a future date without the bother of seeking permission.

In recent years there has been a tendency for charges to rise, so trusts that have been in existence for many years may carry lower charges than those more recently launched, unless the managers have sought permission for an increase. These days, the typical initial charge is between 5 and 6 per cent. Some gilt trusts have a lower charge, around 3 per cent, and cash trusts and index trackers also have a very small or zero charge, while the specialist overseas trusts tend to carry the highest fees.

Out of this initial charge, the managers pay commission to inter-mediaries who sell the trusts for them. The usual amount of commission is 3 per cent, with the rest of the charge going towards the managers' costs, such as advertising. But if you buy direct from the managers rather than through an intermediary, the 3 per cent allowed for commission will still be charged and simply kept by the managers. Sometimes, however, the managers may make a special discount offer. Introductory discounts, of 1 per cent or possibly more for large investments, are quite common during the launch period of new trusts.

The annual charge is commonly between 1 and 2 per cent, though again cash trusts and trackers generally have a lower charge, around 0.5 per cent, while specialist trusts are likely to be at the top end of the scale.

In most cases, the annual fee is taken out of the trust's income, but some trusts now charge it to the capital account instead. This is done to maximise the income that can be paid out, but investors should bear in mind that it will reduce the capital growth from the trust and may ultimately lead to a lower total return. Opponents of the idea have also argued that it is not tax effective: investors stand to receive relatively higher income and lower capital gains, whereas most will be liable to tax on the former and not the latter.

Another point to bear in mind is that the quoted annual management fee may not tell the whole story, as trusts also have to pay out for administration, legal and audit fees. In recent research, the fund considered to be the most expensive had a total expense ratio of over 3.5 per cent, although its annual management fee was only 1.5 per cent. Smaller funds are likely to be the most affected, as fixed costs will have a greater proportional impact.

While it may seem best to go for trusts with the lowest charges, performance can be a more important factor in determining the investment return. Obviously, the higher the charges, the better the performance needs to be for the same result, but over longer periods, differences in performance – as the next chapter will show – can be more than large enough to wipe out the effects of a higher charge.

Normally you should think of holding on to unit trusts for at least a medium-term period, say three to five years. If you buy and sell more frequently, the initial charge on each purchase could start to eat into your returns. However, if you do plan to be an active investor, this effect can be lessened by sticking with one management group. Most managers offer a discount on switches between their own trusts, as an incentive to investors to keep their money within the group. The amount varies from 1 per cent to as much as 4 per cent, which means switching can be done at very little cost.

BID AND OFFER

If you look at unit trust prices in the newspaper you will see that there are usually two quoted, the 'offer' price and the 'bid' price. The offer is what you pay to buy units, while the bid is what you get when you sell. The difference between them is usually greater than the quoted initial charge of 5 to 6 per cent, because the calculations are based on complex rules laid down by the regulatory authorities.

To start with, a trust must have a creation price and a cancellation price. The creation price is based on the value of the shares in the trust's portfolio (valued at their offer price, which is the price at which they could be bought on the market), plus stockbroker's commission and stamp duty. To that is added any cash held by the trust plus accumulated income from dividends and interest payments, and the whole lot is then divided by the total number of units in existence.

The cancellation price is almost a mirror image, being the value of the shares held in the portfolio at their bid price, less the stockbroker's commission, plus cash and accumulated income, again divided by the total number of units.

The full offer price that the managers can charge when selling units then becomes the creation price plus the initial charge. The full bid price, which is the minimum at which the managers can buy back units, is equal to the cancellation price.

The difference between these two is called the full spread and can be as much as 10 or 11 per cent. In practice, of course, few people would be prepared to buy an investment that would immediately drop 11 per cent in value, so the managers normally quote prices somewhere between the two extremes. The 'dealing' spread, which is the difference between the two quoted prices, is typically around 6 or 7 per cent. An illustration of the various prices is shown in Table 6.2.

When a trust is in demand, with new money coming in, the managers are likely to be buying more shares for the portfolio, so the quoted prices will move towards the top end of the range to reflect the costs of this. In this case the trust is said to be on an 'offer basis'.

Correspondingly, when more people are selling the trust than buying it, the managers may need to sell shares to meet the redemptions. The prices will then move towards the bottom end of the range and the trust is said to be on a 'bid basis'.

These price movements within the permitted range stem from the aim to be fair to all investors, particularly those who continue to hold units. For example, if sellers were given too high a price, it would dilute the value of the trust for the remaining unit holders.

As long as you buy and sell on roughly the same basis, it makes little difference where the prices are within the range. But if you buy when the trust is on an offer basis and sell when it is on a bid basis, you will effectively suffer the full spread.

Generally, managers will not move abruptly from one to the other, but will try to anticipate the trend of demand – whether the market is rising or falling – and move gradually over several days. But a very large order can force a sharper movement, so it is possible for the price to move against you quite suddenly.

Table 6.2 *Price calculations*

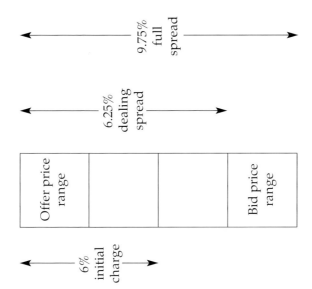

	Maximum offer price	106.00p		
	= creation price + initial charge			6% initial charge
	Minimum offer price	102.67p		6.25% dealing spread / 9.75% full spread
	= minimum bid price + dealing spread		Offer price range	
	Creation price	100.00p		
	= offer value of shares + commission + stamp duty + cash + accumulated income, divided by number of units in issue			
	Maximum bid price	99.37p		
	= maximum offer price − dealing spread		Bid price range	
	Minimum bid price/cancellation price	96.25p		
	= bid value of shares − commission + cash + accumulated income, divided by number of units in issue			

Maximum offer price — 106.00p
= creation price + initial charge

Minimum offer price — 102.67p
= minimum bid price + dealing spread

Creation price — 100.00p
= offer value of shares + commission + stamp duty + cash + accumulated income, divided by number of units in issue

Maximum bid price — 99.37p
= maximum offer price − dealing spread

Minimum bid price/cancellation price — 96.25p
= bid value of shares − commission + cash + accumulated income, divided by number of units in issue

6% initial charge

6.25% dealing spread

9.75% full spread

Offer price range

Bid price range

After several years of discussion and proposals, a single pricing system for unit trusts is finally coming about and may eventually become compulsory. This will harmonise with the system for open-ended investment companies (OEICs), which several groups now offer in place of unit trusts. The idea is that there is just one price quoted for buying and selling; a charge *is* still made, but is shown separately, so should be clearer. A single price is one prerequisite for Individual Savings Accounts (ISAs) to achieve the 'Cat' standard, which is explained in Chapter 9.

DIFFERENT TYPES OF UNIT

Unit trusts may offer either or both of two types of unit: accumulation and distribution. Accumulation units are designed to reinvest any income earned by the trust with a corresponding increase in the unit price. Distribution, or income, units instead pay out the income, usually twice a year, although some pay quarterly or annually.

The difference is simply a matter of convenience. Trusts that have the sole aim of producing capital growth, and those that invest in certain overseas markets, have a very low yield – in the case of Japan, it may be virtually zero. To pay out to every unit holder twice a year could cost more than the income itself, so it is easier to accumulate it into the fund. The managers will, however, send out information on the income that has been accumulated as investors will have to declare it for tax.

Distribution units are used by trusts that are designed for income or a combination of income and growth. Payments are made net of lower rate tax. Some trusts offer to reinvest the income in further units, but this will usually mean paying the initial charge each time. If you do not want the income, and there is a choice available, accumulation units should prove more cost-effective.

When you buy distribution units in a trust, the price will include an allowance for any income that has accrued since the last payment date. So when you receive the next distribution, part of it will represent the income earned since you invested, while the rest is in effect a return of the extra amount you paid for the units. For tax purposes, this portion – known as an 'equalisation payment' – counts as capital; it is not liable for income tax, but will be deducted from the purchase price in calculating any capital gains tax liability.

FUNDS OF FUNDS

A few years ago, a new type of unit trust was introduced, referred to as a 'fund of funds'. This is a kind of 'super trust' which invests across the range of the group's other trusts and thereby acts as a managed fund.

Initially, the concept attracted a fair degree of scepticism but now a third or so of the management groups offer such a trust. The advantage claimed is that it offers the equivalent of an investment management service for relatively small sums. For smaller investors, highly specialised trusts can be too risky, as performance is very volatile and timing – when to buy and sell – is crucial. Through the fund of funds, the investor can obtain a stake in these specialist trusts at lower risk, because the portfolio is spread over a range of trusts and the manager makes the decisions on his behalf.

One drawback is that the fund of funds is limited by the other trusts run by the group. Obviously, it would not be worth while unless the range of trusts it can invest in is fairly broad. But even then it may not be possible to get the best mix, because the individual trusts have their own objectives which may not fit with the overview of the fund of funds. For example, the investment strategy of the Japan trust, which is focused solely on that market, might not be the best approach for the Japanese portion of the fund of funds, which takes a global view. And, of course, if the Japan trust happens to be performing badly, the fund of funds manager has the difficult choice of whether to invest in a poor fund or not to be in Japan at all.

So far, the performance of the funds of funds does not suggest that they have any particular advantage over ordinary international trusts, which also take a global view and are not limited in their investment choices.

CASH TRUSTS

Cash, or money market, trusts are a more recent innovation, born out of uncertain stock market conditions. Unlike the normal run of unit trusts, cash trusts do not involve any risk to your capital, because they invest in fixed capital instruments. In most cases they carry no initial charge and the annual charge is generally only 0.5 per cent.

One aim is to provide a temporary refuge for investors who want to sell holdings in equity trusts when the stock market is falling. The managers benefit because the money stays with the group, while investors may also benefit because they will qualify for any switching discount the group offers if they later go back into an equity trust.

Cash trusts can also provide a higher income than bank or building society deposit accounts. By pooling investors' money into one large fund, the trust can secure top rates of interest on the money market, while the minimum individual investment is generally only £1000 or less. Cash unit trusts were not eligible for inclusion in a personal equity plan, but the new Individual Savings Accounts (ISAs), which began in April 1999, can include a cash element, currently £3000. Several unit trust groups are offering cash trusts in this category, either as part of a 'maxi' ISA or for a 'mini' cash plan. For more information on ISAs, see Chapter 9.

A few cash trusts provide a cheque-book facility for larger investments, so that you can have instant access to your money. Otherwise, if you want to sell, managers are obliged to issue a cheque within 24 hours of receiving the necessary documentation.

INDEX-TRACKING TRUSTS

While most trusts are actively managed, index-tracking trusts – 'trackers' – take a passive line. The aim is to track the movement in one or another stock market index: there are index trusts based on the UK, the US, Europe, Japan, South East Asia and worldwide. One way of doing this is to buy holdings in every stock that is included in the index, but for the USA, for example, this would be impossible, as there are just too many. Instead, the trust will aim for a representative sample in appropriate portions. Generally, trusts do not expect to be spot on every time, but will set a target margin of error.

Not surprisingly, the concept has both its supporters and its critics. On the downside, it does not seem much of an achievement simply to match the index, especially as investors will do slightly worse than that when charges are taken into account. It is also worth remembering that a tracker trust will follow the index downwards as well as upwards, while traditional trusts have the option to go partly into cash to avoid the worst of a fall.

A further point to note is that, among UK funds, some track the All-Share Index and some the FTSE 100. This can make a significant difference, as the FTSE 100 is, by definition, made up only of large companies while the All-Share includes medium-sized and smaller ones. Over different time-periods, one or other will generally come to the fore, depending on which sectors of the market have been performing best.

But both have recently faced problems from large-scale company mergers, in particular that of Vodafone and Mannesmann. The combined company makes up over 11 per cent of the All-Share Index and over 14 per cent of the FTSE 100, yet unit trust rules limit any single holding to a maximum of 10 per cent of the portfolio. So trusts cannot hold shares in this company directly in proportion to its weight within either index; yet this is just what a tracker aims to do.

One solution that several trusts have adopted is to buy a special debenture, which tracks the company's share price and also pays interest. This gives them equivalent exposure to the company, without directly owning its shares. Another possibility is that the rules could be changed. The EU is looking at raising the 10 per cent limit to 20 per cent or even as high as 35 per cent.

But this might create more of a problem than a solution. The advantage of unit trusts lies in their diversification, which helps to spread the risk. Already three large mergers – Vodafone/ Mannesmann, BP/Amoco and Glaxo Wellcome/SmithKline Beecham – account for nearly 30 per cent of the FTSE 100 Index. A change in the rules and a few more mega-mergers could mean tracker funds would be almost entirely made up of half a dozen companies, therefore offering very little diversification and changing the risk profile considerably.

Another possible solution lies in the launch of capped indices to be introduced by FTSE International. To be called the FTSE Cap 100 and FTSE Cap All-Share, these will cap the weighting of any company at 10 per cent and will be reviewed and rebalanced monthly. So fund managers can safely track these indices and be sure not to breach the 10 per cent limit. However, some managers argue that this defeats the objective of shadowing an index, as it does not reflect the true market position.

The argument is likely to rage as keenly as the argument over trackers themselves – whether they are good for investors or not. Supporters point out that many trusts consistently underperform their relevant index; over longer periods, the average performance of funds in any one sector may well be below the index for that market. So while a tracker is never likely to be top of its sector in the performance tables, it is never likely to be bottom either. Trackers can also operate on low charges and have been prominent in recent price competition, particularly with newcomers to the unit trust market.

There is one fund at the time of writing that aims to marry the positive elements of both sides. It is based on the premise that while identifying winners may be difficult, identifying losers is easier. A normal tracker automatically includes all the stocks in the index, for better or worse, but this fund aims to weed out those the manager thinks are definitely for the worse. It is based on the FTSE 100 and the intention is that the 'active passive' approach will allow it at least to match the index, net of its charges, and ideally to beat it.

A more radical proposal was put forward in a report prepared for the Financial Services Authority (FSA) which claimed that active management 'destroys value for investors' by charging more than trackers for generally worse results. The author, an American economist on secondment from the US Securities and Exchange Commission, suggested a new type of fund he called Ariadne, after the character in Greek mythology who led the way out of a maze. This would be largely a tracker, but with up to 10 per cent of its portfolio actively managed, and would guarantee a return not more than 1 per cent below the All-Share Index. If a fund under-performed this mark it would have to compensate investors, using either reserves or an insurance policy.

Not surprisingly, the report created a furore in the investment industry. In particular, critics of the idea asked where the reserves would come from. A tracker, by definition, will not outperform its index, so any reserves could only come from the actively managed portion – but if active management can produce outperformance, it defeats the argument for having an Ariadne fund in the first place. Another issue is cost: UK funds undoubtedly have higher charges than their US counterparts, but the latter are substantially larger and benefit from economies of scale.

Whatever the rights and wrongs of the arguments, trackers received something of an endorsement from the 'Cat' standard that has been introduced with ISAs. Cat stands for cost, access and terms and the standard applies to plans that meet certain criteria in these three respects.

Originally it was proposed that only tracker funds would qualify for the Cat mark for equity ISAs. After representations from both unit trust and investment trust groups, this was withdrawn and any fund that meets the criteria may qualify. However, the cost strictures – no initial charge and a maximum annual charge of 1 per cent – are too stringent for most non-tracking funds, as active management is usually more expensive to administer than passively tracking an index. Hence few groups are offering an actively managed equity ISA that qualifies for the Cat mark. Perhaps because of this, Cat-marked funds have so far had less impact on the market than their supporters expected.

A new form of tracker investment has recently made its appearance in the UK, having already proved popular in the US. Known as a Train – from tradable index security – it comprises a single share in the index itself. The advantage of this is that it is easy to get in and out of the market quickly, which is not the case for a standard tracker holding a whole portfolio of shares. Costs should also be lower. The one fund that has so far been launched is registered in Luxembourg because the rules for retail funds in the UK stipulate a minimum of 20 stocks and Trains technically hold only one. But it is expected that ways may soon be found to introduce UK-based funds.

Another innovation is something called an exchange-traded fund. Again, the idea has been imported from the USA, where several such funds are already up and running. The funds are like a cross between unit trusts and investment trusts: they issue shares, rather than units, and the share price can fluctuate at all times but, like unit trusts, they are 'open-ended', meaning that they can create or cancel shares according to demand. The first one launched, based in Dublin, will track the FTSE 100 Index and up to a dozen more are planned for other major world stockmarket indices.

FUTURES AND OPTIONS TRUSTS

These are a relatively recent development in the unit trust world. The use of futures and options contracts had previously been regarded as potentially too risky for unit trusts – some people felt that if high-risk trusts were allowed, it would affect the general reputation unit trusts had of being relatively safe and thereby discourage investors altogether.

One type uses futures contracts to match the performance of an index. Buying futures is cheaper than buying each individual share, so most of the trust's money can be kept in cash, earning interest, which is paid out as income distributions. The trust tracks only the capital value of the index, ignoring share dividends, but with the interest, the total return should be roughly equivalent.

These are called 'bull' funds and are designed for investors who think the market will rise. There are also 'bear' funds, designed for those who think it will fall, which produce the exact opposite of the index movement: when it falls, the trust price rises by an equivalent amount.

Geared futures and options trusts involve higher risk with the potential for greater reward. For example, a 'two times geared' trust would give double exposure: if the index rises by 10 per cent, the trust price will rise by 20 per cent, but falls will also be doubled. However, as with any unit trust, your loss is limited to your initial investment.

A third type uses futures and options in a hedging role to reduce risk. The effect is that when the market is falling, the value of the fund should fall by less than the index, so that losses are cut, while in a flat market returns should be enhanced. In rising markets, however, the fund may underperform the index, so some growth potential may be sacrificed in return for the protection against a fall.

The mechanics of futures and options contracts are described more fully in Chapter 5.

WARRANT TRUSTS

Spring 1994 saw the launch of the first unit trust to invest in warrants. These may be issued by trading companies, investment trusts and offshore companies and it is intended that the unit trust will hold a mix of all three.

The mechanics of warrants are explained in Chapter 5. The main point to bear in mind is that the price of a warrant is generally much less than that of its related share, but price movements of the two are broadly in line. This means that the proportionate movement in the warrant price will be much greater: if the share price rises, the gain on the warrant can be several times as much, but losses will be similarly magnified.

Because of this volatility, the unit trust should be considered a relatively high-risk investment, although the risk is tempered to some extent by the spread of holdings and the facility to switch heavily into cash if the market is unattractive.

GUARANTEED AND PROTECTED TRUSTS

There is no doubt that, historically, the stock market has provided much better returns than either cash or fixed interest securities. But the short-term volatility of equities puts many people off. Guaranteed and protected trusts attempt to capture most of the upside of equities while limiting, or even eliminating, any losses.

Guaranteed funds have a fixed investment period, at the end of which you are guaranteed your original money back plus a proportion of any growth in the relevant index or indices. The guarantee may be provided outside the fund, for example through a form of insurance policy, for which you will pay a one-off fee at the outset. You may take your money out before the end of the fixed period, but in that case the guarantee is lost and you will simply get back whatever is the current value of your holding. Hence to get the full benefit you must be prepared to lock up your money for the full time.

Protected funds have no fixed term but lock in gains and protect against loss on a rolling quarterly basis. This has the advantage of flexibility, but the returns may be limited. For example, one type uses 'put' options to guarantee that investors will never lose more than 5 per cent of their initial investment over a given period. At the outset it sets a minimum selling price for units that depends on whether the stock market has gone up or down. If the unit price has risen by 10 per cent or more over the period, the minimum price will be set at 5 per cent below the current unit value, locking in some of the gains that have been made. If, on the other hand, the market has fallen, the selling price will be set at 95 per cent of the previous minimum.

Unlike the guaranteed funds, investors can sell their holdings at any time and still take advantage of the minimum price. However, you need to remember that if a fund offers 95 per cent protection, that protection is for a set period of time, such as a quarter or a year. If the market undergoes a long fall, you could lose up to 5 per cent in several successive periods. In other words, while it may be only 5 per cent of your money that is at risk in any one period, over time you could lose substantially more.

The other point to remember about all protection and guarantees is that they come at a cost: the part of your money that is being used to provide the protection is not earning you a return. Moreover, this cost is likely to be highest when you need it most. The more volatile the stock market, the more expensive it is to buy the put options for protection or the insurance to back a guarantee. In fact, some funds are simply not open to new investors at these times, because the cost would be too great. Conversely, this means that when protection is available at a reasonable cost, it may be when you least need it because the market is stable and rising.

One fund, for instance, uses around 14 per cent of the sum invested to buy options, so in a rising market you could lose out on a significant amount of growth. The guarantee is 100 per cent of your money back if you withdraw it after three, five or seven years – but you could lose up to 15 per cent if you withdraw at any other time.

With this fund, the guarantee is based only on your original investment, so if the market rises strongly for a few years the guarantee will effectively become worthless – but you would still be paying for it, in terms of not getting the full benefit of the market increase.

If market volatility is likely to give you sleepless nights, then protected trusts could be attractive. But it is important to make sure you understand exactly what is being guaranteed and what you are paying for, as well as any limits on access to your money.

UNIT TRUSTS AND TAX

In the 1993 Budget, the basic rate of income tax on dividends was reduced from 25 per cent to 20 per cent. Dividends from a unit trust were paid or reinvested net of this 20 per cent tax and the investor received a tax credit for the amount paid. Basic and lower rate taxpayers had no further income tax liability, while higher rate taxpayers had to pay an additional 20 per cent and non-taxpayers could reclaim the 20 per cent paid.

Since April 1999, however, the tax credit has been halved to 10 per cent. The calculation of tax has changed, so that taxpayers are left in the same position as before: higher rate taxpayers having to pay another 20 per cent and the rest paying nothing more. But non-taxpayers no longer have any reclaim facility, meaning their income is reduced.

The new rules for capital gains tax, outlined in Chapter 1, may also affect unit trust investors. Trusts themselves have no liability on their dealings, but investors may be liable on gains made when they sell. These can be offset using the annual exempt allowance, which is £7200 for the 2000/01 tax year. Gains will also be eligible for the taper relief that has replaced indexation – and this is where a problem could arise.

Taper relief starts to apply when you have held an investment for three complete years, building up to a maximum after 10 years. So the longer you hold your investments, the less likely you are to be liable for tax. But if you reinvest dividends, by buying further units, each new purchase will have its own timescale for taper relief. Over 10 years, in a trust with typical half-yearly distributions of income, you would have effectively made 21 purchases, including your original investment. Sorting out any tax liability could become extremely complicated.

The way round this is to buy accumulation units, which automatically roll up dividends and reflect the value in their price. There are no actual new purchases of units, so taper relief will simply be based on the initial purchase. Unfortunately, accumulation units have rather gone out of fashion and are no longer available on many trusts, so unit trust groups may need to rethink this to avoid a nightmare for their investors.

SPECIAL FACILITIES FOR THE INVESTOR

Share exchange schemes

Unit trust groups run various schemes designed to encourage investors to buy their units. Most groups offer 'share exchange' schemes for people who want to sell direct holdings in shares to invest in unit trusts instead. Such schemes have become increasingly popular for privatisation issues.

There will always be a cost advantage to the investor. Occasionally the managers may want to keep your shares for their own trusts, in which case they may pay you the offer price for the shares, or a mid-market price, rather than the bid price less selling expenses which you would receive if you sold them privately. Otherwise, you will be paid the bid price but the managers will either bear the sale costs themselves or offer a discount.

Regular savings schemes

As well as accepting lump sums, many unit trust groups offer regular savings schemes, starting from a minimum of around £50 a month. As a rule there are no penalties for stopping or taking money out, and lump sums can also be added in at any time. Income would not normally be paid out, as the administration would be too complex, so trusts that offer accumulation units are preferable.

Even if you have a lump sum to invest, it can be better to 'drip feed' it into a trust over a period rather than put it all in at once.

Table 6.3 *Pound-cost averaging*

Month of purchase	Unit price	Number of units bought for £50
1	100p	50
2	80p	63
3	125p	40
4	90p	56
5	85p	59
6	110p	45
Average price	98.3p	313 units bought for £300; average price paid: 95.8p

This is due to a phenomenon known as pound-cost averaging. The argument is fairly straightforward: if you invest a bit at a time, you will benefit from times when the price falls because the same amount of money will buy more units. With a fluctuating price, the average cost of units over a period will be less than their average price. On the other hand, if you buy all at one go, the price could be at a peak or a trough, so timing becomes all-important – and few people can be confident of getting it right.

Table 6.3 gives an example of the mechanics of pound-cost averaging, using large price swings to clarify the effect.

Schemes for a regular income

Only a small number of trusts pay a monthly income, but many groups now offer monthly income portfolio schemes. Most trusts pay out dividends two or four times a year, so by packaging together three or six trusts with different distribution dates, a scheme can produce monthly payments.

The trusts in a package may not all pay out on the same day of every month and, more particularly, are not likely to pay the same amount. A refinement is to incorporate a deposit account in the scheme which will collect all the dividends and then pay out level amounts each month.

There are two drawbacks to packaged schemes offered by unit trust groups. First, you are restricted to the trusts of that group, which may not all perform well. Second, the trusts included in the package may not be ideal for your requirements. Several schemes include a gilt or fixed-interest trust, which can boost the income level at the outset but provides little opportunity for capital growth and thereby rising income over time.

The alternative is to put together your own package, choosing the type of trusts you want from different groups. Several professional advisers run schemes of this type or can assemble one to match your particular needs. In some cases you can choose the level of income you want, but you need to remember that if you choose a level higher than the trusts are actually paying out, units would have to be cashed in to make up the difference. Over time this would make progressive inroads into your capital, so you would do better to settle for a lower income to start with and hope capital growth will boost it.

KEEPING TRACK OF YOUR INVESTMENT

Generally, managers revalue at least once a day and prices are quoted in both the *Financial Times* and *The Daily Telegraph*. However, most groups now deal on a 'forward pricing' basis, which means that the deal is carried out at the price set by the next valuation. The remainder use 'historic pricing', which means the price used is that of the most recent valuation, but they must deal at a forward price if it is requested and will also move to forward pricing in certain circumstances, for example if there is a large movement in the market.

So the prices published in newspapers are not necessarily what you will be quoted if you sell that day, but unless a very large deal has just gone through, there is unlikely to be a substantial difference from one valuation to the next. The *Financial Times* indicates whether dealing is on a forward or historic basis, and also shows the cancellation price, so you can see whether a trust is on a bid or offer basis.

Another source of information is the manager's report on a trust, which is usually sent out to unit holders twice a year. Among other things, this will list details of the trust's holdings and any changes made since the previous report; it will also give a commentary on performance and how this ties in with the markets in which the trust invests. Although the information will be somewhat out of date by the time you receive it, it does provide a guide to the general strategy being followed.

How to invest

Investments can be made through an intermediary, such as a bank, stockbroker or financial adviser, or you can deal directly with the unit trust group by telephone or post. Advertisements in the national press may also carry a coupon form for buying units.

Initially, you will receive a contract note, which gives details of the amount invested, the price and the number of units bought, and subsequently you will be sent the certificate. To sell, you can simply send the certificate to the group and a cheque will be issued within a few days.

If you know what trusts you want to invest in, you could consider a so-called 'discount broker'. There are now a number of these that deal in unit trusts, generally advertising their services in the financial pages of the national press such as *The Daily Telegraph.* They offer an execution-only service – they do not give any advice – but will rebate the initial commission, which means that in effect you pay a reduced initial charge. You will, however, pay the same annual management charge, as these brokers make their money from annual renewal commission.

Some professional advisers provide unit trust portfolio management services, usually for a minimum sum of £10,000 or so. These are looked at in Chapter 7.

Buying on the Internet

It is now possible to buy and sell most unit trusts over the Internet. All the large unit trust groups – and many smaller ones – have their own Web sites and so do a number of independent financial advisers and discount brokers.

A recent development is the so-called 'fund supermarket'. Barclays launched a telephone-based version last year, while Prudential's Egg operation has a Net-based service and is due to be followed online by Fidelity, Charles Schwab and Virgin Direct. Like its high street counterparts, the fund supermarket offers products – such as unit trusts, open-ended investment companies (OEICs) and Individual Savings Accounts (ISAs) – from a number of different companies. The idea is that instead of having to visit half a dozen separate company sites or make several phone calls, you can buy a whole portfolio of investments in one place.

The supermarket is also designed to be cheaper, with reduced initial charges – perhaps around 3 per cent instead of 5 or 6 per cent. In addition, there are ancillary services provided, such as a newsline and the facility to check the value of your portfolio. But there is no advice given, so in that respect the service is similar to what you get from a discount broker.

OFFSHORE FUNDS

'Offshore' is a slightly misleading term, conjuring up visions of exotic islands where the very rich go to escape the rigours of taxation. Offshore funds can, indeed, be based in places such as Bermuda and the Cayman Islands, but the more prosaic definition is simply a location that is outside the UK mainland. The traditional bases for funds that might attract UK investors are Jersey, Guernsey and the Isle of Man, but the development of EU regulations has made Luxembourg a popular choice – the Channel Islands and the Isle of Man are outside the European Union (EU) – and more recently Dublin has established an offshore centre.

Offshore funds are collective investments but can take various forms; they may be open-ended, like unit trusts, or closed-ended, like investment trusts. The exact structure and legal framework will depend on where they are based.

Regulation

Moves to allow cross-border dealing in collective investments within the EU have resulted in an array of rules and jargon. For a start, European funds are often referred to by the French acronyms

'SICAV' and 'SICAF'. The former are open-ended funds, which means the size is unrestricted and will increase or decrease according to demand and supply; the latter are closed-ended, which means they have a fixed amount of capital.

Open-ended funds can apply for the status of UCITS (Undertakings for Collective Investment in Transferable Securities), which is granted by the regulatory authority in the country of origin. The main UCITS rules are drafted by the EU, but stipulations on how and where a fund may invest come under local regulations and may vary from country to country. Once a fund has UCITS status, it can be freely marketed throughout member states, subject to marketing rules laid down by each individual country.

The *Financial Times* lists offshore funds as being one of three types: SIB recognised, Regulated and Other. The first category refers to funds that have been approved by the Financial Services Authority (FSA), which means that they may be freely marketed in the UK, in the same way as unit trusts. Funds with UCITS status get this approval more or less automatically.

Funds based outside the EU can also apply for FSA recognition if their country of origin has 'designated territory' status. This is granted by the FSA to countries where the local regulations and compensation scheme arrangements are deemed to be of similar standard to those applying in the UK. From the investor's point of view, if a fund is FSA recognised, it is not too important where it is based, as it will be subject to much the same level of regulation as UK funds.

Regulated funds are those that are authorised under local regulations but have not obtained FSA recognition. This does not necessarily mean that they are less well regulated; it may simply be that the managers are not looking to attract UK investors or, in the case of European funds, that they wish to invest outside the limits of the UCITS rules. These funds can still be sold to UK investors, but only through private placements; they cannot use direct advertising or mailing.

Some countries allow funds to be set up and operated without coming under regulation. These are listed in the *Financial Times* under the heading of 'Other Offshore Funds' and are often aimed at institutional rather than private investors.

Taxation

For a UK investor, offshore funds are subject to one of two tax regimes. The fund may have 'distributor' status, in which case it must pay out at least 85 per cent of its income, which is paid gross but is subject to tax at the investor's normal rate. Any capital gains made on selling out of the fund will be liable to capital gains tax, subject to the usual annual exempt allowance.

Alternatively, the fund may be of the 'accumulator' type, which means all income is rolled up within the fund. No income tax is payable while you are invested, but when you come to sell, all gains are liable to income tax, whether they derive from income or capital growth.

Which of the two is preferable depends on your circumstances. If you are a higher rate taxpayer now, but expect to drop down to basic rate in future, then with an accumulator fund you can defer the tax bill to that point. Alternatively, if you are looking for capital growth, a distributor fund would mean a small tax bill each year, but the bulk of the return would be in capital gains, against which you have the annual tax-exempt allowance (£7200 for the 2000/01 tax year).

The problem with distributor status is that it is only granted for a year at a time, and in retrospect. Although the income distribution rule is fairly easy to comply with, there is another rule that bans 'trading'; this is designed to prevent funds cheating by turning income into capital gains, but the wording is rather vague and funds have occasionally been caught out. If you cash in your holding and distributor status is then refused, you can face an unexpected income tax bill.

Some years ago, when income tax went up to 60 per cent against a capital gains tax rate of 30 per cent, this was a severe penalty. Now that the two rates have been equalised, it is less drastic, but there is still a disadvantage because of the exempt allowance for capital gains tax.

Pros and cons

With so many onshore unit trusts and other funds available, the obvious question is, why look offshore? Originally these funds were primarily aimed at those who were non-resident for tax purposes and could therefore gain a tax advantage; there were few attractions for the UK investor. But the developments in EU regulations, combined with certain restrictions on UK-based unit trusts, have meant that a number of companies are now finding that an offshore base presents greater opportunities.

The major feature that is driving the UK unit trust companies to set up offshore is the facility to pay dividends gross. This is particularly attractive for funds that focus on producing income, such as bond funds and, in future, cash funds. Although the income is ultimately taxable in the hands of a UK investor, there may be cash flow advantages in gross payments, and for non-taxpayers it saves the trouble of reclaiming tax paid.

Another issue is investment flexibility: offshore funds can invest in areas that are not available to unit trusts, such as currencies and commodities. Even where the investments are of the same type, the restrictions may be fewer or non-existent. For example, a unit trust may invest only up to 10 per cent of its portfolio, in total, in countries that are not on the FSA's list of recognised stock exchanges. A Dublin-based UCITS fund, on the other hand, could put up to 10 per cent in each of these countries, and some may be wholly unrestricted.

A potential drawback is that even if a fund is FSA recognised, it does not come under the UK compensation scheme. In some cases, the local regulations may in fact offer a higher degree of protection, but some areas do not operate any compensation scheme. You should always check that the fund assets are held by an independent custodian and, for preference, stick to those run by a well-known name.

Offshore funds are often based on a single price, to which the front-end fee is added, rather than having a bid/offer spread like unit trusts, so they may be slightly cheaper to buy into. Annual charges, on the other hand, may be rather higher than for onshore trusts because, in addition to the management charge, the fund may have to meet the fees of the auditor and the custodian or trustee.

UMBRELLA FUNDS

Umbrella funds, the first of which appeared in 1984, technically consist of a single overall fund which comprises several different sub-funds or share classes. One of the main advantages for some time was that investors could switch their holdings between the different sub-funds without being liable to capital gains tax, which would only arise when they sold out of the whole fund. Unfortunately, this loophole has since been closed and CGT now arises on all switches, just as it would if you moved from one unit trust to another run by the same group.

However, there may still be an advantage in cost terms, as the initial fee will be waived for switches between sub-funds. Some companies also run a parallel portfolio management service, which will look after your investments within the fund and make appropriate switches, but there is an extra charge for this. The main drawback of umbrella funds is that you are committing yourself to just one company, which may not have the best performing funds across the full range.

Another point to watch out for is whether the fund intends to apply for distributor status. This is granted to the umbrella fund as a unit, which means each separate sub-fund must comply with the regulations. If one fails, the fund as a whole fails, which has tax repercussions for the investor as outlined above.

How to invest

As mentioned, funds that have obtained FSA recognition can be freely marketed in the same way as unit trusts, but others can only advertise indirectly, by offering to send out a prospectus. In either case, but particularly the latter, it is probably worth while consulting a professional adviser.

OPEN-ENDED INVESTMENT COMPANIES

While unit trusts with UCITS status can theoretically be sold throughout the EU, in practice they are not attractive to Europeans, who prefer the single price and the tax structure of a SICAV. As a result, several UK companies set up offshore operations, mainly in Dublin and Luxembourg, to run SICAVs. But as SICAVs can be sold in the UK, and the range of funds offered generally paralleled the groups' unit trusts, some questioned whether there was a need to run two separate operations.

Obviously it would have been a considerable loss to the UK investment industry if management groups abandoned unit trusts in favour of offshore SICAVs. So the previous (Conservative) government introduced the idea of SICAV-style funds, known as Open-Ended Investment Companies (OEICs, pronounced 'oiks'), that could be operated and sold in the UK.

OEICs are something of a cross between unit trusts and investment trusts. Like unit trusts, they are open-ended: shares are created and cancelled according to demand, with no set minimum or maximum number. But like investment trusts, they are companies, with quoted shares and a board of one or more directors.

OEICs have no bid/offer spread, but a single price, to which an initial or dealing charge can be added. They may also issue more than one class of share, which may be differently priced or denominated in different currencies. For example, one class may be designed for private investors and another, priced differently and with a different minimum subscription, for institutions. Funds with different share classes run in much the same way as umbrella funds.

The Treasury regulations for OEICs came into effect in December 1996, but details of their tax treatment were not finalised until 1997 and it was only in 1998 that the first funds began to appear. Since then, however, several investment groups have embraced the idea and converted their unit trust ranges to OEICs.

There are two main advantages to OEICs. First, the single price structure, with the initial charge added on, should be simpler and clearer – you can see the charge you are paying, whereas with a unit trust, it is hidden within the bid/offer spread. Second, because OEICs can operate as umbrella funds, several unit trusts can be converted into sub-funds of a single OEIC. This should allow economies of scale and so cut costs.

But there are also drawbacks. Because of the single price, investors can sell out of a fund for a better price than the manager could actually get for selling the underlying shares and if sales are high this will dilute the value of the fund for remaining investors. Hence OEICs can charge a 'dilution levy' in such cases, which effectively brings back the concept of a bid/offer spread.

When unit trusts are converted, there is likely to be some merging, which could mean a change in the asset allocation or investment objective of each trust. It could also bring an increase in charges for some investors; if, for example, a low-cost trust is merged with a higher cost one, the ongoing charge may be pitched in the middle, in which case some investors will benefit while others end up paying more.

Finally, the umbrella structure could raise problems if one of the sub-funds defaults in any way, as the other funds could be obliged to bail it out. This is called 'contagion' and it means that you could be invested in a fund which is doing very nicely and then suddenly find you have lost a chunk of your money to shore up an ailing fund elsewhere in the umbrella. Unit trusts operate individually, so are ring-fenced against this possibility. However, managers claim that the regulatory framework for OEICs means that the risk of contagion is remote and some have put measures in place to meet any deficits that arise, thus preventing any contagion happening.

WHERE TO FIND OUT MORE

The Association of Unit Trusts and Investment Funds produces general performance figures and other statistical data, but does not offer advice or recommendation on individual trusts or management groups. It runs the Unit Trust Information Service, which can provide an introductory booklet, a unit trust user's handbook and a directory of trusts, and can be contacted on 020 8207 1361 or by writing to 65 Kingsway, London WC2B 6TD. The groups themselves also have a range of literature on their own products.

The *Unit Trust Yearbook* is published annually by Financial Times Business Enterprises and contains details of both management groups and all unit trusts available.

Unit trust prices are quoted in daily newspapers such as *The Daily Telegraph* and the *Financial Times;* the *Financial Times* also publishes the prices of offshore funds.

7 Unit Trusts and Offshore Funds (2): The Investment Choice

In recent years there has been a degree of consolidation in the unit trust market, which has slightly reduced the number of companies operating in this field. Nevertheless, the number of trusts has continued to grow steadily, as Table 7.1 shows. With well over 1600 available, it is difficult to know where to start, especially as many have similar aims and specialisations. The best way is probably to decide first what type of trust you are after, and then to choose between the different management groups offering that type.

On the most basic approach, trusts can be divided into four types:

1. trusts whose primary objective is to produce income;
2. trusts whose primary objective is to produce capital growth, either with a general portfolio or specialising in a particular country or sector;
3. trusts that aim to provide a mix between income and growth;
4. cash trusts.

The first three of these groups may invest in the UK or overseas (or, in the case of international trusts, both). The fourth type is in a sense a sub-section of the first, since the aim is income, but cash trusts differ from others in that they do not involve any capital risk.

Table 7.1 *Authorised unit trusts*

Year	Number of trusts	Number of companies
1981	529	93
1982	553	99
1983	630	91
1984	687	102
1985	806	110
1986	964	121
1987	1137	139
1988	1255	153
1989	1379	162
1990	1407	154
1991	1400	157
1992	1456	151
1993	1528	156
1994	1559	162
1995	1633	160
1996	1676	159
1997	1680	153
1998	1739	152
1999	1775	153

Source: Association of Unit Trusts and Investment Funds

UNIT TRUST CATEGORIES

If we look in more detail, the Association of Unit Trusts and Investment Funds sets out 31 separate categories of trust for the purpose of making performance comparisons. These are grouped under five headings, as follows.

Immediate income

Funds principally targeting immediate income.

UK Gilts

Funds that invest at least 90 per cent of their assets in UK government securities (gilts).

UK Corporate Bonds

Funds that invest at least 80 per cent of their assets in sterling-denominated (or hedged back to sterling) bonds, rated BBB- or above by either Standard & Poors or equivalent (Moodys Baa or above). This excludes convertibles.

UK Other Bond

Funds investing at least 80 per cent of their assets in sterling-denominated (or hedged back to sterling) bonds, with at least 20 per cent in bonds rated below BBB- by either Standard & Poors or equivalent, convertibles or preference shares.

Global Bonds

Funds that invest at least 80 per cent of their assets in fixed interest stocks. All funds which contain more than 80 per cent fixed interest investments are classified under this heading, regardless of whether they have more than 80 per cent in any geographical sector, with the exception of the UK (classified under the relevant UK heading).

UK Equity & Bond Income

Funds that invest at least 80 per cent of their assets in the UK, between 20 per cent and 80 per cent in UK fixed interest securities and between 20 and 80 per cent in UK equities. These funds aim to have a yield of at least 120 per cent of that on the FTSE All-Share Index.

Managed Income

Funds should have a maximum equity content of 60 per cent and a minimum gross running yield of at least 120 per cent of the FTSE All-Share gross yield before deduction of management charges. It must also be possible for the income generated to be paid directly to the investor. There is no specific requirement to hold non-UK equities, but assets must be at least 50 per cent in sterling or euros and convertibles are counted as part of the equity content.

Growing income

Funds principally targeting an increasing income.

UK Equity Income

Funds that invest at least 80 per cent of their assets in UK equities and that aim to have a yield above 110 per cent of the yield on the FTSE All-Share Index.

Global Equity Income

Funds that invest at least 80 per cent of their assets in equities (but not more than 80 per cent in UK equities) and that aim to have a yield above 110 per cent of the yield on the FT World Index.

Capital growth/Total return

Funds principally targeting capital.

UK All Companies

Funds that invest at least 80 per cent of their assets in UK equities and have a primary objective of achieving capital growth.

UK Smaller Companies

Funds that invest at least 80 per cent of their assets in UK equities of companies that form part of the Hoare Govett Smaller Companies Index or have an equivalent or lower market capitalisation.

Japan

Funds that invest at least 80 per cent of their assets in Japanese securities.

Japanese Smaller Companies

Funds that invest at least 80 per cent of their assets in Japanese equities of companies that form the bottom 10 per cent by market capitalisation.

Far East including Japan

Funds that invest at least 80 per cent of their assets in Far Eastern securities, including a Japanese content of less than 80 per cent of assets.

Far East excluding Japan

Funds that invest at least 80 per cent of their assets in Far Eastern securities and exclude Japanese securities.

North America

Funds that invest at least 80 per cent of their assets in North American securities.

North American Smaller Companies

Funds that invest at least 80 per cent of their assets in North American equities of companies that form part of the Russell 2000 Index or have an equivalent or lower market capitalisation.

Europe including UK

Funds that invest at least 80 per cent of their assets in European securities. They may include UK securities, but these must not exceed 80 per cent of the fund's assets.

Europe excluding UK

Funds that invest at least 80 per cent of their assets in European securities and exclude UK securities.

European Smaller Companies

Funds that invest at least 80 per cent of their assets in European equities of companies that form the bottom 10 per cent by market capitalisation of the European market. They may include UK securities, but these must not exceed 80 per cent of the fund's assets.

Europe includes all countries in the MSCI/FTSE Pan-European indices.

UK Equity & Bond

Funds that invest at least 80 per cent of their assets in the UK, with between 20 and 80 per cent in UK fixed interest securities and between 20 and 80 per cent in UK equities. These funds aim to have a yield of up to 120 per cent of that on the FTSE All-Share Index.

Cautious Managed

Funds that offer investment in a range of assets, with the maximum equity exposure restricted to 60 per cent of the fund. There is no requirement to hold any minimum percentage of non-UK equity. Assets must be at least 50 per cent in sterling or euros and convertibles count as equities.

Balanced Managed

Funds that offer investment in a range of assets, with the maximum equity exposure restricted to 85 per cent of the fund. At least 10 per cent must be held in non-UK equities. Assets must be at least 50 per cent in sterling or euros and convertibles count as equities.

Active Managed

Funds that offer investment in a range of assets, with up to 100 per cent equity exposure at the manager's discretion. At least 10 per cent must be held in non-UK equities. There is no minimum sterling/euro balance; convertibles count as equities. At any time, the asset allocation may include a high proportion of non-equity assets, such that the fund would qualify for the Balanced or Cautious Managed sector, but the fund would remain in the Active Managed sector insofar as it is the manager's intention to retain the right to invest up to 100 per cent in equities.

Global Equity and Bond

Funds that invest at least 80 per cent of their assets in equities and fixed interest securities (but not more than 80 per cent in UK assets), between 20 and 80 per cent in fixed interest securities and between 20 and 80 per cent in equities.

Global Growth

Funds that invest at least 80 per cent of their assets in equities (but not more than 80 per cent in UK assets) and that have the prime objective of achieving capital growth.

Global Emerging Markets

Funds that invest at least 80 per cent of their assets directly or indirectly in emerging markets, as defined by the World Bank, without geographical restriction. Indirect investment, such as China shares listed in Hong Kong, should not exceed 50 per cent of the portfolio.

Property

Funds that invest at least 80 per cent of their assets in property securities or directly in property itself.

The above sectors also require funds to be broadly diversified within the relevant country, region or asset class. Funds that concentrate solely on a specialist theme, sector or single market size, or on a single country in a multi-currency region, would be included in the appropriate specialist sector.

Capital protection

Funds principally targeting capital protection.

Money Market

Funds that invest at least 95 per cent of their assets in money market instruments: cash or near cash such as bank deposits, certificates of deposit, very short-term fixed interest securities or floating-rate notes. These funds may be either 'money market funds' as defined by the Financial Services Authority, or 'securities funds', as long as they satisfy the criterion of concentrating on money market instruments.

Protected/guaranteed funds

Funds other than money market funds that principally aim to provide a return of a set amount of capital to the investor, either explicitly guaranteed or via an investment strategy that is highly likely to achieve this objective, as well as some market upside.

Specialist sectors

Specialist

Funds with a single sector or single country theme, other than the UK, Japan or US.

Index Bear

Funds designed to track the performance of an index inversely by using derivatives.

Table 7.2 shows some past performance results for each of the categories outlined above. These figures, which are compiled on a regular basis by the Association of Unit Trusts and Investment Funds, show the realisation value of £1000 invested over various time periods in the median fund in each sector – the middle one in the performance rankings, rather than the average.

Past performance, as the saying goes, is not necessarily a guide to the future; as the table demonstrates, different sectors may come to the fore over different periods. It is also important, in looking at figures of this type, to check exactly what they purport to show. Unit trusts are usually shown on an 'offer to bid' basis, which reflects the cash-in value if you had bought and sold on the respective dates. Alternatively, figures may be on an 'offer to offer' basis; this takes out the effect of the price spread and the initial charge, but can give an idea of what the manager has achieved. Statistics are also

Table 7.2 *Past performances of unit trusts*

Sector	Average value of £1000 invested (£)		
	5 years	**10 years**	**15 years**
Active Managed	1901	2749	–
Balanced Managed	1857	2650	5862
Cautious Managed	1586	–	–
Europe excluding UK	2649	3488	11,355
Europe including UK	2396	3558	13,269
European Specialist	2691	3454	9280
Far East excluding Japan	1115	2311	6515
Far East including Japan	1300	1911	5814
Far East Specialist	966	1897	3511
Global Bonds	1203	1668	2674
Global Emerging Markets	1103	1974	–
Global Equity & Bond	1756	2590	6082
Global Equity Income	1967	3062	–
Global Growth	1959	2738	6252
Global Specialist	2169	3569	6787
Guaranteed/Protected	1597	–	–
Index Bear	477	–	–
Japan	1289	1270	4013
Japanese Specialist	1402	1566	5196
Managed Income	1696	2474	–
Money Market	1242	1714	–
North America	2827	4484	7191
North America Specialist	2702	5067	7376
Property	1487	–	–
UK All Companies	2244	3136	7566
UK Equity & Bond	1938	2555	5383
UK Equity & Bond Income	1719	2329	5304
UK Equity Income	1954	2792	7551
UK General Bonds	1495	2107	3563
UK Gilts	1483	2144	3201
UK Smaller Companies	2463	3482	8638
UK Specialist	2166	3064	9086
UK savings £2500 instant access	1140	1513	2213
FTSE All-Share Index	2469	3709	8894
Retail Price Index	1147	1407	1833

Note: A gap indicates that no trusts have been in existence that long. All figures on an offer to bid price basis, with net income reinvested, as at 1 January 2000.

Source: Association of Unit Trusts and Investment Funds

generally quoted with net income reinvested, which compounds the capital growth; if you are investing to earn income to spend, then obviously the capital return will be rather less.

The figures are compared with the returns from a building society and the growth in the FTSE All-Share index and the Retail Price Index. Index comparisons should be treated with caution, as an index does not include dealing costs or the charges encountered with a trust. In the case of an overseas trust, there are also currency considerations; the return in sterling terms may vary significantly from the market trend shown by the index.

INVESTMENT AIMS

The first step in deciding where to put your money is to determine whether you are looking for income or capital growth. The two are not necessarily mutually exclusive; while trusts that go all out for capital growth will not produce any income to speak of, there are others that combine both objectives. Similarly, the strategies pursued by equity income trusts can often produce good growth, even where that is a secondary aim.

INCOME TRUSTS

If you are looking for income, you need to bear in mind that investing in equities will not provide you with very high income at the outset. Even so-called 'high income' trusts may yield only around 5 per cent gross, which, at the time of writing, is much the same as some building society accounts.

The advantage of investing in equities, however, is that they should produce some capital appreciation and a rising income over time, while a building society deposit will be static in value and the income will rise and fall with interest rates.

The income comparison is illustrated in Table 7.3, which shows the gross annual income paid by an equity income trust and a building society higher rate account over a 10-year period. The

Table 7.3   *Annual net income from a UK equity income unit trust, a corporate bond unit trust and a building society account*

£1000 invested 1 January 1990

Annual income

Year	Equity income trust (£)	Corporate bond trust (£)	Building society (£)
1	43	64	98
2	45	61	78
3	43	61	58
4	42	56	34
5	42	59	29
6	45	48	31
7	49	58	24
8	55	59	26
9	58	58	34
10	58	56	22

Note: Figures represent the annual net income paid by the average UK equity income unit trust, corporate bond trust and a building society account with a minimum balance of £2500, 1 January 1990 – 1 January 2000.

Source: Association of Unit Trusts and Investment Funds

building society provided higher income for the first six years, but was then overtaken by the trust, which would also have grown in capital value. The table also shows the gross annual income from a corporate bond trust, which beats the building society after just two years.

It is possible to get a higher initial income from a unit trust by choosing one of the specialist types: those investing in gilts and fixed interest securities, convertibles or preference shares, for instance. These are currently offering a starting yield of 5 to 6 per cent gross. There are also corporate bond funds, which invest in fixed-rate bonds issued by UK companies, which have yields around 8 per cent gross. But with all these trusts there tends to be much less potential for capital growth on the assets, hence the income return is less likely to improve over time.

In general, there is a limit to the amount of genuine income that can be produced, and to go above that level will entail some sacrifice of capital or capital growth potential. A couple of trusts launched in 1993 were specifically designed to convert future capital growth into current income, by the use of options. The trusts invest mainly in blue chip shares and special loan securities, which produce a reasonable base yield, and then also write options, on which a premium is earned. The premium boosts the level of income, but the effect of the options is that any capital growth above 4 or 5 per cent is given up.

Options are also used to limit falls in the capital value, but there is no capital guarantee and in certain market conditions there could be a progressive drop. Of course, this is true of any trust, but with these there is less chance of making it up again in future, since the capital growth potential is restricted. There is also no guarantee on the income: one trust reduced its level from 10 per cent net to 9 per cent.

Even with equity trusts the yield can differ. As a rule, the higher the target yield, the greater the constraints on the manager and the more growth prospects may have to be sacrificed. So trusts with a more modest pay-out now may prove more rewarding in the long run.

But the pursuit of income can work to advantage on the growth side. The yield on a share moves broadly in inverse relationship to its price – if the price falls and the dividend remains the same, it will represent a higher yield. So it may then become an attractive holding for an income unit trust. If the share price subsequently recovers, it will bring a boost to the capital growth on the trust. Of course, as the price rises, the yield will fall, so the manager will sooner or later have to sell in favour of another higher yielding stock. But although he may then miss out on further growth prospects, he equally avoids the danger of hanging on too long and seeing the share price fall back again, so it can turn out to be a useful discipline.

To a large extent, then, if a trust has a good track record for its dividend payments, the capital performance should also be satisfactory. Although past results cannot be relied upon, a consistent dividend history is a fair indication of a manager's ability, as these trusts have a fairly broad range of investment possibilities and are therefore less dominated by market movements than a more specialised vehicle such as a commodity trust.

So the starting-point for choosing an income trust is to weigh up your needs for income today as against income in the future. If you are looking for immediate high income over a short time-span, a fixed interest or preference trust may be suitable. If you are prepared to settle for less now to have more in the future, then think about an equity-based trust or one with mixed holdings. In the latter case, check out the proportions held in ordinary shares as against preference shares or fixed interest securities; again, the higher the content of ordinary equities, the better should be the prospects of a rising income. Another important point is the level of annual management charge. This will normally be paid for out of the trust's income, so the higher the charge, the less will be left to distribute to unit holders.

If the trust is fairly new, you can only go by its portfolio structure and the charges. If it has a track record, you can also check the dividend history; ideally, payments should at least have kept pace with inflation. Finally, check the capital growth; although this may not be your top priority it will underpin the income return.

Overseas income trusts

The bulk of trusts focusing on income are invested in the UK, but there are a growing number based on overseas markets. Some of these invest in particular geographical areas, such as North America or Europe, while others are international in scope. These latter trusts are classified under two sector headings, equity income and fixed interest, which have the same characteristics as the equivalent UK trusts.

The overseas equity income trusts tend to have lower yields than their UK counterparts because the stock markets themselves have lower yields, and the management charge may also be higher, which will detract from the return. You should also bear in mind the currency factor, which can add to the degree of risk involved.

Special schemes

As mentioned in Chapter 6, there are a number of schemes available that are designed to produce a monthly income by packaging together trusts with different pay-out dates. If you are looking for regular income, a package has the advantage over an individual monthly-paying trust – of which there are around a dozen – that a spread of investments gives a spread of risk. There will, of course, be a higher minimum investment than for a single trust.

Set packages have the drawback that there may be little or no choice of which trusts are included, which means there may be a higher fixed interest content than you would like, and also commit you to one management group. The alternative is to put together your own package from among all the income trusts available. If you are prepared to manage with uneven payments, so much the better; aiming to get a similar level of payment on the same day each month will restrict the choice and may mean a sacrifice of overall performance.

GENERALIST TRUSTS

As mentioned, income and growth are not mutually exclusive targets, as there are a number of trusts that offer elements of both, either through a combination of higher and lower yielding equities, or through a mixture of equities with fixed interest securities.

These generalist trusts are often regarded as the plain vanilla of the industry, worthy but dull. Most groups have one, and some even have more than one, but they are rarely likely to be the subject of eye-catching advertisements. The yield is generally in the region of 3 per cent gross and they are expected to show steady, rather than spectacular, performance.

Equity & Bond funds are those that mix equities with fixed interest stocks and have less than 80 per cent in either. The yield can be rather higher than on general funds, depending on the mix of holdings; the greater the proportion of fixed interest securities, the higher the yield but, as mentioned in the last section, this entails lower growth prospects. Most of these trusts, however, steer a middle course between the two in the same way as Growth & Income trusts.

Although they may never top the performance listings, Table 7.4 shows that the returns are not to be scorned. Certain specialist sectors may well do better, but others will do a lot worse, so unless you have confidence in your powers of selection, or sufficient money to put together a range of specialist holdings, a generalist trust can be a good home for a first investment. Equally, if you are building up a portfolio, a general trust can form a stable core, from which you can venture into higher risk holdings.

Table 7.4 *Past performances of generalist funds*

Sector	Average value of £1000 invested (£)		
	5 years	10 years	15 years
UK Equity & Bond	1938	2555	5383
Global Equity & Bond	1756	2590	6082
Balanced Managed	1857	2650	5862

Note: Figures are on an offer to bid basis, with net income reinvested, as at 1 January 2000.

Source: Association of Unit Trusts and Investment Funds

GROWTH TRUSTS

By far the majority of unit trusts available are designed to produce capital growth. They comprise a large variety of types, from broadly based international trusts to those specialising in a particular geographical area, such as the UK or Japan, and those concentrating on a particular industry or market sector. Given this huge range, it is impossible to make generalisations and not easy to set about making a choice. At any one time, different markets will be in the ascendancy, and the time-scale you have in mind for your investment will also have a bearing on where the best prospects lie. However, it is possible to narrow down the choice by considering the following alternatives.

UK versus overseas

Many UK investors naturally incline towards the home market, and there are arguments to support this. For one thing, the returns from a unit trust are in sterling, so if you invest in an overseas trust you are exposed to a currency risk on top of the market risk. Some trusts aim to offset this by using 'hedging' techniques, but that in itself can have certain risks as well as costs.

Second, the stock market will respond to and reflect general factors in the economy, which may be appropriate since your other financial arrangements will be subject to similar influences. On the other hand, the major world economies move very much in line with each other anyway.

Also, any investment in a single market, even one the size of the UK, has limitations in terms of choice of stocks and spread of risk. If you are planning to build up a portfolio of any size, or you already have other UK investments, you should think of spreading your investments further afield for better balance.

International versus single country

If you decide to look abroad, you have the choice between single country trusts and those that maintain a global spread. Single country trusts range from those based on large markets, such as the USA, to much more specialised types; for example, trusts focused on Switzerland or Thailand.

The same arguments apply to investing in a single overseas market as to investing in the UK: there is less spread of risk. This is particularly true in the smaller markets, where there may be a limited number of stocks available. There may also be problems or delays in buying and selling, which can affect performance and add to the risk. For investors seeking to build an international portfolio, perhaps mainly through direct equity holdings, these trusts can offer convenient access to smaller markets; otherwise they give the chance of high rewards if you are prepared to accept high risk. The more cautious investor, on the other hand, will do better with an international trust or a selection of those based on the larger world markets.

General versus specialised

As well as trusts with a geographical specialisation, there are others that focus on a particular industry or market sector. These may operate on a global basis, such as an international technology trust, or within one particular market, such as a Japanese Smaller Companies trust.

Like trusts with a geographical specialisation, these carry a higher degree of risk than a general or international trust. But whereas you could build a collection of holdings in different countries, it would not be feasible to cover every type of industry. Hence the attraction is less to create a market balance among your investments than to inject a higher risk/higher reward element. Smaller companies, for example, are much more volatile than larger ones; they rise faster, but can also fall faster. Similarly, recovery and special situations trusts seek to take advantage of stocks that are under-priced; if the expected improvement occurs, all well and good, but it depends on how well the manager makes his selections. Industry-specific trusts can be even more dramatic; gold trusts, for example, had a phenomenal run in 1980, but subsequently spent a long period in the wilderness.

MANAGEMENT STYLE

Once you have decided where to invest, you then face the choice of management group. Again, there are no easy answers: no one investment strategy is proved to be right or wrong. However, there are certain considerations that may help to sort out what accords with your own views or needs.

Active versus passive

Some managers take a very active approach, turning over the portfolio regularly in the search for value, while others operate on a longer term view. The former may have greater potential – if the manager gets it right – but the dealing costs will be higher and results may be more volatile.

Top down versus bottom up

This refers to the stock-picking approach of the manager. Some start from the top: country first (in the case of an international trust), then industry, then the specific share. Others build up from the bottom, choosing shares they think are attractive, with perhaps overall proportions for sectors or countries.

House style

Some management groups have an overall 'house style' within which the managers of individual trusts operate; this may be simply a matter of the risk/reward approach they adopt or may go further, in that, for example, if particular industries are favoured at a given time, they are represented across the range of trusts. In other cases, each trust manager operates at a very individual level. A house style may impose constraints, but the individual approach could lead to a change of fortune, or at any rate of philosophy, if one manager leaves and another takes over.

Hedging and liquidity

Where a trust invests overseas, the returns – which are expressed in sterling, of course – will be affected by exchange rate movements as well as market trends. In some cases the manager may 'hedge' part of the portfolio to neutralise the currency effects; this can – if it works – protect against losses, although it also means missing out on favourable movements and there is a cost involved. Others take the view that if you buy the market, you also buy the currency, and that the two should not be artificially separated.

Similar views are taken on liquidity. Some managers will move out into cash if the market is falling, while others believe it is up to the investor to decide by staying in or selling out of the trust. Obviously, switching out and perhaps buying back in later would mean the investor faced a new front-end charge, but if the trust goes into cash and subsequently reinvests there will be dealing costs, and there could be a loss if the timing is not judged accurately.

Size of fund

There is a theory that a small trust will tend to outperform a larger one. This has some logic, in that a small trust is more flexible and can therefore respond more quickly to changes in the market – assuming the manager interprets the trend correctly. Large funds operating in a small market may also be hampered by a limited choice of stocks.

Small trusts will obviously tend to hold fewer stocks, but larger ones also vary in whether they are widespread or concentrated. The fewer the holdings in the portfolio, the higher the risk/reward ratio, as a gain or loss in any one holding will have a greater proportional influence.

Location

Some groups run their overseas trusts entirely from a UK base, while others have local offices in the major markets. Naturally, there is much debate over which is better: the objective view from a distance or the 'feel' gained by being on the spot. In fact, those operating from the UK will normally make regular visits to the country and may also liaise with local brokers for information and – particularly in smaller markets – for dealing. Given the sophistication of global communications, one suspects there is not a great deal of difference, and certainly performance results do not point to either approach being consistently more successful.

New launches

One other theory on the relative merits of different trusts is that new launches will do well. This can depend on the reason for the launch and its timing. Some are 'bandwagon' products, investing in a market that is currently rising, in which case they are likely to look good to start with, particularly as they have new money to spend on the most attractive shares, while older trusts in the same market may be stuck with shares that have gone out of fashion.

The ideal timing, of course, is to launch just before a market goes up, to get the full benefit of the rise, but (aside from the difficulty of correctly predicting market movements) it is harder to attract money into a sector that is currently looking dull.

ARE YOU AN ACTIVE INVESTOR?

One important question to consider before choosing a trust is whether you plan to monitor and alter your investment actively or simply want to invest and forget about it. In the latter case, you are likely to do best by sticking to fairly general trusts; the more specialist offerings are more volatile and need to be kept under supervision.

If you expect to be active and switch your holdings around between different trusts, this should influence your choice of management group. Of course, you are not bound to stick with the same group and there are drawbacks to doing so: no one group is going to top the performance tables with every trust it runs. But against that there is the advantage that switches from one trust to another within the same group attract a discount on the front-end charge, which can significantly cut the costs of active investment. So you should look for a group – or perhaps two or three – that has a wide range of funds and offers a good switching discount.

Portfolio management services

If you would like your investments to be actively managed, but lack the time or knowledge to do it yourself, there are a number of advisers who offer portfolio management services. These may be run on a discretionary or an advisory basis. In the first case, you would set out your basic aims, such as income or capital growth and the amount of risk you are prepared to accept, and the adviser would do the rest; you would be kept informed of changes to the portfolio and receive regular valuations, but would not be consulted on each deal.

With an advisory service, the adviser would consult you (and vice versa) before any change was made. The minimum for a discretionary service starts at about £10,000; for an advisory service it is likely to be higher, because of the extra work involved. Charging systems vary; the adviser may operate on the commissions he gets on each trust purchase, but it can be more efficient for both sides to rebate commission and charge an annual management fee.

Broker unit trusts

An alternative to a discretionary management service is a broker unit trust, offered by a number of professional advisers (not necessarily brokers). Often an adviser might be running a large number of individual portfolios on a discretionary basis and making similar investments and changes for each. By setting up a broker unit trust he can consolidate these portfolios into one fund, with a single transaction when he buys or sells, thus considerably reducing the administration.

The trust may invest directly into securities or through a range of unit trusts in a similar way to a fund of funds. In either case, it must have a defined investment objective and strategy and will be governed by the same regulations as an ordinary unit trust. Funds are normally valued daily and the prices are published in national newspapers.

The advantage for the investor is that his money is professionally managed, without the need for him to get involved in each transaction, but he still has access to the fund manager and a degree of personal service that he obviously would not get from the manager of an ordinary unit trust. There is, however, an extra layer of charges, as the adviser will charge a management fee, which needs to be weighed up against the 'added value' in terms of improved performance.

OFFSHORE FUNDS

For the UK investor, the appeal of offshore funds lies largely in the fact that they can offer investment in areas that are not open to onshore unit trusts; in particular, currencies and commodities.

Currency funds can be based on sterling or foreign currencies. Sterling funds can be deposit based, offering the benefits of wholesale money market rates on short-term deposits, or invested in fixed interest securities, which gives the prospect of capital gains – or a combination of both. Foreign currency funds operate in a similar way, but have the added dimension of exchange rate movements against sterling, which can generate capital gains or losses.

Some companies offer a range of funds based on different individual currencies, with free switching between them. As a rule, though, single currency funds are high risk; markets move fast and timing is crucial to the end result. Unless you have a particular reason for wanting exposure to a certain currency, or have a large amount to invest that can be spread over several funds, you may be better off with a managed currency fund or a management service linked to a range of funds.

Commodity funds are also not for the faint-hearted. Where onshore unit trusts invest only in the shares of commodity-linked companies, offshore funds may additionally use commodity futures contracts or invest directly into the commodities themselves. The outlay required and the risk involved are rather less than if you undertook the same investments on your own behalf – you can only lose the money you put into the fund, whereas with direct investment you could be committed for further sums – but unless you are an inveterate gambler, this type of investment should only be considered within larger portfolios and then only for a small proportion.

Points to watch for with offshore funds are the level of charges, which may be smaller initially but larger annually than for onshore funds, and the tax status. As explained in Chapter 6, offshore funds may have distributor or accumulator status. In the first case, at least 85 per cent of the fund's income must be distributed and will be taxed at the appropriate income tax rate in the hands of the investor, while capital gains will come under the standard CGT rules. In the second case, all income is rolled up within the fund and no tax is due while you remain invested, but when you sell out, all profits will be taxed as income at your highest rate.

With foreign currency funds, for example, most of the benefits come from capital gains, so distributor status is advantageous; when you sell, you can make use of the annual CGT exempt allowance before you need pay any tax. With sterling funds that generate interest, accumulator status allows the tax bill to be deferred, which will be a benefit if your tax rate is likely to fall in the future.

8 | Investment Trusts

Investment trusts are not trusts, but companies. Their aim in life is to invest their capital somewhere else – in other company shares, in fixed-interest securities and the like. Investors who buy investment trust shares are, therefore, getting a 'slice of the action' of a whole portfolio of shares for the price of one. In this respect, they are similar to unit trusts (with which they are often compared and contrasted) and certainly their basic reason for existing is identical: to provide the small investor with a spread of risk for a modest outlay.

This spread of risk is legally insisted upon by the fact that, to qualify for the tax treatment described below, investment trusts cannot invest more than 15 per cent of their assets in any one security, meaning a theoretical minimum portfolio of at least seven. In practice, trusts are likely to have anything between 40 and 200 holdings. The exceptions to this rule are the shares of other investment trust companies, which themselves will automatically provide a spread of risk. They must also distribute at least 85 per cent of the income they receive from their investments to their shareholders.

THE TAX POSITION

Investment trusts are similar to unit trusts in that liability to tax on any gains they make belongs to the shareholder, rather than the company itself. This means shareholders can realise up to £7200 of gains (in the 2000/01 tax year) before being liable to tax.

On the income side, dividends from other companies in which the trust invests are paid net of basic rate tax to the holders of the investment trust shares. Non-taxpayers can reclaim the tax; higher rate taxpayers will have to pay more.

Do investment trusts have a unique selling point? The answer is yes, they have several, some of which may be attractive to investors, others possibly offputting.

THE SHARE PRICE AND THE DISCOUNT

The major difference between investment trusts and unit trusts is that the former are 'closed-ended' funds of money while the latter are 'open-ended'. Unit trusts expand and contract according to the demand for them; if demand outstrips supply, new units are created; if supply exceeds demand, units are cancelled. Investment trusts, on the other hand, have a fixed number of shares.

This difference in structure has a practical effect on prices. The price of units in a unit trust is directly related to the value of its underlying investments, while the share price of an investment trust moves up and down according to the demand for it – just like the share prices of other quoted companies.

In fact, if you totted up the value of holdings in an investment trust's portfolio and divided by the number of shares in existence, the result (known as the net asset value) is almost certain to be different from the share price. Occasionally the share price is higher, in which case it is said to be at a premium. More commonly it is lower, which is described as a discount. At the time of writing, the average discount for all investment trusts was around 15 per cent.

Why should the share price stand at a discount? One reason is technical. As a going concern, the investment trust's portfolio is valued at mid-market prices – halfway between bid and offer; but if it were to be liquidated or taken over, the valuation would move to the lower bid basis and there would also be professional costs involved in winding it up. However, the major part of the discount is explained by supply and demand. If the shares of a trust are in demand, the discount will narrow or the price may even move to a premium; if the trust is out of favour, the discount will widen.

There is some debate over whether the discount is a benefit or a drawback. The argument in its favour is that it means you are buying a stake in more shares than you are paying for. For example, if the discount stands at 10 per cent, then every £90 you invest in the trust effectively represents £100-worth of the shares in its portfolio. On the other hand, if the discount is still the same when you come to sell, you will lose the 10 per cent again.

The discount can be thought of as an extra layer of risk – or reward. At one level you have the opportunity to gain or lose with movements in the value of the underlying portfolio. On top of that, you will gain if the discount narrows between the time you buy and sell, and lose if it widens. Broadly speaking, if the market is rising and the value of the portfolio is going up, the trust is likely to be in greater demand and the discount will narrow, so you gain twice over. Conversely, when the market is falling, demand drops off, the discount widens and you lose twice over.

While you should be cautious about buying a trust that is already on a very low discount – the expectation being that it will widen – it would be wrong to place too much emphasis on the discount. The manager's ability to produce good performance is likely to be a much larger factor in the investment return.

One other point about the discount is that if it gets too large the trust can become vulnerable to a takeover. An institution can offer an attractive price to shareholders while still leaving plenty of scope to make profits for itself. A case a few years ago was the Globe investment trust, which was standing at a 20 per cent discount when it was taken over by Coal Board Pension Funds.

After a spate of new issues in 1995, discounts widened quite a bit and this was exacerbated by some heavy selling by institutions. As a result, returns diminished and investment trusts, on average, underperformed both unit trusts and markets. This led to some consolidation and takeover activity and the sector as a whole has been seen as somewhat under siege.

But investment trusts are fighting back. Part of the problem is that as investment trusts cannot be directly advertised, many private investors are not familiar with them. The Association of Investment Trust Companies has taken a strong lead in developing initiatives to raise their profile and to improve value for shareholders – both indirectly, by improving what is called corporate governance, and directly, through measures to reduce discounts.

Share buy-backs

Two developments in particular have helped investment trusts to recover. One is the advent of Individual Savings Accounts (ISAs), which have replaced personal equity plans (PEPs). The PEP rules required a trust to be at least 50 per cent invested in the European Union to be fully qualifying, a criterion many trusts did not meet. ISAs have no geographical restrictions, which is especially good news for the large generalist trusts that invest globally and which are often well suited to smaller private investors.

The other benefit came from the removal of advance corporation tax in April 1999, which eased the way for share buy-backs. Although investment trusts are essentially closed-ended, this is one way in which they can influence the number of shares in existence. It means, quite simply, buying back their own shares, which should have two effects. First, reducing the number of shares on the market closes the gap between supply and demand, so the discount should narrow. Second, since shares can be bought at a discount, buy-backs should enhance the net asset value of the trust. Both these effects will benefit continuing shareholders.

Gearing

The 'magnifying' effect of the discount is itself a form of gearing. But investment trusts can go one better than that: unlike unit trusts, they can borrow money to invest, alongside the shareholders' funds. If, for example, you can borrow money at 10 per cent, and invest it in something that goes up 50 per cent in a year, then you have magnified the profits. (Needless to say, if the stock you are investing in goes *down*, you will have magnified your losses.) An example of how gearing can work in your favour is shown in Table 8.1. In this case, the borrowing is in the form of a debenture stock.

Golden rules for stockmarket success

Over time, the stockmarket has shown the greatest and most consistent ability to create real wealth. If you had placed £100 in the companies which broadly made up the London Stock Exchange in 1899 and reinvested gross income, by the end of 1999 it was worth a staggering £1,285,872. To put this in perspective, a deposit of the same amount in cash would have been worth only £12,805* over the same period.

The charts below show very clearly how different investments rewarded investors over time. It is worth taking a moment to look at these charts carefully, because, if history is any guide, the decision on how to allocate your capital between the main areas of investment will play a very important part in determining your future wealth. We firmly believe that most investors should have some exposure to stocks and shares in their portfolios, whether as individual share-holdings, or through a unit trust, investment trust or with profits bond.

In its purest form, buying a share enables you to take a stake in a company and participate in its profits by way of dividends, and in its growth by way of an improvement in the share price. There is nothing to beat the excitement and feeling of involvement that holding shares can bring. If you buy shares in companies that

LONG TERM RETURNS FROM DIFFERENT TYPES OF INVESTMENT

	Average annual real return (%p.a.)		
	80 years	20 years	10 years
Investment	1918–1998	1979–1998	1989–1998
Deposit	1.5	4.3	4.7
Fixed Interest	2.4	7.3	8.7
Equities	8.0	11.8	11.1

Return is adjusted for inflation and includes capital gains and income without deduction of tax.
*(Source: Barclays Equity Gilt Study 1999. Offer to Bid. Income reinvested). Please note that equity investments do not give the capital guarantee of a deposit. The PIA do not regulate National Savings.

The table shows the recent value of £10,000 invested into the stockmarket, deposit and property, at the beginning of each year. It clearly demonstrates that the biggest factor in generating returns is time. Despite markets moving up and down early investments do best.

TIME NOT TIMING

Date	FT All Share Index	FTSE 100 Index	Halifax Solid Gold A/c	Halifax UK House Price Index
1/1/87	£48,911	£34,996	£21,738	£18,561
1/1/88	£45,777	£34,263	£20,073	£16,034
2/1/89	£41,744	£32,732	£18,565	£11,934
1/1/90	£31,097	£24,226	£16,859	£11,605
1/1/91	£34,843	£27,381	£15,155	£11,542
1/1/92	£29,187	£23,542	£13,914	£11,956
1/1/93	£24,517	£20,619	£13,034	£12,965
3/1/94	£19,282	£17,169	£12,465	£12,809
2/1/95	£20,739	£19,146	£11,973	£12,841
1/1/96	£16,909	£15,909	£11,470	£13,024
1/1/97	£14,688	£14,251	£11,074	£12,012
1/1/98	£11,934	£11,429	£10,648	£11,516

Based on £10,000 Investment offer to offer, excluding income to 18/10/99, source Micropal. Halifax Solid Gold Account rate for £25,000 investment in a 30 day notice account.

*Please note that equities and equity indices do not afford the same guarantee of capital as provided by a deposit with a bank or building society. Source: Barclays Capital

you know and understand, you can derive a competitive advantage over so-called experts. The legendary US investor Peter Lynch found that kids in high school consistently beat the experts hands down by investing in companies they knew and understood. They could spot trends long before they filtered their way through to the experts in their ivory towers. The shrewd investor keeps their eyes and ears open as they go about their everyday activities and ask themselves who will benefit from the trends they spot.

With investment, the most important factor is to keep time on your side. The sooner you start investing, the better your final prospects for wealth. If you have already left it too late, make sure your nearest and dearest avoid the same mistake. Shares can be an excellent way to get youngsters started on the savings habit. If you are stuck for a present for a child, why not buy a small shareholding in a company or product close to their heart, or with a relevant shareholder perk. You can invest and designate the account for a child. Rather than spending the money on the latest Manchester United kit, an equivalent shareholding will generate pride, a sense of ownership, and as the Report and Accounts make attractive reading to genuine fans, they might just develop sound commercial instincts too. Another idea is Bloomsbury Group – publishers of the popular Harry Potter series, this share comes with the added attraction of a perk offering 30% discount to share holders. Investment Clubs are also a great way to get started, with social attractions as well as financial. As long as you do not over-commit yourself, it is never too early to get started on the stockmarket.

Of course, the stockmarket presents pitfalls as well as opportunities, but happily there is now more information on investment than ever before. The internet offers a rich seam of information, with continuous news feeds and broker reports and forecasts. However, treat this information with caution. As mentioned above, information that is already in the market usually gives you only hindsight. What investors need for stockmarket success is foresight.

The Economist magazine recently published some excellent research on the attractions of investing with foresight rather than hindsight. If you invested just one dollar in the year 1900 in the asset class which provided the best returns over the next twelve months, and reinvested it each year in next year's winner, it produced a staggering $9.6 quintillion (seventeen noughts) by the year 2000. Even after taxes and dealing costs, the dollar invested with perfect foresight would be worth $1,300,000,000,000,000. In stark contrast, the same dollar invested in the **previous** year's best investment would be worth just $290 after taxes.

This research neatly illustrates some golden rules of investment. They are as follows:-

Past Performance is no guide to the future. When the investment bug bites, it is human nature to look at the 'hot stocks' and top performance charts. Try and resist buying yesterday's winners. Broker reports and comment often reflect information which is already in the market place, and hence already reflected in the price.

Aim to pick Tomorrow's Winners. To do this, you need to avoid hype, avoid fashion and look carefully at the underlying reasons which will determine success. Aim to get rich slow – but get very rich.

Keep dealing charges to a minimum. Just look at how the Foresight fortune was diminished by taxes and dealing costs. If you are buying shares, ensure costs are low and good value. If you are buying unit trusts, ISAs or With Profits bonds, either make sure you have the best advice, or the best discounts.

Use every tax shelter possible. If you can hold your equity investments in an ISA or pension, and charges do not eat into the tax savings, then make sure you take advantage of such tax breaks.

Think long term. Time, not timing has often proved to be the investor's best friend.

Peter K Hargreaves.
Chief Executive Hargreaves Lansdown plc.

(*source Barclays Capital. Please note that equities and equity indices do not afford the same guarantee of capital as provided by a deposit with a bank or building society).

Table 8.1 *Gearing on an investment trust*

Capital structure of trust:

4,000,000 5% debenture stock	£4,000,000
6,000,000 £1 ordinary shares	£6,000,000
	£10,000,000

Assume the portfolio doubles in value over five years and that the debenture stock is repaid at the end of that time. The effect is as follows:

	Year 1	Year 5
Value of portfolio	£10,000,000	£20,000,000
Less debenture stock	£4,000,000	£4,000,000
Assets attributable to 6,000,000 ordinary shares	£6,000,000	£16,000,000
Net asset value per ordinary share	£1	£2.67

Thus, while the portfolio has increased by 100 per cent, the assets attributable to each ordinary share have increased by 167 per cent (from £1 to £2.67).

Charges

Unlike unit trusts, investment trusts do not have an initial charge as such, though there are dealing costs when you buy shares just as there are with the shares of other companies. There is also an annual management charge, which tends to vary across the different categories: general trusts carry a charge of around 0.3 per cent of the asset value, while on specialist trusts it can be as much as 1 per cent. Newer launches have also tended to have higher charges than the older established trusts, but even so, they compare well with unit trusts.

INVESTMENT CHARACTERISTICS

The closed-ended structure of an investment trust, mentioned above, influences the management style as well as the share price.

While the unit trust manager must accommodate new money coming in or demands for units to be redeemed, the investment trust manager is working with a fixed pool of assets, regardless of how shares are being bought or sold.

As with the discount, the closed fund has its supporters and its critics. In a rising market, new money attracted into a unit trust can be used to snap up good opportunities, while the investment trust manager may not be able to move so fast. But in a falling market, a unit trust may have to sell its better holdings to meet redemptions, while the investment trust is insulated.

This insulation allows the investment trust manager to make more speculative decisions. Indeed, investment trusts do not have the same restrictions on their holdings as unit trusts – they can invest in unquoted shares and the smaller stock markets around the world that are not yet approved for unit trusts. Obviously these can be more risky, but, with no redemptions to worry about, the manager can afford to take a long-term view.

INVESTMENT RANGE

From the start, investment trusts had an international outlook. Many were set up in Scotland, which had a long history of looking abroad for opportunities. This is still reflected in today's trusts, which currently number around 340.

One of the problems in classifying investment trusts is that their investment scope is generally much more loosely defined than is the case with unit trusts. Another difficulty for investors is that the older trusts, in particular, often have names that have little to do with their aims: Scottish Mortgage, for instance, is an international general trust with no particular focus on either Scotland or mortgages.

Some guidance is given by the categorisation used in performance measurement. This divides trusts into 20 different sectors, as shown in Table 8.2. In most cases, the definition is that a trust has at least 80 per cent of its assets in the particular sector, but in the case of Smaller Companies, the minimum is 50 per cent, and for Venture and Development Capital it is simply 'a significant proportion' in unquoted companies. International trusts have the broadest definition, of having less than 80 per cent of assets in any

WHERE DOES THE 'SMART' MONEY INVEST?

A professionally managed portfolio of assets such as an investment in stocks and shares is really the only long-term option open to private investors seeking a real return that will not only match inflation but will also offer genuine opportunities to beat it and maintain the real value of your capital.

Historically, stockmarket investments have consistently outperformed deposit-based savings accounts. This fact has not been lost on the 10 million or so UK investors who now hold shares. An investment in stocks and shares can, of course, also prove volatile in the short term as stockmarkets are subject to ups and downs reflecting movements in economic confidence or the impact in changes in taxes and interest rates.

REDUCING STOCKMARKET RISK

Investment trusts offer one of the safest ways to invest in the stockmarket. By investing in dozens if not hundred of companies they reduce the risk by pooling investors' money to achieve a wider spread of stockmarket holdings. You can therefore invest safe in the knowledge that your money is in the hands of a professional investment manager.

Although available to private investors, investment trusts have commonly been referred to as one of the best kept secrets in the city – a secret almost the exclusive preserve of investment institutions such as pension funds and life assurance companies. Recent research has now confirmed that only 8% of private investors in the UK have discovered the attraction of investment trusts by investing some of their capital or regular savings in these vehicles.

INVESTING TO MEET FUTURE NEEDS

Since investment trusts are less risky than investing directly in shares, they can be used to meet a range of important financial objectives: repaying a mortgage, meeting school fees, funding university education, retirement planning or covering an important expense such as a family wedding.

Meeting these objectives successfully does require prior planning. Investment trusts should be considered a medium to long-term investment so you can ride out any short-term dips in the market. You must also be prepared to see your investment fall in value as well as rise. Nevertheless, the long-term returns you can expect from an investment trust are extremely attractive compared to, say, traditional savings accounts.

There are so many different investment trusts to choose from that you can usually find one that meets your needs precisely. You can take your pick from trusts which are designed to maximise capital growth, those that aim to produce income and trusts which produce both. Furthermore, you can choose from trusts which aim to produce a good steady return from investing in blue-chip companies, or trusts which are more adventurous and invest in small, growing companies or in very specific areas of the market.

MINIMISING YOUR TAX BILL

On 6 April 1999 the government replaced Personal Equity Plans ('PEPs') by Individual Savings Accounts ('ISAs'). As with PEPs, all income and capital gains within an ISA are free of tax. However, instead of the annual PEP limit of £6,000, the annual limit for maxi ISAs has been set at £7,000 for the tax-year 2000–2001 and £5,000 for each tax year thereafter. The government has guaranteed that ISAs will remain in place for ten years. This means that over the next ten years it would be possible for an individual to invest £54,000 (£106,000 for a couple) in a tax-free account.

ISAs give you more choice over where to invest than with PEPs. Investment trusts can be held within the stocks and shares component of an ISA and you will have the freedom to choose whichever ones you prefer. PEPs and ISAs are probably the best-known tax-saving devices and should, in most circumstances, be your first port of call for investing to meet future long-term needs.

You should also bear in mind that if you have a number of different PEP plans with different managers you may find that the performance varies and charges differ from plan to plan. It may prove more cost efficient, therefore, to consolidate them with one PEP manager where you can get good performance at lower charges. It may also enable you to balance your overall holdings. If you are unsure whether consolidation through a PEP/ISA transfer is right for you, you should take professional advice.

REPAYING YOUR MORTGAGE

The first major financial transaction most people undertake is buying a house.

Most mortgage lenders offer "interest only" mortgages where you pay monthly interest payments to the lender and you make your own arrangements for repaying the debt whenever and however you want.

Investment trust savings schemes and ISAs offer a convenient and flexible way to pay off a mortgage. Monthly savings can be increased, decreased or suspended as your financial circumstances dictate and, by investing in a range of different investment trusts over the period of the mortgage term, you can ensure that you are not reliant on the fortunes and investment skills of one management house.

If your investment trusts perform well, there is the possibility of paying some of your mortgage off early and reducing the total interest payable on the loan. Once your mortgage is completely paid off, you might be left with a surplus lump sum from your investment trusts which you can spend as well.

INVESTING FOR CHILDREN

Every parent wants their child to get a good start in life. That generally means a good education and a clean slate financially. Investment trust savings schemes are ideal products to consider investing in for your children: perhaps to build a nest egg for their adult life, or a means of funding school fees or university costs. The structure of investment trusts and their low costs mean investment trusts have particularly good long-term potential for growth. This makes them perfect investments for children, where you are planning for years rather than months ahead.

Nevertheless, the costs of paying for your children's education can put a severe strain on your finances. Paying fees out of income requires a substantial salary, particularly if two or more children are to be educated. The solution is to save in advance. The best investments for school fees planning depend to a great extent on the time horizons and risk outlook of the saver. Investment trust monthly savings schemes and ISAs can be a relatively painless way of funding for future education costs. Since you are spreading the cost of the investment, a savings scheme will put less of a squeeze on your finances than trying to scrape together a lump sum.

Another increasingly common option is to buy zero dividend preference shares ('zeros') issued by split-capital investment trusts. Rather than paying out a regular dividend, zeros are a low-risk investment which pay out a pre-determined capital amount at the end of the fixed life of the split-capital trust. The return is not guaranteed but is a low-risk investment because this particular class of share is normally first to be repaid from the assets of the company.

PLANNING FOR RETIREMENT

Providing ourselves with adequate retirement provision is becoming increasing important. Although many of us may not want to think about retirement, or believe it is too far away in the future to worry about, it comes to all of us fortunate enough to survive the rigours of middle age and reach the autumn of our life. Unfortunately, too few people currently enter retirement with enough savings to ensure they are financially secure.

Retirement is well worth planning for in advance. It can span nearly a third of your lifetime, and it is a time when you should be doing the things you never did in your working life, such as going on cruises and long overseas holidays.

Investment trust pensions may not be a particularly familiar option to many people. Their low cost, flexibility and performance potential make them worth serious consideration. There are a handful of packaged pension schemes available from investment trust management houses. Unlike most traditional personal pensions, these investment trust schemes have transparent, low charges. In most schemes, these include an initial set-up charge, government stamp duty for buying the trust shares and a modest annual management charge.

You can also gain investment trust exposure through a self-invested personal pension (SIPP). These schemes allow you to choose the assets that go into your personal pension plan. Rather than be restricted to insurance company funds, you can opt to buy other investments such as investment trusts, other shares, unit trusts and gilts. Although flexible, most SIPPs are only appropriate for people able to make larger contributions. This is because charges tend to be fee based, which means the greater the investments you make, the smaller the impact of the charges on your pension fund growth. Taking professional advice on how best to organise your pension is highly recommended because it can be a complex operation.

John Yule is the marketing director of Friends Ivory & Sime Investment Trusts

We called our new range ZeroCharge™ for one obvious reason.

Have you clicked yet?

Find the new ISA, investment plan and PEP transfer plan from Ivory & Sime Investment Management at

www.itszerocharge.co.uk

or call us on 0845 600 6166

ONE YEAR GROWTH UP TO 333%*

its investment trusts
the easy way to invest in the stock market

Table 8.2   *Investment trust categories and average performance*

Comparative return to investor from £1000 invested over various periods

Sector	1 year	3 years	5 years	10 years
International General	120.0	160.3	212.4	384.9
International Income Growth	112.1	135.7	192.4	311.2
International Capital Growth	146.3	197.3	237.7	411.9
UK General	116.3	155.8	219.4	351.5
UK Capital Growth	126.8	139.2	208.8	349.7
UK Income Growth	97.1	134.0	177.8	314.7
Endowment Policies	103.9	122.2	–	–
Commodity & Energy	129.4	89.6	110.2	–
High Income	92.9	148.2	184.1	304.7
North America	123.3	161.8	238.6	417.4
Far East excluding Japan	194.3	97.0	97.4	201.2
Far East including Japan	150.9	100.5	102.8	175.7
Japan	207.8	212.1	165.7	250.5
Property	107.1	135.2	176.3	132.0
Europe	164.0	219.5	338.8	411.4
Emerging Markets	149.4	94.0	132.0	126.4
Smaller Companies UK	177.0	174.5	245.6	343.7
Smaller Companies International	220.1	259.2	347.7	493.3
Closed-end Funds	143.3	178.4	233.3	181.3
Venture & Development Capital	133.9	148.7	216.5	335.1
FTSE All-Share Index	109.9	159.4	231.1	378.5
MSCI World Index (£)	123.4	185.1	244.3	364.4
Retail Price Index (previous month)	102.3	108.1	114.0	139.4

Note: Investment trust figures are calculated on an offer to bid basis with net income reinvested, over periods to 31 March 2000.

Source: Association of Investment Trust Companies

one geographical area, and split capital trusts are the most complicated type, with various different share classes.

The variation in scope between trusts within the same category means that performance comparisons are not necessarily on a like with like basis, but to give a general guide to investment returns, Table 8.2 shows the average for each sector, plus a few key indices, over periods to the end of March 2000.

HOW TO INVEST

Investment trust shares can be bought through a stockbroker, bank or other authorised dealer. When a new trust is launched, the company must publish a prospectus in at least one newspaper. In some cases, a full prospectus is published, including a coupon to apply for shares; otherwise there will be a contact address given from which you can obtain the full prospectus and an application form.

If you have only a small amount to invest, the minimum commission charged by stockbrokers would be disproportionately high and a much cheaper route is through a savings scheme, of which there are currently 45 available, covering some 225 trusts. The first scheme was launched in 1984 and the concept has proved highly successful at attracting private investors into investment trusts.

Despite the name, savings schemes can be used for lump sums as well as regular investments. The minimum can be as little as £20 a month or £200 for a lump sum. Dealing costs are very small – usually 1 per cent or less – because investors' money is pooled within the scheme to buy shares in bulk. In some cases this means that dealing takes place only once a month, so it is a good idea to find out when the deadline is. This and other information on savings schemes can be obtained from the AITC.

It is increasingly possible to buy investment trusts on the Internet, either through a broker or directly from the management groups, through a savings scheme. Web site addresses are given in the monthly information service available from the AITC, details of which are given at the end of this chapter.

Share exchange schemes

As with unit trusts, several companies offer share exchange schemes through which you can swap holdings of equities for investment trust shares. The company will sell the shares on your behalf and may either bear the selling costs itself or offer a special discounted charge. The charge for buying into the investment trust will normally be at the low savings scheme rate, but may be waived altogether.

KEEPING TRACK OF PRICES

Investment trust prices are published daily in newspapers such as *The Daily Telegraph* and the *Financial Times*. The Association of Investment Trust Companies publishes a monthly information service, usually around the third week of the month. This gives two sets of performance figures: the total return on £100 invested as measured by the trust's net asset value – which gives an idea of what the manager has achieved in isolation from share price movements; and the share price total return on £100. In each case figures are over one, three, five and ten years. It also gives a host of statistical data, including the geographical spread of trusts, the total value of assets, the share price, the net asset value, the discount, the gearing potential, the gross yield and the annual growth in dividends as measured over five years. In addition there is information on savings schemes and personal equity plans and a contact list of names and addresses for the management groups.

VARIATIONS ON A THEME

Limited life trusts

Whatever the so-called 'advantages' of the discount, some companies have seen it as a drawback, and they have decided to get round it by offering 'limited life' trusts. These have either a fixed redemption date, at which point the company will be wound up and its assets realised at full market value, or a series of dates – perhaps once a year – at which shareholders have the option to vote for the winding-up of the company.

Either strategy has the advantage that the discount is unlikely to stray up too far; there can be a drawback, however, in that it means fund managers cannot be as far-sighted in their investment policy as they would with an ordinary investment trust.

Split capital trusts

Split capital trusts started out in the 1960s with the aim of accommodating two types of investor within the one trust: those who were seeking high and growing income, but had little or no interest in capital growth; and those seeking capital growth, with no desire for income. This was achieved by having two classes of share: income and capital. More recently the concept has been expanded and split capital trusts may now also include zero dividend preference shares, stepped preference shares and highly geared ordinary shares. All split capital trusts have a fixed life-span, although shares can be bought and sold at any time.

The original type of income shares offer high income during the life of the trust and a fixed redemption price when it is wound up. The nearer the trust is to its winding-up date, the nearer the share price is likely to get to its redemption value, but meanwhile it may stand above that, reflecting expectations of future income. So if you hold the shares to redemption there may be a capital loss.

A newer type of income share may get a proportion of the assets at winding-up, on top of the fixed redemption price, but only after other classes of share have taken their entitlements. In contrast, 'annuity income' shares have only a nominal redemption value, perhaps as little as 1p, so there is a built-in capital loss, but meanwhile they receive all the income generated from the trust's portfolio. Finally, highly geared ordinary shares, which are found in 'hybrid' trusts paired with zero preference shares, have no fixed redemption price but receive the surplus assets after the zeros have been paid off, and meanwhile receive all the trust's income.

Income shares are suitable for investors seeking high and rising income, particularly if they are non-taxpayers or can hold the shares tax free within a personal equity plan. The highly geared ordinary shares are better suited to experienced investors who are prepared to accept a capital risk in return for potentially high rewards.

Capital shares normally receive no dividends during the life of the trust, but at winding-up they get all the remaining assets after the prior claims of preference and income shares have been met. There is thus a risk involved, but the chance of very good returns. Zero dividend preference shares, on the other hand, have a fixed redemption value and take top priority at winding-up. The return is not guaranteed, as the trust will have to generate sufficient assets to meet the liability, but the risk is very low.

Stepped preference shares offer a combination of income and capital returns, with a fixed redemption value and a fixed rate of annual dividend growth. As with zeros, the returns are not guaranteed, but the risk is small.

Split capital trusts offer a lot of potential for investors who have specific capital or income needs, or are prepared to take on higher risk for potentially high returns. However, because of their complex structure it is important to be sure exactly what each type of share's entitlement is, and what the likelihood is of its being met – for example, what growth rate the trust will have to achieve between now and the winding-up date to repay the various classes of share.

Warrants

Around 97 trusts currently have warrants available and new launches sometimes offer a free warrant for every so many shares you buy. A warrant is not itself a share, but gives you the right to buy a share at a fixed price at some point in the future.

The terms, which are set when the warrant is issued, specify the 'exercise price', at which the future share can be bought, and the 'exercise date', on which the option can be taken up. This may be a particular day, or a period between two dates, each year up to the final exercise date. There is no obligation to buy at any point and obviously it will only be worth while if the exercise price, plus the original price of the warrant, compares favourably with the current price of the share.

Of course, once the final expiry date has passed, the warrant becomes worthless. But during their life warrants can be bought and sold just like the shares themselves, so warrants can be bought as investments in their own right, with the intention of selling at a profit, rather than exercising the right to buy shares.

The warrant price is generally much lower than the share price, but its movements are proportionately greater. This is known as the gearing, the level of which is measured as the share price divided by the warrant price. The higher the gearing, the greater are the potential risks and rewards of the warrant. Two other features to look for in choosing a warrant are the premium – the amount by which the warrant price plus its exercise price exceeds the current price of the underlying share – and its remaining lifespan, up to the final exercise date. The longer the lifespan, the higher the

ICON

PERSONAL SHARE DEALING

on the Internet

Putting you in
the dealer's chair

Now you can have direct access to the London Stock Exchange - at the click of a mouse!

With full access to over 2100 quoted UK shares, the ICON Share Dealing Service is simple to operate with up to the second share prices and the very latest market information.

All you have to do is to register, select a share to buy or sell, type in how many you require and request a price - then simply click the 'deal' button and watch the trade happen before your eyes - nothing could be easier!

The 'ICON' share dealing service is provided by James Brearley & Sons Ltd, a long established stockbroker offering a wide range of additional services including execution-only dealings, discretionary portfolio management, PEP's, ISA's, traded options advice and dealing, high interest bank accounts and personal finance planning.

Details of the 'ICON' personal share dealing or any of the James Brearley services can be found by visiting their website on:

www.jbrearley.co.uk
or call **01253 629444** for a brochure

JAMES BREARLEY & SONS LIMITED
STOCKBROKING & INVESTMENT MANAGEMENT

On-Line investments to revolutionise share trading

The past year has seen an explosive growth in real-time systems and long established stockbrokers, James Brearley & Sons, are at the forefront of the new share trading revolution.

The system, which is surprisingly simple to operate, is known as the ICON Personal Share Dealing service giving direct access to the London Stock Exchange with up to the minute prices for over 2000 UK quoted shares. Clients can check the valuations of their own portfolio at any time.

When clients register they are given their own secure password which enables them to contact the site; their screen displays their own portfolio with up to the second values and there is a Hotlist window showing the current prices of shares not held but of interest. Dealing is particularly easy, just select the share, type in how many to buy or sell then request a price. If the price is acceptable, click the 'deal' button and watch the trade being done. The portfolio changes within 2 seconds of pressing the deal button to show the new position.

Roger Brearley, Chairman of the Stockbroker Group said "The response to the new ICON service has been tremendous; in addition to the numerous UK calls, we have had enquiries from Europe, America and the Far East. That's the beauty of on-line share dealing which is accessible to all parts of the Globe. Our service is available to both new and existing clients and as one of the smaller stockbrokers, we can avoid the delays and problems that larger organisations have reported".

One distinct advantage James Brearley has over its larger rivals is that it offers a support service for queries from on-line clients. "There are no hidden extras – what you see is what you get," says Roger Brearley. "We must be one of the lowest priced services available for on-line dealing with an annual fee of just £25 and a flat £20 commission to trade over the Internet and if there are any initial problems we can offer advice through our usual Stockbroker channels".

Investors can now go shopping for shares in the Internet with ICON services putting you in the dealers chair so you can tap into the stock market on-line at any time, 24 hours a day.

Another advantage of the ICON system is that it always tries to better the market price and you will receive the benefit when this applies, although there is no guarantee that a price better than the market will be obtained.

Orders placed outside market hours must have a price limit and will be dealt with after the next market opening. Limit orders, whether placed prior to market opening or when the market is open, will lapse at the normal close of business on the day they are first actionable.

"We've found that when clients open an ICON account, they really enjoy being in the hot seat and being completely in control of their own portfolio" says Roger, "and they can keep a watchful eye on which stocks they are interested in by referring to the ICON Hotlist".

James Brearley & Sons, an independent company, was established 80 years ago. The 'ICON' direct dealing system is the most recent addition to the comprehensive service they provide for the private investor. The Firm's core traditional business is, however, one of managing clients investments on either a Discretionary or Advisory basis, with qualified advisers available to offer personal attention. Although the new 'ICON' share dealing service has proved very popular, James Brearley also accept numerous telephone execution deals as most clients do not yet have web access. Full details of the groups services including PEPS and ISA's, high interest bank accounts and pensions are available on the James Brearley Website. The site also provides news, share recommendations and links to other information providers.

With direct access to the Market, James Brearley operates at the heart of the investment industry. As a member of the London Stock Exchange the company has direct access to the stock market for buying and selling shares.

A stockbroker's principal activity is in providing their clients with sound advice for which demanding professional qualifications are required. James Brearley & Sons are bound by the rules and regulations of the Securities & Future Authority which demand very high standards of professional conduct.

The range of services can be tailored to suit individual circumstance and the flexible approach offered by James Brearley & Sons Ltd is welcomed by their many clients. Financial services offered by James Brearley & Sons include executions only dealings, discretionary portfolio management, PEP's, ISA's, traded options advice and dealing, high interest bank accounts and personal finance planning.

James Brearley & Sons was established in 1919 in Blackpool, celebrating its 80th Anniversary in 1999. There are branch offices in Blackburn, Burnley, Carlisle, Kendal, Lancaster, Preston, Southport and Stockport all of which offer the same high standards of professionalism.

Prospective clients can sample details of all James Brearley's services by visiting their website on www.jbrearley.co.uk

A brochure is available "ICON Personal Share Dealing" by contacting:

James Brearley & Sons Ltd, 56/60 Caunce Street, Blackpool FY1 3DQ.

Telephone 01253 629444.

Fax 01253 751522.

e-mail icon@jbrearley.co.uk

acceptable premium: there will be more time for the share price to increase and represent a profit over the exercise price.

One other point to bear in mind is that warrants do not entitle the holder to any dividends. This means there will be no income tax liability, while capital gains will come within the annual £7100 capital gains tax allowance. The exceptions are subscription shares, which do pay an annual dividend, but currently there are only a couple of trusts that issue these.

TRADED ENDOWMENT TRUSTS

A handful of specialist trusts invest in what are known as traded, or second-hand, endowment policies. As explained in Chapter 10, a policyholder who no longer wishes to keep an endowment may be able to sell it for a better return than its surrender value. The new owner then pays the premiums for the remaining term of the policy and receives the pay-out on maturity.

These trusts do just that. At their launch, they buy up a large number of policies with similar maturity dates and then pay the premiums on them over the next several years. When the policies mature, the trust is wound up and the profits are split among the shareholders.

The trusts pay no dividends, which means that, like zero dividend preference shares, they can be attractive to higher rate taxpayers. There is no ongoing income tax to pay and the profits at maturity may fall within the annual capital gains tax exemption allowance. With some of the trusts, the policies are chosen to mature over a five-year period and profits are then distributed in each of those five years, which makes it more likely that they will be covered by the allowance.

Because there is a set pay-out date, the trusts can be useful for meeting particular obligations, such as school fees. Of course, you could invest directly in second-hand endowments for the same purpose, but there are two advantages of doing it through a trust. First, it is more flexible, as you can change your mind and sell the shares at any time, and second, the trusts can be held in an Individual Savings Account (ISA) for further tax-efficiency.

Over the last few years, these trusts have been very successful. They can be viewed as fairly low risk: the underlying policies are invested in property and fixed-interest securities as well as equities, so are less exposed to stock market volatility, and because they are several years old they already have annual bonuses allocated to them that cannot be taken away. On the other hand, insurance companies' annual bonus rates have been falling lately, owing generally to the effects of lower inflation, which may have a dampening effect in future.

LLOYD'S TRUSTS

The well-publicised losses of the Lloyd's insurance market led, in October 1994, to a new approach to attracting capital: allowing investment by limited liability companies. This engendered the launch of a new family of investment trusts.

Lloyd's trusts invest primarily in equities, gilts, bonds or some mix of these. As with ordinary investment trusts, the shares can be bought and sold on the stock market and some of the trusts qualify as holdings for a personal equity plan. In addition, the trusts will use their portfolios to underwrite Lloyd's syndicates, which they may do to a limit of twice the capital involved.

In theory, then, investors' money will work twice over. The underlying portfolio will generate dividends, and offer the potential for capital appreciation, in the ordinary way. On top of that, a proportion of any underwriting profits will be passed on to the shareholder. However, because Lloyd's accounts take three years to complete, these profits would only come through in dividends in the fourth year from launch.

The downside is that there are also two ways of losing money. The underlying portfolio may fall in value, while any underwriting losses that are sustained will have to be met by selling assets. But the risk is mitigated by the fact that there will be a time limit on claims for the contracts underwritten, which is not the case for existing Lloyd's Names, and also because, with limited liability, you can never lose more than you invest.

At the time of writing there are about 15 such trusts. A number are fairly small and not very frequently traded, hence there has been no significant movement in share prices to indicate whether the concept is a successful one or not. Information and analysis have also been scarce, partly because these would involve analysing all the underlying Lloyd's syndicates to which the trusts are exposed, which is a highly specialist and lengthy procedure.

The decision on which syndicates to support is obviously a major factor in the potential investment return. The larger trusts have tended to spread themselves across the market, while some of the smaller ones have taken a more specialist approach. To some extent this selectivity can be an advantage; while a large spread should in theory reduce risk, in practice it also reduces choice and makes monitoring more difficult.

Costs are also a consideration. Fees and commission have to be paid to Lloyd's, Lloyd's members' agents and other advisers to the trust, as well as the trust manager, all of which will reduce the returns for investors.

So even if you are prepared for the risks – which means being prepared to lose your entire investment – picking a trust is not straightforward. One way around this is a 'fund of funds', which invests in a selection of the trusts available. Otherwise, you should certainly consider taking professional advice.

VENTURE CAPITAL TRUSTS

Venture capital trusts (VCTs) were first announced in the 1993 Autumn Budget, but there then followed a year of consultation before details were given in the 1994 Budget. The first trusts were launched in 1995.

There were already a number of investment trusts that specialise in the venture and development capital sector. What is different about the new ones is that in return for meeting specific investment criteria, they will offer considerable tax concessions.

For investments of up to £100,000 a year, there is front-end income tax relief of 20 per cent if you subscribe at launch, no tax on dividends and no capital gains tax on sale profits. There is also rollover relief – capital gains tax on profits from other assets will be deferred if the proceeds are reinvested in a VCT, although it will have to be paid when the VCT shares are sold, unless the money is further reinvested into another VCT. The criterion for all these concessions is that the VCT shares must be held for at least five years.

For its part, the VCT must, within three years of being set up, have 70 per cent of its holdings in qualifying companies – broadly, unquoted trading companies. Investments may include loans, with a minimum term of five years, but at least half the portfolio must be in ordinary shares.

Venture capital is by its nature a risky area – many new ventures quickly bite the dust. On the other hand, VCTs spread the risk, as they invest in a selection of companies and can invest up to 30 per cent of their portfolios outside the venture capital sector – in blue chip shares, say, which would significantly reduce the overall risk. Moreover, the tax reliefs are attractive, although in exchange you are locked in for five years.

There are three main points to consider if you are thinking of investing in a VCT. First, you should look at where it is investing. There can be considerable differences between seed-corn investment, where money is put into companies at a very early stage of their development, and expansion finance, which covers a later stage. The latter tends to be less 'exciting': the potential returns are smaller, but the risk level is also lower. Second, you should look at the management group's track record in the sector, as experience is even more crucial here than in other investment areas. Finally, there are the charges. These are likely to be higher than for the average investment trust, because of the quantity of research needed into each company the trust invests in, although the US practice of charging performance fees seems unlikely to catch on in the UK.

HEDGE FUNDS

Hedge funds are a special kind of investment fund that aims to make money no matter which way the market is moving. If, for instance, the manager expects a share to fall in price, he will 'sell it short', which involves borrowing shares to sell, in the expectation of buying replacements later on at a lower price. If the manager expects a share to rise in price, he can simply buy and hold it in the normal way.

Although hedge funds can be relatively low risk, they can also be very high risk – one American fund, Long-Term Capital Management, got into serious trouble in 1998 and had to be bailed out at a reported cost of over $1 billion. Minimum investments also tend to be very high, so on the whole these funds are not for the average private investor. But Finsbury Asset Management runs an investment trust that invests in hedge funds. The company claims it produces a return that is roughly in line with the MSCI World Index but with only half as much risk.

LIFESTYLE PRODUCTS

Until recently, investment trusts were viewed purely as vehicles for investment or saving as an end in itself. But in practice, as discussed in Chapter 1, many people have a specific reason for saving – perhaps their children's future or their own retirement. Some investment trust groups are now responding to this by designing 'lifestyle' products that serve a particular purpose.

This has been prompted in part by new rules, introduced in January 1995, for the disclosure of charges on financial products. This tends to be a disadvantage to insurance companies, whose products have traditionally involved 'front-end loading' of charges, in contrast to investment trusts and unit trusts, which take a flat charge from each investment. As a result, investment trust companies have seen opportunities to compete in new areas.

Pension plans are one example. The plans are underwritten by insurance companies, as they must be administered by an authorised pension provider, but the underlying investment is into investment trusts. The advantages over insurance companies' own plans are that costs tend to be lower and charges are not front-end loaded, which means contributions are generally more flexible – they can be altered, or stopped and restarted, without incurring penalties.

PEP mortgages were also offered by some investment trust companies. Now that PEPs can no longer accept new money, existing plans have generally been rolled over into the new Individual Savings Accounts (ISAs). However, the lower investment allowances for ISAs and the fact that they may have a limited life have made them less attractive than PEPs were for mortgage purposes. Hence there may be no further expansion in this area, but it seems likely that investment trusts will continue to develop in other fields.

WHERE TO FIND OUT MORE

The primary source of information is the Association of Investment Trust Companies (AITC), Durrant House, 8–13 Chiswell Street, London EC1Y 4YY. The Association produces a free information pack that provides a booklet on buying investment trust shares plus details of all trusts, savings schemes, personal equity plans and the addresses of the management groups. In addition, as well as a statistics leaflet, it publishes free fact-sheets on:

- ☐ how investment trusts work;
- ☐ investment trusts and risk;
- ☐ investing for income or capital growth;
- ☐ investing for children;
- ☐ investing for a mortgage;
- ☐ investing for a pension;
- ☐ investment trusts and Individual Savings Accounts (ISAs);
- ☐ split capital trusts;
- ☐ warrants;
- ☐ discounts;
- ☐ share buybacks;
- ☐ investment trusts and the Internet.

For more comprehensive coverage, the AITC offers a monthly information service, which includes statistical data on the trusts, performance figures and a list of contacts for the management groups. Subscriptions are available on a full monthly basis, at a cost of £35 a year, or quarterly, for £20 a year.

For more details, there is an enquiry line on: 020 7431 5222.

9 Individual Savings Accounts and Personal Equity Plans

In 1997, the new Labour Government announced that personal equity plans (PEPs) and tax exempt special savings accounts (TESSAs) were to be ended in favour of a new savings vehicle, the Individual Savings Account (ISA). PEPs had been in existence for 10 years, having been announced in the 1986 Budget and introduced on 1 January 1987, while TESSAs had been around since January 1991.

Under the original rules, PEPs would have simply ceased to exist. Up to £50,000 could be transferred from PEPs to an ISA during a six-month transition period, but any savings beyond that level would revert to being taxable. There was also to be a £50,000 lifetime investment limit for ISAs, so anyone who already held this much in PEPs would have no further tax-free saving opportunity. However, after strong representations from the investment industry, the Chancellor relented in the Budget of March 1998. Since the start of the 1999/2000 tax year, it has no longer been possible to make any further contributions to PEPs, but existing plans may continue and do not affect the contribution limits for ISAs.

ISA RULES

ISAs have been available since 6 April 1999 and may include any or all of three elements: stocks and shares, cash, and life insurance. The overall investment limit for the current 2000/01 tax year is £7000, with a limit of £3000 for cash and £1000 for insurance.

The stocks and shares element may include any of the investments previously allowed for PEPs: shares, unit trusts, investment trusts, fixed-rate bonds, preference shares and convertibles. There is no longer any distinction drawn between 'qualifying' and 'non-qualifying' as regards where a fund invests, so unit trusts and investment trusts may be included up to the full limit regardless of their geographical scope. Shares from an approved profit-sharing or share option scheme may be transferred into a plan at their market value, but 'windfall' shares from a building society or insurance company conversion may not be put into an ISA.

The cash element includes all types of bank and building society accounts, plus taxable National Savings products and supermarket savings accounts. You may also transfer in the capital, but not the interest, from a maturing TESSA and this will not count towards the annual investment limit.

Finally, the insurance element can include any type of single premium life assurance policy or one on a recurrent single premium basis. It must be written on the sole life of the investor – joint life policies do not qualify – and must not be a pension or annuity plan, although it can offer additional benefits such as critical illness or accident cover. It must remain in the ISA for its full term or it will automatically cease to exist – you cannot count it in one year and out the next. However, if it matures or is surrendered, the proceeds can be used to take out a new policy or policies without counting towards that year's investment allowance.

Unlike with PEPs, investors may take out more than one plan a year – and this is where it gets complicated. Plans are of two types: 'maxi' ISAs, which must have a stocks and shares element and may also incorporate either or both of cash and insurance; and 'mini' ISAs, which cover any one of the three elements. In any one tax year, you may have *either* one maxi plan *or* up to three minis, one for each element, which may be with the same or different providers.

However, to ensure that the overall investment allowance is not breached, there are individual limits for each type of mini: the normal £1000 for insurance and £3000 for cash and £3000 for stocks and shares. So, for instance, if you put £1000 into a cash mini plan, you may put no more than £3000 into a stocks and shares mini, but if you take out a maxi plan, you may put in £1000 in cash and top up to the full £7000 with stocks and shares.

The investment limits apply to money going in during the course of a tax year. So if you invest to the limit and then take some money out, you cannot replace it until the next tax year. Nor can you switch funds between the different elements of the plan: money that you invest in a cash element, whether in a mini or a maxi, cannot later be transferred into insurance or stocks and shares, for instance.

The tax position is also more complicated than for PEPs. The easy part is that you will have no income or capital gains tax liability and will not have to declare ISA holdings on your tax return. Within the plan, a 10 per cent tax credit will be paid on the dividends from UK shares for the first five years of the scheme, up to April 2004. This is less generous than the old regime for PEPs, where the tax credit was worth 20 per cent. What is more relevant is that it is also less than the effective tax saving on cash deposits, which will continue to be 20 per cent. In other words, cash and other interest-paying funds will be a more tax-efficient holding in an ISA than stocks and shares for basic and lower rate taxpayers. For higher rate taxpayers there will still be a significant tax benefit on dividends.

The picture grows murkier when it comes to funds that pay both interest and dividends. Under the rules, a fund must be at least 60 per cent invested in fixed interest stocks, such as corporate bonds, gilts and the like, to qualify as interest-paying. If it falls below this level, all income will be classified as dividends, regardless of where it comes from, and the tax credit will be just 10 per cent. As a result, a number of fund managers have been reviewing their income funds and tweaking the portfolio if fixed interest holdings have been just under the 60 per cent mark.

Another difference from PEPs is in the way a plan can be set up. ISAs may be opened with a gift from someone else, whereas a PEP could only be opened by an investor personally, using his own

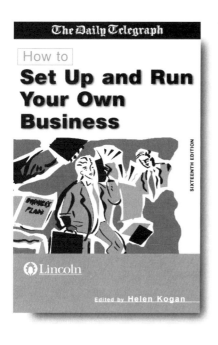

money. It is also possible to open an ISA by telephone or over the Internet, instead of the written application that was required for PEPs and TESSAs, although written forms are still likely to be most common.

ISAs have no statutory lock-in period – you can take your money out at any time without losing any tax benefits – and no minimum subscription, apart from whatever the plan manager may impose. Finally, the scheme is guaranteed to run for at least 10 years, with a review after seven years to decide if and how it should continue.

The Cat standard

One of the government's main aims in introducing ISAs is to encourage more people to save. To give people confidence that an ISA is suitable, it has drawn up criteria for a quality mark for plans, called a 'Cat' standard. This stands for cost, access and terms and it involves particular requirements for each of the three ISA elements. These are summarised in Table 9.1.

Table 9.1 *Criteria for the Cat standard*

Plan type	Cost	Access	Terms
Stocks and shares	No initial charge, annual charge of no more than 1%	Minimum investment no more than £500 lump sum or £50 a month	Unit trusts, investment trusts and OEICs that are at least 50% invested in EU equities
Cash	No charges for withdrawals or transfers	Withdrawals within seven working days	Interest rate no less than 2% below base rate; no limits on frequency of withdrawals
Insurance	Annual charge of no more than 3%; no other charges	Minimum premium of no more than £250 lump sum or £25 a month	After three years surrender value must at least match premiums paid in

The UK All-Share Index-Tracking ISA

114.9%*

fund growth in the last five years

NO initial charges ▶

NO withdrawal fee ▶

ONLY 0.54% ▶ total annual charges

Choosing an ISA? Check the fund

Choose our UK Index-Tracking ISA for a wealth of tracking experience and an outstanding record for growth.

Looking for real growth potential from an ISA? Look no further. The Legal & General UK Index-Tracking ISA invests in a fund that's grown by 114.9%* in just five years. And with annual charges of only 0.54% – more of your money will be working for you from the start.

So why not call us, visit our website or return the coupon now?

0800 092 0092

Please quote ref: E27DF18. 8am to 8pm weekdays, 9am to 5pm weekends.
For your protection, we may record and monitor calls

www.LandG.com/uk5

✂ -

YES I would like more information about the Legal & General UK Index-Tracking ISA. Occasionally, we may tell you about other products or services offered by the Legal & General Group of companies that we believe may be of interest to you. If you would prefer not to receive this carefully selected information, please tick here ☐.

E27DF18

| Title   Initial   Surname |
| Address |
| |
| Postcode   Date of birth |
| Tel. No: Home |
| Tel. No: Work |

Legal & General

Post to: Legal & General Direct Limited, FREEPOST SWC0467, Cardiff CF24 0GY.

Initially, the Cat mark for stocks and shares ISAs was to be restricted to index-tracking unit trusts – investment trusts were to be excluded, along with all actively managed funds. However, after representations from the industry, the final rules widened the scope to include any fund that is at least 50 per cent invested in the European Union and meets the cost and minimum investment criteria. In practice, the restriction on charges is very difficult for a non-tracker fund to meet, as active management is generally more expensive than passive: it requires greater research, for one thing, and administration is likely to be more complex. As a result, there are fewer actively managed Cat-marked funds than there are trackers.

Perhaps the biggest objection to the concept of the Cat standard is that it will be misunderstood as some kind of official endorsement. Many felt it was inappropriate for equity funds, because performance can be far more important than charges in determining the actual return to an investor. The fear was that investors might see the Cat mark as some kind of promise of performance and that there could be a severe backlash if and when the market fell. This was especially true when the Cat mark was confined to trackers; because they appear to be so straightforward, it is easy to forget that they will track the index *down* as well as up. The concern is enhanced by the fact that Cat-marked plans will mostly be sold direct – through newspaper advertisements, for example, with no advice given, as the low charge leaves little scope for commission to be paid.

Certainly, research that has been conducted has tended to suggest that there is much less awareness and understanding of the Cat standard than there is of ISAs themselves. This is despite the many column inches that have already been devoted to the subject in newspapers, focusing on the arguments for and against. However, now that plans have been up and running for over a year, investors may become more familiar with the concept. Awareness may also increase if the idea is extended to other areas; the government is proposing to set similar standards for the new stakeholder pensions.

b^2 have taken the hard work out of starting a tax-free ISA. Just fill in one simple form – or even do the whole thing over the phone – and one of the best performing ISAs on the market will be yours. Since its launch in October 1998 the Market Track 350 Account has grown savers money by over 37% – giving savers a tax-free profit of £1,850 on a £5,000 investment. So cut out the hard work. Call b² for a jargon-free information pack, quoting B4301, or visit our website.

ISAs from b²

www.b2.com
0800 62 62 62

TYPES OF PLAN

With the changes to the Cat standard and to other ISA details not finalised until late 1998 or even early 1999, providers had relatively little time to perfect their plans before the official launch date on 6 April 1999. Nevertheless, a surprising number were available from the word go and the number of providers has proliferated since then. Many of them are unit trust and investment trust companies but there are also banks, building societies, stockbrokers, Marks & Spencer Financial Services and even supermarkets.

By far the most popular element is stocks and shares. Under the rules, this must be incorporated into maxi plans and just over half the maxis on offer at the outset were based on stocks and shares only. Most of the rest had a cash element, but very few included insurance. Mini plans showed the same pattern of favouring stocks and shares but eschewing insurance. This is still the case at the time of writing.

A few investment companies, such as Standard Life, also operate a bank, so can offer a savings account as the cash element. Most, however, are offering cash unit trusts. While these can be just as attractive as savings accounts, investors need to remember that they cannot switch from these into equity-based trusts. When cash trusts were first launched, it was mainly as a temporary safe haven for periods of stock market volatility, a way for the companies to hang on to investors' money when they might otherwise have taken refuge in a bank or building society. The idea was that when the jitters were over, they could switch back to an equity fund with a discount on the initial charge. But under ISA rules, money invested in the cash portion of a plan must remain in the cash portion; even in a maxi plan, you cannot switch between the different elements.

Many of the major investment companies have eschewed the Cat mark, on the grounds that margins are so tight that the product would either be a loss leader or need huge volumes of sales to be profitable. Evidence to date is that investors have not particularly sought out Cat-marked plans, although this may change as the concept becomes better known.

DISCOUNT ISAS AND UNIT TRUSTS THROUGH BETTER INVEST DIRECT

Saving you money, and helping you make money

As a buyer of the Daily Telegraph Lump Sum Investment Guide, you are undoubtedly one of the growing number of people throughout the UK who wish to gain greater control over their financial destiny. And that means you can also save yourself hundreds of pounds in set-up charges, commission payments and fees.

Many people seek advice from Independent Financial Advisers. And, in return for that advice, when you buy a financial product the IFA is entitled to commission from the investment company that supplies the product. For ISAs and unit trusts, this generally equates to around 3% of the amount invested.

Reduce costly set-up charges

If you have spent time carrying out your own research, you may decide that you do not need independent advice, and you may want to go direct to the investment company in an attempt to avoid commission payments... not a good move. All that happens is that the investment company pockets the commission. What's more, whether you go through an IFA or you go direct to the investment company, you will expect to lose a further 2% or more in initial set-up charges. On an ISA investment of £7,000, these commission and set-up charges will equate to as much as £367, in effect making your investment worth only £6,633 on Day One.

Benefit from commission rebates and extra discounts

But, by buying your ISA or unit trust through Better Invest Direct, you can save between 3% and more than 5% - Better Invest Direct rebates all initial commission to which it is entitled as an IFA, and it is able to negotiate further discounts with investment companies. In some cases, this can mean no initial charges at all. And, importantly, Better Invest Direct does not charge handling fees.

Not only does this mean that your investment is working harder for you from the start, it also gives you the ability to change from one investment to another without reducing the value of your investment. This is ideal for PEP transfers if you feel that your current PEP is not performing well.

So, how does Better Invest Direct earn a living? Investment companies generally make an annual charge of around 1.5% on your ISA or unit trust, irrespective of whether you go through an IFA or go direct to the investment company. We have simply agreed to receive 0.5% of this amount, which would normally be retained by the investment company anyway.

The normal value of your investment, therefore, is unaffected by what Better Invest Direct earns from the investment company. And just think about the long term benefits, say over five years, of saving, for example, £350 on set-up charges in Year One! That saving could be worth significantly more after just a few years.

A wide range of financial products from all leading investment companies

Better Invest Direct has saved thousands of investors hundreds of thousands of pounds in the last year. To find out more about how we can help you save money on literally thousands of ISAs, unit trusts, OEICs and PEP transfers from all of the leading investment companies, simply call our Investor Hotline on 0800 169 3604 or visit our web site at www.betterinvestdirect.co.uk.

Richard Wood

Richard Wood is Managing Director of independent financial advisers Better Invest Direct Limited, a member of Investment Strategies (UK) Limited which is regulated by the Personal Investment Authority. Call Better Invest Direct's Investor Hotline free on 0800 169 3604 for further information.

CHOOSING AN ISA

In principle, the ISA rules offer greater flexibility than there was with PEPs. Instead of just one plan a year, with one provider, you can have up to three, with three different providers, if you opt for the mini route. But in practice the rules harbour pitfalls for the unwary and ideally you need to think about your full year's investment intentions before you open any plan.

Mini plans look attractive because you can spread your money between different providers, choosing each for its particular strength. The drawback is that the investment allowances are more tightly drawn: £3000 for stocks and shares, £3000 for cash and £1000 for insurance. So if you put just £1 into a cash mini, for example, you will be able to put only £3000 into stocks and shares. If you put that same £1 into the cash part of a maxi, you could put up to £6999 into stocks and shares. To make the most of your allowance through mini plans, you would have to put exactly £3000 into cash, £3000 into stocks and shares and £1000 into insurance.

Of course, you may not expect to have £7000 available to invest, but if your circumstances alter, you will not be able to change your mind. Once you have made your choice, you can only switch between plans of the same type, so you are stuck with the decision for the rest of the tax year.

But maxi plans are not without drawbacks of their own. First, they mean all your investments are with one provider, so there is less spread of risk. Second, as mentioned above, many maxi plans on the market offer stocks and shares only, while few provide the full choice of all three elements. Third, in choosing a plan, should you go for the provider with the best performance record for the stocks and shares element or the highest interest rate on cash? Few institutions specialise in both these areas, so a maxi plan is always going to be a compromise, probably based on which element is most important for you.

Charges and performance

Charges are clearly relevant, as they will influence the returns you get. As with PEPs, plans based on unit trusts make no charge other than that on the underlying funds, but these can vary quite signifi-cantly, from zero to around 5.5 per cent for the initial charge and from 0.5 to 1.5 per cent for the annual charge.

Plans that carry the Cat mark are guaranteed to have no initial charge and an annual charge of not more than 1 per cent. This undoubtedly looks attractive, but you have to consider what you are getting in return – if the charge has been cut, perhaps a service has also been cut. In the case of tracker funds, for example, it is the manager's judgement that has been taken out of the equation – and supporters of trackers would argue that this is no bad thing! But whether or not you agree, it is worth remembering that the Cat-marked trackers currently available are all based on the UK stock market. If all your other investments are UK-based – such as your house, your pension and even your day-to-day savings – you might want to put your ISA holdings further afield, for the sake of a balance of risk.

The other point about Cat-marked plans is that they are likely to offer little, if any, commission, because the low charges leave no margin for it. Hence there may be no advice available, unless you are prepared to pay a fee for it. If you know what you want, well and good; if not, and you want advice, you should consider whether you prefer to pay for it via a higher up-front charge or a specific fee.

As regards performance, most of the current stocks and shares ISAs are based on existing unit trusts and investment trusts, so you can check the track records of the individual funds. As the saying goes, past performance is not necessarily a guide to the future and today's league leaders are not always the heroes of tomorrow, but a consistent past record is a reasonable indication of potential. Other points to consider are the overall investment philosophy of the plan manager and whether the attitude to risk broadly accords with your own.

Growth versus income

Normally, the choice between investments that focus on capital growth and those designed to pay income depends purely on your own circumstances. The retired, for example, may be looking for income to supplement a pension, while those in mid-life may be seeking growth now to provide income in the future.

183

Tax can also be an influence. If you are a higher rate taxpayer then, all else being equal, you should be better off with a growth investment, perhaps cashing in part of it to provide an 'income' if necessary. That way you can benefit from your annual capital gains tax exempt allowance, whereas you would have to pay tax on all actual income received.

The conventional wisdom with PEPs was that if you held both income and growth investments, the income ones should be given preference for Pepping. This was based on the reasoning that capital gains tax is not an issue for the average investor, so there is more benefit in saving income tax.

However, the picture for ISAs is a little more complicated. The tax credit on dividends is now half what it was for PEPs, and ISAs can also include cash and insurance products that were not part of PEPs. In fact, the greatest tax saving now comes on cash deposits and other investments that pay interest rather than dividends, so in terms of pure tax-efficiency these should be given first priority – assuming you were going to hold them anyway. But if your focus is wholly on growth, then you should stick to it for your ISA. After all, if you are investing over a long term, even quite modest savings can build to a level where capital gains tax could come into play.

Self-select plans

As with PEPs, you can have a self-select ISA if you want to make all the investment decisions yourself. This allows you to mix funds from different management groups or even different types of investment, such as unit trusts, investment trusts and individual shares.

It is not entirely do-it-yourself, because you must have an authorised plan manager providing the ISA 'shell'. These plans are mainly offered by banks and stockbrokers, which will generally charge a fee for the administration. This means it can work out more expensive than an ISA from, for instance, a unit trust group, which will absorb the administration cost within its own fund charges. Fees may be on a flat rate or percentage basis and can vary considerably between managers, so it is worth shopping around. Watch out, too, for additional costs: you can expect to pay dealing costs to buy or sell shares, but some managers also charge for

If you don't want advice, you don't need to pay for it.

Using a discount broker can save you hundreds, even thousands of pounds on your investments. If you don't want advice from a financial advisor, you could invest directly with a fund management or life assurance company. However, if you do, you will invariably pay the full initial charge. This can often be 5%, or even more of the amount you invest. **If you use a discount broker, you do not receive advice, but the initial charge is far less, in some cases removed altogether.** This is because the discount broker gives up most, or all of its initial commission. It is also able to secure additional discounts on your behalf because of the high volume of business it deals with.

The following are typical examples of discounts and savings offered by discount brokers on a lump sum £7,000 Maxi ISA investment.

Company	Initial charge	Discount	Saving
Aberdeen	4.25%	4%	£280
Gartmore	5%	4.75%	£332.50
Fidelity	3.25%	3%	£210
Jupiter	5-5.25%	4%	£280
Invesco	5.25%	5%	£350

So, how does a discount broker make any money? If your investment doesn't pay renewal commission, it retains part of the initial commission. This is usually between 1% and 2%, depending on the type of investment and the amount invested. However, most unit trust (or OEIC) managers pay renewal commission to brokers on ISAs and PEPs. Renewal commission (sometimes referred to as trail commission) is normally paid every six months, in arrears. The amount paid is usually 0.5% per annum of the value of your investment. It is funded from the 1% - 1.5% annual management charge.

Because investments tend to be held long-term, e.g. five years or more, renewal commission payments can be worth more than initial commission. If the average PEP/ISA investor has a portfolio worth £25,000, with modest growth, renewal commission could be worth £750 over five years. **The average investor is a valuable customer to the discount broker.**

Renewal commission is designed to meet the costs of servicing your investments. So, what after-sales service can you expect from your broker? Unfortunately, most brokers do not offer very much after-sales service.

Discount broker CommShare realised that an opportunity existed to set itself apart from other discount brokers by offering services for renewal commission. **Uniquely, it offers investors the opportunity to share renewal commission for five years.** It also offers an optional fund monitoring service, which can be paid for out of the investors' share of commission.

Briefly, this is how it works. If you buy an ISA (or transfer a PEP) using CommShare, you receive the same level of discount on the initial charge that could typically be obtained through other discount brokers. For the next five years, CommShare allocates any renewal commission received to an account set up for you. Annually, you will receive a statement setting out the total amount of renewal commission received, your share of this total (between 30% and 50% depending on the total collected), optional fund monitoring fees and the net payment due to you. The net amount is paid to your bank account by direct credit.

Example:

Total Renewal Commission Received

£125.54

Cash Rebate at 40% of £125.54

£50.22

Less Fund Monitoring Fees £10.00

Amount due to Investor £40.22

Accompanying this statement is a detailed breakdown of renewal commission received from each company and fund performance information. Performance information is included for each of your funds, where renewal commission has been received, and where information is available using Standard & Poors Micropal database.

It is possible to offer these services on your existing portfolio of investments. Most fund managers and life assurance companies pay renewal commission to provide ongoing service to you. They pay it to your choice of servicing broker. This is regardless of the broker who arranged the investment, or whether you originally dealt with the investment company directly. If you want to appoint CommShare to service your portfolio of investments, it is a simple case of completing authorisation forms, which are forwarded to the relevant companies. This means that you could appoint CommShare as servicing broker for all your existing PEPs/ISAs

paying renewal commission, enabling commission sharing and service on your entire portfolio.

On an average portfolio of £25,000, and assuming fund growth of 7% per annum, a typical investor would benefit from payments amounting to more than £370 over 5 years. This is of course in addition to annual fund performance information and the option to participate in a fund monitoring service.

Summary

- If you don't want advice, you don't need to pay for it.
- Investing directly with a fund company or life assurance company will not normally save you any money.
- Using a discount broker could save you up to 5% of your initial investment.
- Using CommShare will save you both initial and ongoing charges, and you will receive an ongoing service.

Please note that not all investments pay renewal commission. Also, a number of companies, albeit a small minority, will not transfer renewal commission from one broker to another.

If you would like to find out more about the services that CommShare offer, you can call to request a free PEP/ISA information pack, using a freephone number:

0808 100 50 45

Or, you can write, using a freepost address:
CommShare Ltd
FREEPOST SEA 1943
Marlowe House
109 Station Road
Sidcup
Kent
DA15 7ET

holding unit trusts or for collecting dividends. Finally, check what services are offered in return for the fee.

Buying on the Internet

Buying on the Internet was not possible for PEPs because a physical signature was needed on the application form; however, this requirement was relaxed for ISAs. Many unit trust and investment trust groups now offer ISA information on the Internet and several allow you to invest online. In fact, at the end of the tax year, there was a considerable amount of investment online, right up to the midnight deadline on 5 April.

Some firms require you to print out the application form and send it by post, or to send a cheque by post even though you can complete the application form online. Others, however, provide the whole process online. All personal information is encrypted and, in many ways, the process is actually safer than using the post. Payment is by Switch or other debit card, rather than credit card, and you will also need to give your National Insurance number, which is required to open any ISA.

ISA facilities

With the first plans little more than just off the starting-blocks, it is too early to know what, if any, special facilities might be developed. But one issue that has been raised is the question of ISA mortgages. In principle, these could work in much the same way as PEP mortgages and there might be an added benefit from the wider investment scope of ISAs, which would allow a portion of the savings to be held in cash for safety.

However, there are two concerns over ISA mortgages. One is the lower annual investment limit – currently £7000 as against a total of £9000 for PEPs – and the other is that they are only guaranteed a 10-year life-span, although that could be extended when the time comes.

For people who already have a PEP mortgage, providers have generally offered a choice between an ISA and an ordinary savings scheme for continuing contributions. But they have been more circumspect about attracting new business and, currently, ISA mortgages are not being promoted as a facility.

PERSONAL EQUITY PLANS

Since 6 April 1999, when ISAs were officially launched, it has not been possible to put any new money into PEPs. However, existing plans can be continued and will have the same tax benefits as ISAs. You may also switch money from one plan to another and, indeed, one provider has announced its intention to launch new PEPs just for this purpose. So it may be worth reminding yourself of the various types of PEP that are available.

Types of plan

☐ Managed PEPs are the largest category and the easiest option if you are not a particularly experienced investor or have a fairly modest sum invested. The most common are those offered by unit trust and investment trust groups, which give you a choice of funds, but generally only from their own range. A few, some-times referred to as multi-PEPs, include funds run by a number of different managers. There are also managed PEPs that include shares, usually run by stockbrokers. These are likely to be more expensive, as there may be initial and annual plan charges as well as dealing costs, whereas basic unit trust plans generally have no charges other than those on the trusts themselves.

☐ Advisory PEPs are those where you choose the holdings, but the plan manager offers advice. They are available from stock-brokers, investment managers and independent advisers and generally can include any of the investments that are eligible for a PEP. Plan charges and dealing costs are important in choosing a plan, as are the quality and availability of the advice offered – for example, whether the manager will sometimes contact you with suggestions or if it is always up to you to take the initiative.

☐ Self-select PEPs are the nearest you can get to a do-it-yourself plan. There must, as always with PEPs, be an authorised plan manager, usually a stockbroker, but all the decisions are yours alone. As with advisory PEPs, charges and dealing costs will be prime considerations when choosing a plan, but you should also check the scope of holdings allowed, as some managers may exclude unit trusts and investment trusts or shares outside the FTSE 100 Index.

☐ Corporate PEPs are set up by companies, via a plan manager such as a bank or stockbroker, chiefly for their own shares. A few may allow other shares to be included, but for the most part these are one-company affairs aimed mainly at employees and existing shareholders.

☐ Corporate bond PEPs, not to be confused with the above, were first seen in 1995 and invest in fixed-rate bonds issued in sterling by UK companies with terms of five years or more. They may also include preference shares and convertibles, but not gilts. Their attraction is that they offer a relatively high income, currently up to about 9 per cent, but in general the higher the income the lower the quality of the bonds, hence the greater the risk. There is also likely to be limited potential for capital growth, so these PEPs are best suited to investors whose main need is income.

☐ Single company PEPs are based on the shares of just one company, but the choice of company can be changed at any time. While PEPs were still open to new investment they carried their own contribution allowance, in addition to that for a general PEP, and must still be kept separate. In other words, if you do not have one already, you cannot open one with money from a general PEP; if you do have one, you can only switch it into another single company plan. As with all PEPs, charges are an important criterion when choosing a plan and you should also check whether the selection of the company is up to you or the plan manager.

To switch or not to switch?

Although you cannot add new money to any PEPs you have, it is still worth keeping them under review. It may be that the plan manager's attention is focused on the new ISAs, to the detriment of its PEPs; this could mean that the level of service deteriorates.

Alternatively, as it may become more expensive to run PEPs, with no new money coming in, charges could be raised. Or it may just be that performance is not all it should be.

Whatever the reason, you should not be afraid to vote with your feet and switch to a new plan manager, but there are two caveats to keep in mind. One is that there will be a cost involved: possibly an exit charge from your existing plan, plus an initial charge on the new one, although providers keen to lure money from their rivals may be offering discounts.

The other concerns 'consolidation'. With the ending of PEPs as regards new money, there has been an increased interest in the transfer market, with a focus on the merits of consolidating all your existing plans into a single new one. (If you hold both general and single company PEPs, they cannot be lumped together, so in this case consolidation would be into two plans, one of each type.) The argument is that you will then have just one statement to cover all your holdings, which will help you to keep track of them, and any other paperwork will be greatly reduced.

While this may sound attractive, once you have consolidated plans you will not be able to separate them again in future. For example, if you currently have five separate plans with different providers and you transfer them all to one new provider, they will be amalgamated into a single plan. If you wanted to transfer again in future, you would only be able to move the whole amount to one new plan; you could not split it between several plan managers.

For this reason, 'multi-PEPs', which include the funds of several different managers within one plan, have been trumpeted as the best of both worlds. The advantage is that you can spread your money among a number of fund managers, and change your selections when you want, but still have just one lot of paperwork. However, these PEPs tend to be more expensive, as there are plan charges on top of those on the underlying funds. If you are an active investor and switch holdings regularly, a multi-PEP could be cost-effective as switching costs within the plan are relatively low. Otherwise, this could be a pricey way of getting a consolidated statement, which your adviser, if you have one, should be able to provide for you in any case.

IGNORING YOUR PEPS CAN DAMAGE YOUR WEALTH!

We do not often have time to focus on our personal finances so move to the PEP Consolidation Company to simplify your PEP investments.

Why should you be looking at your PEP holdings?

It could have been up to thirteen years ago that you invested in your first PEP. So much can change: your investment aims, the number of funds or shares in your portfolio and your attitude to risk, and they can all affect the suitability of your portfolio. However, that review could be the catalyst in achieving a savings goal or a regular income with all the tax advantages of a PEP. Are you just finding all the paperwork and information you are sent by your PEP managers a complete nightmare?

Have a think about the following:

1. *Have your investment objectives changed?*

   Look at whether you require a regular income (for example if you have retired) or would prefer to accumulate your investment to achieve a future goal (for example to pay for your childrens future schooling or university tuition). **PEP Consolidation provides the solution with just one income payment from all your funds.**

2. *Do you have a concentration of investments in one area?*

   It may be that each year you come to the end of the tax year and invest in a rush to beat the end of tax year without reviewing the spread of your investments. As your portfolio of PEPs has built up over the years (and hopefully grown) so you need to take

a look at the overall picture to see if you have the right balance No one fund group offers a total solution. **The PEP Consolidation Company enables you to invest in any fund of your choice, providing the solution.**

3. *Has your attitude to risk changed?*

   It may be that you were working when you made your first investment in a smaller companies PEP (a higher risk objective). Now five years later, with retirement approaching and paying off the mortgage, that money may be more suited in a UK blue chip fund where you can be more sure of its stability. Look at your commitments, income and cash flow and try and make a decision as to how much risk you should take. **Switch to any fund simply and easily with the PEP Consolidation Company.**

4. *Are your investments performing unsatisfactorily?*

   You should receive a statement every six months from your PEP manager and from this you will get a general idea as to how well your investment is performing. It is a good idea to compare this performance with other funds with the same objective. Even if your fund has performed badly, it may be that the rest of the funds in that sector have performed even worse. Also give your investment a chance to prove itself. We all know the cautionary saying "the value of your investment can go down as well as up" but in the long-term the likelihood of this happening can be considerably lessened. **With the PEP Consolidation Company you receive one simple valuation for all your investments allowing simple comparisons to be made.**

If you've answered yes to any of the above then you should take your review a step further and talk to your IFA so that you can start amending your portfolio and choosing funds to suit your needs. There are so many funds claiming to be number one using varying time periods and investment sectors (as decided by the regulatory body in case you've ever wondered) to help their statistical analysis and then of course you could check whether that number one fund is in the number one quartile, decile or overall. This is where your IFA will have all the fund knowledge that you don't have the time or resources to process.

It's easier than you think

You may have realised that it is time to make a few amendments but is it really worth the effort to move things around? When it comes to changing your portfolio you will be surprised to know that Fund managers expect your investment objectives to change with time.

For example, say you want to move a fund from PEP manager Alpha to 6 different funds and fund managers through a transfer. All you have to do is complete the PEP Consolidation transfer application form, include the name of your investment in Alpha in the space provided and detail the new funds you require. It's easier than writing a cheque and in future, you will only have to switch funds – no more PEP transfers.

If the funds of your PEP manager have performed well, but you require a wider choice of funds, you may decide to stay with the same funds but switch into PEP Consolidation to give you the greater access you may require for the future. Once you are on board, further changes can save you money on exit/entry charges due to advantageous dealing arrangements with the PEP Consolidation Company. Changes only require a simple written confirmation.

Take some extra time to ensure that your PEP holdings suit your investment needs. Review your investments, decide on your long-term goal and talk to your IFA about changing your portfolio where necessary. The actual transfer and switching of funds to the PEP Consolidation Company can in most cases be achieved quickly and easily and could substantially increase the performance of your PEP portfolio.

The Benefits of The PEP Consolidation Company

- Huge range of funds
- Discounted switches between funds
- Growth, Income and Specialist funds
- Consolidated statements
- Internet valuations
- Simplified paperwork

Contact us:
The PEP Consolidation Company, 16 St John Street, London, EC1M 4NT

Telephone 020 7454 0704;
Facsimile: 020 7367 0689

Visit our website: www.eurolife.co.uk We can recommend an Independent Financial Adviser who is a member of IFAP in your area.

We strongly recommend that you seek independent financial advice before making any investment decisions

---

KEEPING TRACK OF YOUR INVESTMENT

Prices of unit trusts, investment trusts and shares are quoted in newspapers such as *The Daily Telegraph* and the *Financial Times*. This can give you a general idea of how your investments are performing, although the actual value of your PEP or ISA may be affected by plan charges or dealing costs. More accurate information will be given in the statements and valuations sent out by the plan manager, usually at half-yearly intervals. Managed plans may also provide reports on the companies or trusts included in the plan, plus newsletters or commentaries on the investment strategy.

10 | Life Assurance and Friendly Society Investments

Within the last generation, life assurance companies have become sizeable players in the savings market. This is not to say that they have abandoned their traditional role of supplying straightforward protection products such as term assurance, or the savings-plus-protection vehicles such as endowment plans. In fact, this range has been expanding, with the introduction of the likes of critical illness insurance and long-term care plans.

But the fact remains that insurance is generally sold rather than bought, so to maintain a healthy flow of new business, insurance companies have been broadening their horizons in the investment field. Many have associated unit trust companies, but they are also competing for lump sum investments with their own products.

This chapter looks at the main types on offer. Single premium bonds are a version of collective investments, like unit and investment trusts, that provide smaller investors with a stake in a large portfolio of assets, thereby spreading risk. Annuities are income-producing vehicles and are also put to use in 'hybrid' plans, which aim to produce a fixed level of income plus the prospect of capital growth. They therefore offer greater opportunities than fixed capital investments such as building society accounts, but with a measure of capital risk.

Second-hand endowments are policies that have been sold by their original holders and provide a lump sum route into what is traditionally a regular savings product. Fourth, the chapter looks at friendly societies, which have similarities with life assurance companies but certain tax advantages.

Finally, there is a review of health insurance products. While these are obviously not investments as such, they can protect your ability to enjoy the fruits of your investments.

SINGLE PREMIUM BONDS

Single premium bonds – so called because they are based on a one-off contribution – offer a broad investment choice and a spread of risk for sums starting at around £1000. Although technically they include an element of life assurance, it is relatively small – often it is simply the current bid value of the bond. This means that the investment potential is maximised rather than money being siphoned off to pay for life cover.

The bonds can be invested in a wide range of underlying funds operated by the company. These are similar to the various categories of unit trusts; for example, there are equity funds covering the UK, North America, Europe, Japan and the Far East, as well as broadly based international funds. There are also types that are not found among unit trusts, such as managed funds, with profits funds, currency funds and, to a large extent, property funds.

Managed funds invest in a mixture of equities, fixed interest securities and property, thus giving the widest possible spread of assets and risk. For this reason, they are the most popular, appealing both to very conservative investors and to those who prefer to leave all the investment decisions to a professional. There can, however, be considerable differences between one managed fund and the next, depending on the investment strategy adopted.

Essentially, there are two types: those that have a more or less set division between equities, fixed interest and property, which are sometimes called 'three-way' or balanced funds; and those where the manager takes a more active role in determining the proportions. A fairly recent trend is to offer more than one managed fund with differing degrees of risk; for example, Adventurous, Balanced and Cautious (or Conservative). The Adventurous fund will have a higher proportion in equities, which carry the highest risk/reward prospects, while the Cautious fund will lean more towards fixed interest securities.

In theory, a more actively managed fund should produce a better return by responding to changes in market conditions, but equally there is more scope for wrong decisions. The three-way fund, on the other hand, is likely to produce steadier, if unexciting, returns. Some examples of the past performance of managed funds are shown in Table 10.1.

In the late 1980s and early 1990s, property funds were in the doldrums, thanks to the sliding fortunes of the property market, and many shrank considerably in size. But from mid-1993 performance started to improve, as demand increased with the upturn in the economy. At the time of writing, expectations are for steady, if not spectacular, growth in both the commercial and residential sectors.

The drawback of property funds is that they are unwieldy – property cannot always be sold readily, so the portfolio cannot easily be adjusted to changing market conditions. Managers also reserve the right to delay making repayments to investors for up to six months, to avoid having to sell at a loss to raise cash quickly. In practice, such a delay has only ever been imposed on funds invested in residential property, while the bulk focus on commercial property. Smaller funds are often invested instead in the shares of property companies, which are more tradable, although the returns are subject to different influences.

Table 10.1   *Past performance of balanced managed funds*

| | Percentage increase in fund value over different periods | | |
	1 year	3 years	5 years
Best	22.72	60.68	104.12
Average	4.64	35.20	68.73
Worst	–6.23	12.41	24.30

Note: Figures are on a bid-to-bid basis, with income reinvested, to 28 April 2000.

Source: Standard & Poors Micropal

With profits funds, like managed funds, are invested in a mix of assets, but instead of the value of your holding depending on the value of investments in the underlying fund, with profits funds work by adding bonuses. The bonus rate is declared annually and depends on the investment profits made by the fund, but a part of these is usually held in reserve to boost rates in bad years. So there should be a 'smoothing' effect on market fluctuations, which reduces the risk. Some companies set a minimum guaranteed bonus rate and there may also be a terminal bonus, although this is not guaranteed.

Companies also reserve the right to make a 'market value adjustment' when money is paid out or switched to another fund. This would arise if the actual investment performance has not matched up to the value that has been credited, and is designed to protect continuing investors in the fund. Although this is likely to apply only in the early years – and is not normally applied on death – it does detract from the apparent safety of these funds.

TAXATION

The taxation of bonds is governed by the rules applying to assurance companies. As regards the underlying fund, this will pay tax on investment income and is also subject to capital gains tax on profits from the disposal of assets, hence the fund will set aside a reserve against future liabilities. The tax paid by the fund cannot be reclaimed, which is a major drawback for non-taxpayers.

Basic rate taxpayers have no tax worries on their own score – their liabilities are covered by what the fund has already paid. For higher rate taxpayers, however, it is a different – and rather complex – story. To start with the good news, up to 5 per cent of the original investment can be withdrawn from the bond, free of tax, each year for 20 years – this counts as being a return of capital. If the allowance is not used every year, it can be carried over, so if, for instance, you take nothing out in the first year, you have 10 per cent to play with in the second, and so on. The bad news comes at the end, when you cash in the investment. Tax is then assessed by a procedure known as 'top-slicing'. First, the total profit made from the bond is calculated, taking into account any withdrawals that have already been made, and the resulting amount is divided by the number of years for which the bond has been held. This figure is then added to your income for the year in which you cash in the bond to determine if you are liable to higher rate tax. If so, the higher rate will be applied to the whole of the profit made, and you will have to pay the difference between that and the basic rate tax which has already been paid.

There are two ways to mitigate the tax bill. If you can, you should put off cashing in the bond until a year when you are a basic rate taxpayer – after retirement, perhaps. Then you will have no further liability. You should also opt for the bond to be split into separate segments, each of which is effectively a policy in its own right; some companies do this automatically, others may do it on demand. The advantage is that if you want to withdraw more than the 5 per cent allowance, you can cash in all of one segment, which gets more favourable tax treatment than making a partial withdrawal above the limit.

BONDS VERSUS UNIT TRUSTS

Bonds and unit trusts have certain similar characteristics – both offer low-cost access to pooled funds and charges are comparable. Hence there has long been debate about their respective merits for investors.

One drawback of bonds is that capital gains tax is paid by the life assurance company on profits within the bond. With unit trusts, the capital gains tax liability falls on the investor, which hitherto has generally been an advantage. The new capital gains tax rules, described in Chapter 1, complicate the picture somewhat. Life assurance companies are still subject to the old regime, with index-ation, while investors come under the new system, with taper relief. If you have already used your exempt allowance, taper relief may be worth less than indexation, particularly if you have switched your holdings from time to time and so not held any for very long. In this case, bonds may be a better option. However, most investors will be able to make use of the exempt allowance, currently £7200 for the 2000/01 tax year, which tips the scales towards unit trusts.

Against this, the returns from a bond are treated as having had basic rate tax already paid, whereas in practice the charge incurred by the insurance company may be well below 20 per cent. Hence the returns may be higher than could be achieved on unit trusts. There is also the annual 5 per cent tax-free withdrawal allowance, which is useful for higher rate taxpayers. If you can cash in at a time when you are subject only to basic rate, and if you are also already using your capital gains tax allowance on other investments, bonds can be tax efficient.

Of course, unit trusts can be held in an Individual Savings Account (ISA), up to the current investment allowance of £7000. In this case, there will be no income or capital gains tax to pay. Bonds can also be held in an ISA under the insurance element, but only up to a value of £1000 a year, so if you are investing more this may influence the choice.

The other main attraction of bonds is the facility to switch between different underlying funds at low cost and without any tax liability. If you move from one unit trust to another, there may be a capital gains tax liability and you will have to pay a new front-end charge; even with a discount offered for staying with the same management group, this is likely to be at least 2 per cent. Bonds generally offer one or more free switches per year, after which there is a small charge of perhaps 0.5 per cent. Of course, you are restricted by the range of funds offered by the company, and it is unlikely that any single company will top the investment tables across the board.

For different investors' needs and circumstances, one or other product is likely to have the edge, so it is a good idea to seek advice before you commit yourself.

VARIATIONS ON THE BOND THEME

Guaranteed equity bonds

Guaranteed equity investments were born out of the disillusion with the stock market of many smaller investors after the 1987 crash. At first sight, they seem to be the perfect investment: they guarantee to return a high percentage of any increase in a given stock market index over the investment period, or your original capital if the index should fall.

However, you need to check the small print to be quite sure what you are being promised, as there are a number of variations on the theme. The investment period is commonly five years; if you take your money out before then, you normally forfeit the guarantee and there may be early surrender penalties as well. So if the market starts falling just before the end of the period, you could lose all the gains made up to then. Some products have a periodic 'lock-in' facility, whereby gains to date are consolidated into the guarantee; while others average the index value over the last 6 or 12 months, to protect against a last-minute fall.

In several cases, the guarantee applies only to the capital growth in the index, which means the income from share dividends is sacrificed. Over longer periods, this can be quite a lot to give up.

The message is that guarantees only come at a price, but these bonds can be attractive for short periods if you are nervous of stock market movements. For larger sums, though – say £10,000 upwards – you could put together your own package to offset risk, so it is worth taking independent advice.

High income bonds

These are another fairly recent idea, stemming in this case from the plunge in interest rates during 1993, which was a severe blow to building society investors dependent on income.

The bonds generally run from three to five years, during which time they provide a guaranteed level of income – recently this has been as much as 10 per cent a year gross. They also offer some form of promise on the capital return at the end of the term. This varies from bond to bond, but recent issues have been along the lines that the original capital will be returned in full, as long as a particular stockmarket index does not fall by more than a specified amount during the term. The two favoured indices recently have been the Eurostoxx 50, which comprises 50 of the largest European companies, and the Nasdaq 100, an American index that mainly covers technology companies.

The bonds use quite sophisticated derivatives to provide these guarantees and it is not always crystal clear exactly what is being promised. In fact, these products have come in for quite a bit of criticism. Firstly, it is argued that the payments made are not truly income, but are made out of capital. Secondly, the regulatory authorities have not been happy that the risk to capital is always adequately explained in the literature.

Certainly it can be complicated. For instance, some bonds available at the time of writing promise that you will get back your original investment *either* as long as the index does not – at any time during the term – fall by more than a set percentage *or*, if it does fall by more than that, it subsequently recovers so that, by the end of the term, it is at or above its starting level. As an example, if the index started at 100, you might be promised your money back as long as it never fell below 75 or, if it did, it was at 100 or higher at the end of the term.

This sounds like a reasonable safety net, especially as the companies cite records showing that the relevant index has never fallen by that much in the past. However, if the unexpected happens and the index does fall through the safety net, your return can fall quite sharply. A typical example is that you would get back your original investment, less 1 per cent for every 1 per cent fall in the index and less all the income you had had. So you might get back only around half of what you had invested – and in the worst case, with some bonds, you could get back nothing at all.

So you do need to check the downside very carefully and decide if you can stomach the risk. Of course, if you need a 10 per cent annual return to live on, and you can only get 5 per cent interest from a building society, you are probably going to have to take some risk. At least with the bond, if all works out well, you will retain your capital, whereas, if you leave the money in a building society and draw out more than the interest it earns, your capital will shrink over time. But you should also remember that you will effectively be locked in for the full term; if you want to withdraw your money early, any guarantees will be invalidated and there may also be some form of penalty charge.

Distribution bonds

These are bonds designed to pay out the dividends accumulated by the underlying fund, so that investors can receive an income without cashing in holdings. They tend to focus on UK equities and gilts, which offer higher dividends than overseas securities.

The income is free of tax for basic rate taxpayers, and also for higher rate payers as long as it is within the 5 per cent annual allowance. But they share with other bonds the drawback that the fund itself is liable to capital gains tax and income tax, which cannot be reclaimed by those not liable.

Personal portfolio bonds

These are bonds that allow you to have your own choice of investments held within the medium of a bond. They are designed for sizeable investments – around £50,000 upwards – that would normally be managed by a stockbroker or financial adviser. Because the investments are held within a bond, investors can avoid tax until the bond is cashed in. Moreover, many of these bonds are held with offshore life companies that are not themselves liable to UK tax.

But now the Chancellor has cracked down – and severely. Since April 1999, holders of these bonds have been liable to a tax charge on 'deemed gains' of 15 per cent of the premiums paid into the bond in any year plus the total deemed gains from previous years. As a result, most insurance companies have stopped selling the bonds.

BROKER BONDS

Broker bonds are offered by a number of independent financial advisers, not necessarily insurance brokers as the name suggests. They had their origin in the early 1980s, when advisers who managed bond funds on behalf of clients used the power of proxy to make block switches instead of making the same move individually for each client.

Broker bonds have moved on a long way since then. The concept is that clients' money is pooled into one fund, which the adviser will manage, moving it between underlying funds to make the most of current market conditions. These funds can be 'fettered', meaning they are invested with just one life company, or 'unfettered', which means they can be invested across a number of companies, depending on where the adviser sees the best prospects. The latter are more common and offer greater scope for the adviser to give added value, compared with an individual bond.

The advantages of a broker bond are that you have your investment professionally managed, without being required to approve every move, but still have access to the person doing the managing, which would not be the case if, say, you simply put your money into a life company's managed fund. In return, you will be faced with an extra layer of charges levied by the adviser.

So can performance justify the extra cost? A report published by the Personal Investment Authority (PIA) showed that the performance of broker funds had generally been poor, well below that of similar life funds and unit trusts. The PIA stopped short of banning broker funds, but advisers who offer them must meet a performance benchmark comparable to the average fund in the relevant sector, or write to clients with an explanation if they fail to do so. They must also have passed the appropriate exam, must inform clients of a possible conflict of interest in recommending their own funds and must reconfirm the fund's suitability for the investor on an annual basis.

As a result of these strictures, the broker fund market halved in value in the space of just two years. It has been rumoured that the regulatory authorities would like to see an end to them altogether.

ANNUITIES

Annuities are a means of transforming capital into income. The basic concept is simple: you pay a lump sum to a life assurance company and in return you get an income, at a predetermined level, for the rest of your life. A basic annuity is irrevocable; once you have given up your capital, you cannot have it back.

Annuities operate rather like a mirror image of life assurance. Instead of paying out a lump sum when you die, they pay an income until you die. So the older you are, the fewer payments are anticipated and the higher the rate will be. For this reason, annuities are not normally suitable for anyone under about 65; the income offered would be too low to justify giving up the capital for good.

Table 10.2 *Annuity rates*

Purchase price £100,000	Level income (£)	Inflation-linked income (£)
Male 60, single life	8085	5904
Female 60, single life	7619	5093
Male 70, single life	10,912	8760
Female 75, single life	9742	7072
Male 60, female 60, joint life	7480	5028
Male 65, female 65, joint life	8273	5868

Note: The table shows gross annual rates assuming payments are made monthly in arrears, without guarantee.

Source: The Annuity Bureau, May 2000

The income from an annuity is taxable, but only in part. A portion of it is treated as being a return of your original capital, and is therefore tax free, while the rest will be taxed as income at your normal rate. The capital element is determined by scales laid down by the Inland Revenue, based on your age; the older you are, the shorter the likely payment period, so a higher proportion of the return will be treated as capital. However, new scales were brought in at the beginning of 1992 – previously they were based on mortality tables that were around 40 years old, when life expectancy was lower than it is today. The new scales reduced the capital element for any given age, making the after-tax return rather less attractive than before. Examples of current rates are shown in Table 10.2.

One exception to this tax rule is an annuity bought with money from a pension fund. This is known as a 'compulsory purchase annuity', because you are obliged to buy it (though you may still have a choice of companies to buy it from), and it is wholly taxable as income. Ordinary annuities that you buy voluntarily are called 'purchased life annuities'.

VARIATIONS OF ANNUITIES

The main failing of a basic annuity is that it dies with you. To take an extreme example, if you handed over £100,000 and died the very next day, your estate would be £100,000 the poorer and the insurance company equally the richer. For insurance companies,

Annuities – 2000

An annuity is a lump sum investment which provides income for the rest of your life and is mainly appropriate for those of retirement age or above. It is an insurance policy which can be invested in different ways. The insurance return is based on how many years the insurance company expects you or any jointly insured to live. In addition, your monies are invested either in a fund that provides a guaranteed income or in a with-profit or equity-based fund where some variability of income may occur.

An annuity is a simple insurance product and, if you are looking for a guaranteed income annuity, the best buy is almost always from the company providing the highest rate of return. But the returns vary greatly from company to company and the one that offers the top rate for males may be poor value for females or joint lives. You need to shop around and be specific about what you want.

Annuities can be purchased either with the capital from both personal and insured company pension funds or with private capital - a purchased life annuity. Purchased life annuities offer particularly attractive returns for those with a high income need who are over 70 years old and in relatively good health. Pension annuities can be bought by retirees from their chosen company. This is called the Open Market Option. All retirees should exercise their Open Market Option even if this subsequently proves that their current company is best for them. You will only know you have got the best if you have exercised your option to research the market.

NEW OPTIONS IN ANNUITIES

Over the past few years higher income has become available for smokers, people suffering ill health or those who have worked in hazardous environments.

- **Standard enhanced annuities** – for smokers, or those who have undergone operations or are over-weight, but individual medical assessment does not take place.

- **Individual enhanced annuities** – where individual medical assessment helps to determine the income level - these are particularly helpful in more severe cases. Income can be increased by anything up to three or four times the "normal" annuity level.

These enhanced annuities are currently available with guaranteed income annuities only although this may change in the future.

WHERE TO INVEST YOUR ANNUITY FUND

Investing in long-term gilts enables insurance companies to offer guaranteed income returns and this traditional annuity has proved beneficial to the policyholder over the past 20 years as interest rates and inflation have on average steadily fallen. This beneficial effect has disguised the fact that a fixed interest fund may not be the most appropriate investment vehicle to produce income over 20 or more years for the average retired couple.

The dramatic fall in gilt yields has highlighted the importance of the investment decision and how to best achieve your income objectives for the rest of your life. For a rapidly growing number of people, the answer is to be found in with-profits or equity-linked annuities where the performance of the under-lying investments is likely to reflect the performance of the economy as a whole including any resurgence in inflation.

Some recent press coverage has questioned the desirability

of purchasing an annuity with a pension fund. However, for 95% or more of retirees the most efficient use of the capital built up in a pension fund is to annuitise that fund into lifetime income as long as you don't restrict your investment decision. The with-profit or unit-linked annuity provides for many a viable answer to the investment decision.

It is worth noting that the age at which the best value of insurance return is obtained from an annuity is between 64 and 68 for a man where the spouse is up to seven years younger. The insurance return is best at this age for two reasons. Firstly, competition amongst insurers for business in this age bracket, and secondly, the small additional effect from those who the insurance company expects to die earlier. The additional benefit from those who are unfortunate enough to die earlier than the average - the "mortality drag" effect - reduces as you get older.

Guaranteed income annuity rates may be at a historically low level but converting capital into income is as important as ever when interest rates from building societies and bank accounts and other sources of income in retirement are also at very low levels. A with-profit or unit-linked annuity may well be the answer.

An annuity is a very simple concept. However, ensuring that you purchase the one most suited to your need and providing the highest income is complicated and requires expert advice, particularly as many annuity providers deal only through independent financial advisers.

Some help is available in your living room via BBC2 Ceefax, page 260. These rates, provided by Annuity Direct, allow you to track what is happening to annuity returns in the weeks leading up to your purchase.

Stuart Bayliss, Director, Annuity Direct - The Retirement Income Specialists

For a free guide to retirement planning, please phone or use the coupon on our advertisement

premature deaths make up for clients who live unexpectedly long, but for your heirs it could be a serious blow.

There are several ways of overcoming this problem. First, the annuity can be guaranteed for a certain period, such as five or ten years. Payments will then be continued for that time, regardless of whether you die sooner. In practice, if the annuity-holder dies, the insurance company may offer his heirs the option of commuting remaining payments to a lump sum.

Second, if you are married but have no other dependants, you could opt for a joint life, second death annuity. As the name implies, this will continue paying income until the death of the second partner.

Third, you can ensure that you (or your estate) at least get back the original outlay through a capital protected annuity. If at your death the income payments so far are less than the purchase price, the insurance company will pay over the difference. All of these options cost money, in that the rate will be reduced. Rates for women will be lower again, as they have a longer life expectancy.

Annuity rates are also affected by how often the income is paid, whether it is paid in advance or in arrears, and with or without proportion. The latter refers to the position if you die between payment dates – whether or not a proportion of the next payment is made. Obviously, it hardly matters if payments are monthly, but for annual income it could be useful. If you have no heirs and are in no immediate hurry for money, an annuity payable yearly in arrears, without proportion and with no guarantees would give the best possible rate.

Another drawback of the basic annuity is that the income is fixed for life and therefore vulnerable to inflation. It is possible instead to have an increasing annuity, under which payments rise each year, either by a fixed percentage or in line with, say, the Retail Price Index. Two further, much less common, options are with profits and unit-linked annuities, where the income is linked to an investment fund. This means it is dependent on the fortunes of the stock market, so while the long-term trend should be upwards, it can fluctuate from year to year. Both this and the increasing annuity will give a lower income at the outset than the plain level type.

HYBRID PLANS

One variety not mentioned above is the temporary annuity, which pays out for a fixed period of time rather than for life. These have little application by themselves, but are often used in packaged schemes offered by life companies. Sometimes called 'hybrid' or 'back to back' plans, these combine different products with the aim of providing a reasonable level of income plus the prospect of capital growth.

Plans fall into two types. With one, the lump-sum investment is used to buy a 10-year annuity; payments from this are used to fund the premiums for a 10-year endowment policy, while the surplus provides a running income. At the end of the 10 years, the maturing endowment should provide a return of the original capital. With the second type, part of the original lump sum buys a temporary annuity to provide income, while the rest is put into an investment such as a bond, unit trust or personal equity plan, again designed to return at least the original capital at the end of the term.

Some of the packages around now are quite sophisticated. With the second type, for example, you may be able to choose the level of income you want, either by adjusting the amount put into the annuity or by taking additional income from the second investment. But there are two important questions to ask. First, what return would there be if you died during the term? The annuity will normally die with you, so the return may be less than you invested. Second, what rate of growth is needed from the investment to return the original sum, and how realistic is this? Remember that the higher the income you take, the less money will be left to build up capital.

One other point is that the package will usually combine products from the same company, which may not be good for both annuities and investments. You might get a better deal by putting together your own combination from different companies.

SECOND-HAND ENDOWMENTS

These are with profits endowment policies that have been sold by their original holder before maturity owing to a change of circumstances. They can be bought either through auctions or through 'market-makers' – firms that buy up policies to sell on to investors. When you buy a policy the details stay the same – it is still based on the life of the original owner – but you take over responsibility for paying the remaining premiums due. These can usually be commuted to a lump-sum payment, but this is not always beneficial; the discount offered may be negligible and the policy will become non-qualifying in status, which means there may be a tax liability on the maturity proceeds.

While policy auctions have been around for decades, market-makers are a fairly new phenomenon. The market, however, is expanding fast, as selling a policy can give a much better return than the surrender value. For the investor, a second-hand policy can be attractive if you need a lump sum at a specific time in the future; for example, to meet school fees or for retirement.

Policies will normally have run for around two-thirds or more of their total term, so in addition to the basic sum assured, they will have built up bonuses that, once they have been allocated, are guaranteed to be paid at maturity. In some cases, the value of the sum assured plus bonuses can be as much as the purchase price, so your profit then depends on the level of bonuses allocated during the remainder of the term and the amount of the remaining premiums.

The price is determined by the current value of the policy, its original term and the period remaining, the future premiums and the seller's mark-up. Sellers usually quote an anticipated rate of return at maturity, but whether this will be achieved or not depends on the future pattern of bonus rates. The recent trend has been downward, and since most policies bought have fairly short terms to run – between three and ten years – it is not likely that they will pick up again significantly.

Unless you already have some experience in this area, you would be wise not to buy at auction. Like car auctions, they can offer bargains, but you could equally end up paying over the odds if you lack the specialised knowledge. Similarly, policies issued by 'top name' insurance companies offer the safest prospects though they may not be the cheapest. It is usually worth taking some professional advice.

FRIENDLY SOCIETIES

Friendly societies have been around for a couple of centuries. In some respects their operations resemble those of insurance companies, but on a smaller scale, as they have been subject to tight restrictions on their activities. However, the Friendly Societies Act 1992 opened the way for expansion and most societies incorporated in 1993. This means that they may own assets directly instead of through trustees and may set up subsidiary companies that can manage unit trust schemes and personal equity plans or do insurance broking. They are also due to be brought under the Policyholders' Protection Act, which has not previously applied to friendly societies.

The societies' chief advantage over insurance companies is that they can issue tax-exempt policies, which invest in funds that are free of income and capital gains tax and pay the proceeds tax free to the investor. These are 10-year plans designed for regular savings, but many offer a lump sum version, using an annuity from which payments are drip-fed into the plan over its term.

The bad news is that there is a limit on the premiums that may be paid into these plans and this in turn has meant that charges have tended to be relatively high. Since 1994, this limit has been £25 a month or £270 a year. The tax concession will also be undermined by the changed rules for tax credits on the dividends from UK shares, although the 1998 Budget confirmed that friendly society policies would receive the same 10 per cent credit as PEPs and ISAs until 2004.

Investors may take out only one plan each, but children are also entitled to have plans, so a family of four are able to invest up to £1200 a year through monthly savings. Plans do not always have to cease at the end of 10 years: some offer the choice to continue paying premiums or to take an 'income' by making regular withdrawals.

PRIVATE HEALTH CARE

What would be the use of the highest return on a lump sum investment if you were not healthy enough to enjoy it – or worse, not around at all?

According to research commissioned by PPP healthcare group, 51 per cent of those polled rated health as their most important priority, ahead of personal relationships and financial security. There is a strong argument for using some of your spare funds to pay for private health care in one form or another to ensure a reasonable quality of life. However, as there are several different types of health insurance, it is important to sort out which one is relevant to your needs.

Private medical insurance (PMI)

Currently, some 15 per cent of the population has some form of private medical insurance. Sales were fairly static during the 1990s, although moderate growth is expected in the future. Certainly the number of providers has grown; there are now around 25, offering a wide range of products.

These fall into three broad ranges: low-cost, middle-range and up-market policies. The more you pay, the more coverage you buy. At the top end of the spectrum are plans that include fully comprehensive dental treatment, childbirth, full refund for specialists' fees and outpatient treatment.

Their annual costs vary from about £600 a year to over £6000 for a comprehensive family plan. Scales of charges generally depend on your age, where you live and what level of benefits you choose. At the lower end, for example, some types of treatment may be excluded from cover, while for others there is a cash limit. On the most expensive plans, a full refund will be given for most expenses, including, for example, the cost of a parent accompanying a young child. Plans may also pay a daily allowance if you have treatment under the National Health Service.

The choice can be somewhat baffling at first glance as the industry players seek to differentiate themselves and establish competitive advantage. There are also derivative products that have a minimal level of cover or may be intended only to meet the cost of major surgery, dental care, hospital costs or accidental cover. As with all insurance, there is the question of whether certain types of cover are really necessary, to which the counter argument is: 'You won't know whether you need the cover until it's too late.'

One of the problems in picking out just how much cover you need to take out in money terms is knowing the cost of the care itself. As examples, a consultation with a doctor could cost £150, an X-ray £200, having your tonsils out could come to over £1500 and major heart surgery might run to well in excess of £5000. Charges can vary significantly between different types of hospital and different parts of the country, so it may be worth while checking out your local facilities.

How to choose

It is important to research the market. At the end of this section (page 219) is a list of the major players and their telephone numbers. They will all be pleased to send details of the plans they offer and premium rates. You can also find surveys of plans in financial magazines such as _Planned Savings_ and _Money Management_.

A useful reference book is _Laing's Review of Private Health Care_, for which details are given on page 220. This lists a range of useful information about the PMI market and also the names of specialist brokers.

Brokers who really understand the market and the differences between the products and who keep up to date with what is going on can be a real help in cutting through the information undergrowth to find the most appropriate policy.

Permanent health insurance (PHI)

If you are employed, your employer may provide sick pay for a period of time if you should suffer a long-term illness that prevents you from working. Thereafter, however, you might have to fall back on state benefits, which are fairly limited. It is therefore worth considering PHI – and even more so if you are self-employed.

PHI provides replacement income after a set 'deferment' period that can be as little as four weeks, but is typically six months – the period for which Statutory Sick Pay is provided. There are special versions designed specifically to cover mortgage payments, but a standard PHI plan will pay up to 75 per cent of your gross earnings (or 90 per cent of net earnings). The shortfall is deliberate; if a plan were to provide as much as you normally earn, so the argument goes, there would be no incentive for you to return to work.

The cost of a plan depends on factors such as your age, occupation, medical history and the length of the deferment period you choose, as well as how much cover you want. It may also depend on the way the plan defines 'inability to work'. The best is that you are unable to do your own normal job, but some policies stipulate that you must be unable to do your own job or any other to which you are suited – meaning that you may be obliged to go back to work in a different, and perhaps less well paid, position.

As long as you qualify for payments, they will generally continue until you are able to go back to work or up to your normal retirement age. A good plan will also pay a proportionate amount if you return to work in a lesser capacity or part time.

Critical illness insurance

Whereas life assurance will pay out a lump sum if you die, critical illness insurance will pay out if you suffer a serious illness. The range of illnesses covered can vary between policies, but the core ones – and those most often claimed for – are heart attack, cancer and stroke.

As a stand-alone policy, critical illness insurance has been fairly little taken up since the first plan was launched in this country in December 1986. However, it is becoming increasingly common as an option on a mortgage plan and in this context it seems to have struck more of a chord.

With today's pace of development in medicine, there is much more likelihood of suffering a critical illness than of dying during one's working life. It is also an insurance that is particularly relevant to those without dependants since, unlike life assurance, the person taking out the policy stands to benefit personally. For both these reasons, it should become more popular as it becomes better known.

Long-term care

Long-term care insurance is an even newer development than critical illness cover. The idea is to take out cover in early or middle life that will pay for nursing home care in old age, should it be needed. Under the current rules for state benefits, the local authority will pay nursing home costs only if your total assets, including your home, are less than £8000. Between £8000 and £16,000 there is a sliding scale and over £16,000 you are entitled to no help at all.

Despite this, long-term care insurance has yet to take off. One problem lies in the design of plans: since the need for care could continue indefinitely, and the cost is therefore open-ended, plans are either very expensive or have restrictions on the benefits. Another problem is that people are reluctant to buy insurance for something they may never need, especially when any potential benefits may be 20 or 30 years away.

Mixing and matching

One way in which insurers have tried to add to the attractions of healthcare plans is to combine more than one benefit. Critical illness insurance, for example, is often sold in combination with life assurance and there is at least one plan available that also includes long-term care insurance and a measure of private health insurance. The advantage of this is that it may help to cut the costs, but the drawback is that the benefits will only be paid once. So if you make a claim for a critical illness, you will no longer have any life assurance, whereas with two separate plans you could have both.

Contacts for the main providers

Abbey Life 01202 292373	BCWA 0117 9293742	BUPA 0800 289577	Clinicare 01438 747733	Cornhill 01483 552975
Halifax 0800 142142	MFIA 01162 362420	Norwich Union 0800 142142	Provincial 01539 723415	Exeter Friendly Society 01392 75361
Healthcare Agencies 01753 532092	Nationwide 0800 335555	Permanent Direct 01923 770000	Saga 01483 553553	Guardian Direct 0800 282820
Johnson Fry Healthsave 020 7451 1000	NPS 01536 713713	PPP healthcare 0800 335555	Staffordshire 01902 317407	Guardian Health 01303 853400
Lloyds 0800 750750	Northern Bank 01232 333361	Prime Health 01483 553553	Sun Alliance 0800 374351	WPA 0500 414243

Further reading

- *Laing's Review of Private Healthcare*, 1996, Laing & Buisson (London).
- *Money Management* magazine.
- *Planned Savings* magazine.

11 Retirement Planning

Pension planning can be as complex as any other investment described in this book and twice as important. Once you retire, your income will very largely depend on the investments you have built up during your working life and a pension can be the core element. It may seem out of place in a book devoted to lump-sum investment, as pension planning is (or should be) chiefly a matter of regular saving. But there are three good reasons why it should have a prominent place in any investment strategy.

1. Very few people have the maximum possible pension provision. In fact, it is estimated that fewer than 2 per cent of members of company-run pension schemes will retire on the maximum two-thirds of final salary that is allowed by the Inland Revenue. This can arise because the company scheme is not geared to producing maximum benefits, or because the employee does not put in a sufficient number of years of service. Most people, indeed, are likely to end up with a far lower pension than they expect or imagine.

2. Pensions are extremely tax efficient as an investment. All contributions, to whatever type of plan, qualify for tax relief at the highest rate of income tax you pay and the funds in which they are invested are themselves free of all income and capital gains tax. In addition, when you retire, you can take part of the proceeds as a cash lump sum, tax free; the exact proportion depends on the type of pension you have and when it dates from.

3. There have been a host of developments in pensions legislation in recent years, aimed at improving private provision

and, alongside that, reducing the burden on the State. As a result, there are now greater opportunities to make your own pension arrangements, through lump-sum investments as well as regular savings.

PERSONAL PENSIONS AND COMPANY SCHEMES

Personal pensions came on the scene in July 1988 and are open to anyone who has earnings that are not already covered by a company pension scheme. That includes not only the self-employed, but also those who have freelance earnings in addition to a main job – or, indeed, in addition to a current pension. Moreover, employees have the choice of opting out of a company scheme and taking a personal pension instead.

On the face of it, this is not an attractive choice. For a start, if you take a personal pension, all the costs fall on you – both the charges of the plan and the payments into it. Your employer may make a contribution to it, but there is no obligation for him to do so.

Then there are the benefits to consider. Many large company schemes operate on a 'final salary' basis; this means that the pension is equivalent to a proportion of your salary at the time of leaving the company, typically one-sixtieth per year of service. Should runaway inflation suddenly double your salary, or investment performance not measure up to expectations, that is the company's problem. With a personal pension, all the risk is on your head: you will only get what you put in and the investment growth it achieves.

On top of this, a company scheme will normally offer additional benefits: life assurance, should you die before retirement, which can be up to four times your annual salary; a widow's or widower's pension, of up to two-thirds of your own prospective pension; and guaranteed or discretionary increases in your pension once it is being paid. In fact, since April 1997, it has been compulsory for final salary schemes to provide increases in line with the Retail Price Index up to 5 per cent.

Under the rules, employees who opt for a personal pension are still eligible to have life assurance through a company scheme, but again, there is no obligation on the employer to provide this. If you decide to go it alone, you will have to think in terms of paying for all these benefits yourself.

So why consider a personal pension? The most important reason is job mobility. If you leave a company, your pension entitlement is based on your years of service to that point and your final salary at the time of leaving. Since the beginning of 1985, companies have had to revalue these preserved rights by the lesser of the inflation rate and 5 per cent, which means so-called 'frozen' pensions have been somewhat thawed. But higher rates of inflation, or promotional salary increases, can still make this entitlement look pretty feeble.

Alternatively, you can take a transfer value out of the scheme to put into a new company scheme or a private arrangement. However, transfer values are usually conservatively assessed, so each time you move you are likely to lose out. In contrast, a personal pension can be continued intact across any number of job changes, so, for younger people in particular, it can be a much more stable means of building up benefits.

Companies are also turning increasingly from final salary to 'money purchase' schemes, which are less of a financial commitment. Instead of promising a pension based on salary, these schemes build up a fund of money for each employee which is then used to buy a pension at retirement. This is similar to the way a personal pension operates, so if your employer is prepared to contribute to a personal pension in place of the company scheme, you could be no worse off.

There are limits on the contributions you are allowed to make to a personal pension, which start at 17.5 per cent of annual earnings for those under 35 and increase with age to a maximum of 40 per cent. There is also an overall earnings cap on the calculation, which for the 2000/01 tax year stands at £91,800. If you do not use the full contribution allowance in one year, the rest can currently be carried forward for up to six years. So if you find yourself with windfall cash, you may be able to tuck away a sizeable lump sum by picking up unused allowance from past years. However, significant changes are planned to come into effect from April 2001 that could see the carry-forward allowance abolished, or at least financially reduced. So, if you have the opportunity, you should certainly consider using it now while it is still available.

FINANCIAL PLANNING IN RETIREMENT

Planning for retirement should ideally start many years in advance. For reasons that are well-known, people are living longer and three distinct life phases are recognised today: education, work and retirement (euphemistically called the "grey phase"). The so-called grey phase can be as long as your working life. Therefore, financial decisions at the point of retirement are crucial and may have a major impact on your standard of living for the rest of your life.

Your finances in retirement depend to a large extent on sound planning, which begins with fundamentals such as budgeting income against known levels of outgoings. Included in these calculations is the mortgage, if you still have one. Now MIRAS has been abolished should the mortgage be repaid? Can you obtain a safe return on your capital higher than that which you pay to your lender? What type of mortgage is it? Are there redemption penalties for repaying early? All of these are important questions to ask. The same considerations apply to loans and debts.

The making of a will is also part of sound planning. It is not only important to make one, but to keep it updated. Should you die "intestate", it may well be that your estate will not be dispersed in accordance with your wishes, and your family could suffer as a consequence.

Your income in retirement may come from a number of sources. These days many people receive not only a state pension or pensions, but benefit from a company or personal pension arrangement. In connection with the state pension, it is advisable to complete a DSS Form BR19 in order to obtain a forecast as to your likely benefit. This is a relevant exercise for everyone, but particularly married women if they have not built up pension eligibility in their own right.

In the current tax year (2000/01) the basic state pension is £67.50 each week. If you are in a company pension scheme or have a personal arrangement, you may need to consider whether or not to take part of your pension in favour of a tax free lump sum. If you have a personal pension or AVCs, shop around to obtain the best annuity rate, rather than automatically opting for the pension quoted by the company you have saved with.

Inflation is a major threat to those in retirement. The average rate of inflation in the last 50 years has been 6.5%; at this rate capital loses approximately half its true value over 11 years – a frightening thought if you are going to be in retirement for, say, 22 years. Even at the current lower rate of nearer 3% the spending power of your money falls by nearly a quarter within 9 years.

People approaching retirement sometimes mistakenly think that they will be less affected by tax than during their working life. Unfortunately, retired people receive no special tax treatment. Whilst certain people may receive higher allowances (due to age, for example) tax levels are still the same as when you were working. Prior to retirement it is advisable to complete a Form P161 "Leaving Service : Getting a Pension for the First Time", which may be obtained from your local tax office. By completing this, you will ensure that your tax coding will reflect your changed circumstances, and you will not pay more tax than is necessary. Tax is a key element in planning for retirement, and getting it right can help to make your money go further.

Your home is another important factor in retirement. Some people elect to sell and realise the equity in their property by purchasing a smaller home. Those who wish to stay, but ideally would like to use the equity in the home in order to supplement income, may consider a number of plans (usually called Home Income Plans) currently available. However, this is a specialist area, and needs very careful consideration and guidance before proceeding.

As far as investing capital is concerned, the sensible approach is to divide it into separate segments: some for easy access, to cover contingencies which may arise in future, some for income in order to supplement your pension/s and some for growth to combat the effects of inflation in the medium to long term. Building Society and bank deposit accounts are likely to be the most suitable for easy access, but look out particularly for those with postal, telephone and internet facilities which are likely to offer a higher level of interest than their High Street counterparts. When considering products for income and growth, there are primarily three options: i) invest for maximum income, with less emphasis on capital growth, ii) invest for maximum growth, with less emphasis on income or iii) invest for a balance of income and growth. Naturally your personal objectives will determine the correct balance for you. This book describes the various investment vehicles that are available to you.

Not surprisingly the majority of people will need professional help with financial planning for retirement, not just initially but on an ongoing basis, to ensure that their objectives are still being met, perhaps within changed circumstances. There is huge choice when it comes to seeking assistance. However, advisers are divided into two categories; firstly, tied agents or company representatives who may only recommend their own group's products, and secondly independent financial advisers (IFAs) who may choose across the spectrum of products and providers. Apart from knowing which category your adviser comes into, other points to consider before acting on any advice are:

1 How is the adviser remunerated (fees or commission).

2 Have you received the recommendations in writing.

3 Ensure you fully understand the products and key features including applicable charges.

4 Make cheques payable to the organisations with which you are investing your capital not to the adviser.

5 What is the ongoing review procedure to monitor performance and report back to you.

Types of plan

Personal pensions are available from insurance companies, banks, investment trust groups and unit trust groups and offer a variety of investment choices: with profits, unit-linked, deposit-style and investment and unit trusts. Deposit-type plans offer maximum security with the lowest growth prospects and are suitable mainly for those very close to retirement who need to know their capital is safe. With profits plans invest in a mix of assets and aim to smooth out fluctuations, thereby offering a balance between risk and reward. Unit-linked, investment trust and unit trust plans provide direct exposure to the equity market through a range of funds, which themselves offer different levels of risk and growth prospects. Broadly speaking, the further you are from retirement, the more risk you can afford to take, in return for the likelihood of higher growth.

One other type of plan, which first appeared in 1990, is the self-invested personal pension. This is a 'do-it-yourself' option that gives you a free choice of all allowable investments, which include equities, unit trusts and investment trusts, insurance company funds, deposit accounts and commercial property. These plans are geared towards larger investors, and would not normally be cost-effective for lump sums of less than about £50,000. The attractions are that you are not tied to the investment fortunes of one company and there is generally a fixed fee structure which is economical for very sizeable sums.

Pensions mis-selling

Personal pensions were eagerly embraced by the financial service industry and also widely promoted by the government of the day through television adverts that stressed the extra money your plan would receive if you contracted out of the State Earnings Related Pension Scheme (SERPS). Unfortunately, amid all this fervour, a lot of people opted out of their company schemes to take personal pensions, to their detriment. In the last few years there has been a massive operation to check sales of personal pensions and, where appropriate, to compensate anyone who was wrongly advised.

This has focused attention on the failings of personal pension plans and, in particular, on the high front-end charges that many carry. The government is now looking to overhaul the whole pensions area, with a new State Second Pension (SSP) scheme to replace the current State Earnings Related Pension Scheme (SERPS) and the introduction of stakeholder pensions and Pooled Pension Investments (PPIs).

THE STATE EARNINGS RELATED PENSION SCHEME AND THE STATE SECOND PENSION

At the end of 1998, the government issued a Green Paper on pensions. One of the main provisions was that the State Earnings Related Pension Scheme (SERPS) is to be replaced with a new State Second Pension (SSP). SERPS will not accept any new contributions or members after 2002, but those who have already accrued SERPS benefits will get them as promised.

The new SSP is particularly designed to help the low paid. Anyone earning less than £9000 will be treated as if they were earning at least this much when they retire and will have a total pension worth at least 20 per cent of average earnings. There will be a guaranteed minimum pension which will be linked to earnings, unlike the current basic state pension, which is linked to prices. The SSP will also credit contributions on behalf of those who are not working because they are caring for children or for sick or elderly relatives.

Currently, anyone who is self-employed is automatically excluded from SERPS. The government is consulting as to whether they should be allowed to join the SSP, in exchange for higher National Insurance contributions. Everyone will be entitled to an annual statement, covering both state and private provision, showing how much they have paid in, what the costs are and how much they can expect to get when they retire.

Until the SSP is brought in, the employed can still decide whether to be in SERPS or to contract out of it. In return for giving up your rights under SERPS, you receive a rebate on your National Insurance contributions which you may invest in a personal pension. If you are in a company pension scheme, this is the only type of personal pension you are allowed.

Since April 1997, the National Insurance rebate has been based on your age, varying from 3.4 per cent up to 9 per cent. Broadly speaking, this should make contracting out attractive for men up to their mid-50s and women up to their mid-40s or so. But income should also be taken into account; for those earning less than about £11,000, the charges on a personal pension may outweigh the gains from the rebate. It is also important to remember that a plan based only on the rebate is not going to produce an adequate pension. So if you are not also in a company pension scheme, you should be making further contributions of your own.

STAKEHOLDER PENSIONS

The 1998 Green Paper also provided details of the stakeholder pensions which the Labour Party had first announced in its manifesto. These are due to be introduced in 2001 and are aimed especially at those who are not in an occupational scheme. Almost all companies that do not offer a pension scheme will have to give employees access to a stakeholder plan, although they will not be obliged to contribute to it themselves.

The schemes may be run by unions and other collective organisations and will be supervised by trustees. They will be answerable to the scheme members and will keep a check on aspects such as performance and charges. Plans will have to meet certain criteria: no penalties for stopping contributions or switching schemes; a minimum contribution of £20; and an annual charge of no more than 1 per cent. Any advice not included within the 1 per cent charge must be paid for separately. Alternatively, there should be a 'decision tree' to help people assess their options, and schemes themselves may offer general advice or a facility for low-cost individual advice. In particular, plan managers will have to offer a 'difficult' investment option for those who do not want to make their own choices.

Those who join a stakeholder scheme will be able to opt out of the State Second Pension scheme (SSP) in return for a National Insurance rebate that will be paid into the scheme. For those earning between £9000 and £18,500, the rebate will be worth 9 per cent on the first £9000 and 2.5 per cent on the balance of their earnings. Those earning more than £18,500 will have no specific incentive to opt out of the SSP, but from 2007 the SSP will provide only a flat rate pension, with contributions based on a salary of just £9000, so there will be no great incentive to be in it either.

Contributions to stakeholder plans may be up to £3600 a year without evidence of earnings and will attract tax relief at your normal rate. At retirement, the fund will be treated in much the same way as a personal pension is currently: you will be able to take up to a quarter of it as a tax-free lump sum, while the balance must be used to buy an annuity, which will be taxed. You may, however, continue to contribute to the plan for up to five years after you retire. You may also – in a significant departure from previous pension rules – save up to £3600 a year in a 'third-party' plan for the benefit of a spouse or child.

So, should you consider a stakeholder plan and, if so, should you wait until it is introduced or take out a personal pension now? Waiting is not generally to be recommended in the case of pensions – Table 11.1 shows how the amount of pension produced by a given level of contributions is reduced the later you start. But if you open a plan now, you should make sure it is flexible enough for you to keep your options open. The Personal Investment Authority (PIA) has given a strong message to companies that pensions sold now must not penalise anyone who switches out when stakeholder plans arrive. As a result, many have already restructured their plans, moving from front-end loading, where charges are levied heavily in the initial years, to level loading, where they are evenly spread throughout the term. Level loading does not necessarily reduce costs – over the longer term they could actually be greater – but it does mean that early contributions do not all disappear in charges, so transfer values, if you want to switch out, should be much better.

Whether it will be worth switching to a stakeholder plan is hard to say as yet. The current suggestion is that these plans could be cheaper and more flexible than personal pensions, but the latter are

Table 11.1 *How much should you put into a pension plan?*

The columns show what level of pension (expressed as a percentage of final salary) can be expected, assuming that contributions of 10 per cent of salary are made each year.

Age now	Pension[a] at age 65	
	Male %	Female[b] %
30	58.9	53.4
35	47.6	43.2
40	39.5	35.8
45	28.7	26.0
50	20.6	18.7
55	14.7	13.3

Note: [a] These figures assume a 2 per cent 'real' growth rate on the pension fund, and that pension contributions keep pace with salary increases, ie they are always 10 per cent of salary. They also assume that all of the fund is taken as a pension, rather than a proportion as a lump sum.
[b] The figures for women are lower at all ages because pension rates are lower for women (they live longer).

Source: Allied Dunbar

likely to change if there is serious competition. Already there are plans offered by unit trust and investment trust groups that have level charges and no penalties for stopping or altering contributions. You should also consider the features and services provided – these may be at a minimum to keep costs low – and the likely performance.

POOLED PENSION INVESTMENTS (PPIs)

The idea of the Pooled Pension Investment was announced in January 1999 and it is due to be introduced in April 2001. It is not a separate pension scheme as such, more a way of investing for a pension: essentially it is a tax-free 'wrapper' for an investment through a unit trust, investment trust or OEIC. In fact, it is a sort of cross between a pension and an ISA and was originally dubbed a 'LISA' – Lifetime Individual Savings Account – but the government wanted a more serious name and eventually settled on Pooled Pension Investment (PPI).

PPIs can be used for personal pensions, company schemes and additional voluntary contributions and will be subject to standard pension regulations. The usual contribution limits will apply, tax relief will be given at your highest rate and you will not be allowed access to the money before retirement. When you do retire, the fund will be used to buy an annuity in the normal way. The advantage claimed over current pension arrangements is that PPIs are expected to be flexible and cheap, although there will be no statutory limit on charges as is proposed for stakeholder plans.

ADDITIONAL CONTRIBUTIONS

As mentioned, you cannot make contributions to a personal pension if you are a member of a company scheme. You can, however, make extra payments through an Additional Voluntary Contributions (AVC) scheme. This can be an in-house scheme provided by your employer or a free-standing plan operated by an insurance company.

Why should you do this? The answer is that a company scheme can fall short of the ideal for a number of reasons: it may offer less than the standard one-sixtieth per year of service; the final salary assessment may not include extras such as bonuses and overtime payments; it may not provide the maximum possible death benefits or spouse's pension. Most of all, if you change jobs, you will not clock up the necessary number of years of service, and benefits from previous employment may be partly or wholly frozen.

The choice between in-house and free-standing schemes depends on your circumstances. Briefly, an in-house scheme is convenient, as payments are usually deducted directly from salary and the employer will bear the plan charges; but a free-standing scheme can offer a wider investment choice and is yours to take from job to job.

Members of company pension schemes can put in up to 15 per cent of earnings a year, tax free. Compulsory contributions are normally around 5 to 6 per cent, so there is plenty of scope for making AVCs. However, while it is possible to have a single premium plan – to which you can make one-off payments as and when you can afford it – the allowance cannot be carried forward from year to year, so there is less scope for large lump-sum payments than there is with a personal pension.

An alternative route to building up savings for retirement is an Individual Savings Account (ISA). Unlike in the case of a pension, there is no tax relief on the money going in, but there is greater flexibility: the investment limits are generally higher; you can get the money out whenever you like; and all the proceeds can be taken as cash, whereas an AVC can only be used to provide income. The two are not mutually exclusive: to maximise savings, you can have an ISA in addition to an AVC.

HOW MUCH TO SAVE

The chief drawback of pensions is that you cannot draw on the money until you reach a minimum age – currently this is 50 for personal pensions and normally 60 for company schemes, but the government is, at the time of writing, proposing to increase minimum pension ages in the interests of helping older people to find, or remain in, employment. Other investments may be difficult to convert into cash, but a pension is by nature non-negotiable. Hence most of us contribute only grudgingly – on average, around 4–5 per cent of earnings.

A glance at Table 11.1 shows how inadequate this can be. Even contributing at 10 per cent a year, starting at age 30, will not produce the maximum allowance of two-thirds' final salary at 65. This is based on a fairly conservative assumption for investment growth, but the truth is that the danger of over-funding is pretty remote, while under-provision is extremely common.

On top of that, you may not want to soldier on to the age of 65. If you retire early, not only will you have accumulated fewer rights from a company scheme, say 35/60ths instead of 40/60ths, but most schemes also levy a penalty, often up to 6 per cent a year. Hence there is all the more reason to plan now for your future leisure.

The good news is that pension plans are becoming much more flexible. Many insurance company products will allow you to switch without penalty from, say, a free-standing AVC to a personal pension if your employment circumstances change, and contributions can be made in the form of occasional lump sums instead of, or in addition to, regular savings. So there is no excuse for not acting!

WHERE TO FIND OUT MORE

The financial pages of newspapers run frequent articles on pension issues, as do specialist magazines. For specific suggestions on your own circumstances, you should think of consulting a financial adviser.

There are also a number of bodies that can offer certain types of information and help. The Occupational Pensions Advisory Service can advise on the rights of members of company schemes and can be contacted on 020 7233 8080. To track down pension entitlements you may have from past employment, contact the Pensions Register on 0191 225 6393. If you have any disputes that you cannot resolve with your pension provider, there is the Pensions Ombudsman's Bureau on 020 7834 9144, or, for aspects of personal pensions, the Insurance Ombudsman's Bureau on 020 7928 7600.

12 | Tangibles and Other Investments

This chapter looks at alternative investments that do not fit into any of the categories covered so far. Chief among these are 'tangibles', which, as the name implies, are physical objects rather than financial instruments. They can be highly specialised – rarity is often a key factor in their value – and may therefore require a high degree of expertise. Hence investors should be prepared either to do considerable research on their own part, or to put their trust in an expert. Tangibles also tend to be less liquid than financial investments, partly because there is not always a ready market, and partly because of indivisibility – you can sell a small parcel of shares, but you cannot sell one arm of an antique chair.

TANGIBLES

Tangibles are extremely wide-ranging and can be categorised in a number of ways, but a broad breakdown can be made as follows.

Objects of intrinsic value

This would include items such as precious metals and gemstones whose value is determined more or less by objective criteria rather than any artistic or cultural merit. For this reason, they can be easier to get to grips with, though an understanding of the market is still useful.

Arts and crafts

This group covers items such as paintings and antiques, ranging from furniture to silver or porcelain. Specialist knowledge is more or less essential and some objects may need particular storage conditions. Security and insurance are also important considerations; it is worth checking out specialist art insurers, who can offer better rates with fewer specifications on security measures than the big general companies.

Collections

Collectable items range from those with recognised markets and dealers, such as stamps and coins, to the more esoteric, such as matchboxes and beer mats. The latter, of course, are usually collected for pleasure rather than financial gain, but even in the former case, enthusiasm for the subject is often the key to financial success; the essence of a good collection is that the items have been hand-picked, rather than simply thrown together, so that the sum is greater than the parts.

Other items

Tangibles that do not come into the above categories include, for example, jewellery, exotic rugs and classic cars. Like collectables, these are often bought for pleasure rather than investment gain; for the latter purpose, specialist knowledge or advice is desirable, as the most aesthetic objects are not necessarily the most financially rewarding.

Although there is such a wide variation in types, tangibles do have some common characteristics, which should be borne in mind if you are buying primarily for investment purposes.

1. They produce no income, which can be an advantage to higher rate taxpayers, but meanwhile they involve running costs for storage and insurance. Hence the prospects for capital gain should be enough to finance this ongoing 'deficit' as well as producing a profit.
2. While some tangibles such as gold and precious stones have intrinsic worth, in many cases the price depends on current

supply and demand rather than 'face' value. This in turn may be influenced by fashion as much as market trends, as well as economic factors such as inflation that detract from financial alternatives.

3. Some items, especially collectables, may not be freely marketable, so money invested should be truly 'spare' capital that you will not need access to in an emergency.

4. Because the markets are often limited, with little competition, dealing costs or mark-ups may be high, so you need to invest over a longer term before there is an appreciable profit.

PRECIOUS METALS

As alternative investments go, precious metals have a certain glamour, but investors should not get too carried away with the glitter. Investment value and beauty are two very different characteristics; jewellery, for example, may have increasing value but should not be considered purely for investment purposes, because the retail mark-ups are high and the cost of the workmanship involved can outweigh the intrinsic value of the metal.

Both gold and platinum can be bought in the form of bars and coins. Gold is the more popular choice with investors; while platinum is much rarer, and is underpinned to some extent by industrial demand, it does not have the same history as gold of being seen as the ultimate store of value and haven in troubled times.

In the UK, the one-ounce gold Britannia coin is minted for investment purposes. Other options are the South African Krugerrand and the Canadian Maple Leaf; there are also sovereigns, which are smaller, but these are not always available singly – a minimum purchase might be 20 coins.

An important point to bear in mind is that if you buy coins in this country they will be subject to VAT at (currently) 17.5 per cent. This can be avoided by buying offshore, usually in the Channel Islands, and this can be arranged through a high street bank. On top of the price of the coin, you will also have to pay a dealing charge and transportation costs, including insurance while the coins are in transit.

To continue to avoid VAT, the coins will need to be held offshore, which the bank will do for you. This is also convenient in terms of security, but it does of course mean further charges, for both storage and insurance. Together these would currently come to around £100 a year upwards, depending on the number of coins and their value. Furthermore, any urge to see your treasure should be resisted, as this can incur yet another charge, on top of your own travelling costs.

Given that there are these various running costs, and no income being generated, gold is only attractive if there are good prospects of capital growth. The increasing sophistication of 'hedging' instruments such as futures and options has meant that gold is no longer the prime refuge from inflation that it once was. After the 'gold rush' of 1980 the metal spent many years in the doldrums. In 1997 it hit a 12-year low.

An alternative way of investing in gold is to buy shares in gold mining companies, either directly or through a unit trust. These tend to move ahead of the price of the gold itself and are even more volatile: over 1995, the gold price went up 7 per cent, while share prices rose by a massive 44 per cent. Offshore funds are another possibility; these may invest in shares, physical gold or gold futures, so will respond to different market factors.

There are also both onshore and offshore commodity funds, the former investing only in shares of associated companies, while the latter can include direct investment; these may include some exposure to gold, but within a spread of holdings, which can reduce the risk. Finally, you can buy gold options, but these are not currently traded in London, so the dealing cost is relatively high.

DIAMONDS

Diamonds share some of the characteristics of gold: a hard-headed approach is needed, and jewellery should be ruled out for purely investment purposes, because too much of the cost relates to the settings and there is also the fashion element, which can affect the value. Again, it is best to buy and store the stones offshore, which a dealer can arrange for you, but there will be storage and insurance costs.

Diamonds offer rather more scope than gold to pick and choose what you want, because there are a wide range of grades. Stones are categorised by the 'four Cs': cut, colour, clarity and carat (in other words, weight). Each of these may be good, bad or somewhere in between, so there are various possible permutations which will influence the current price and the future prospects.

The conventional rule is that investment stones should be at the upper end of the scale in each category, as quality stones are more likely to hold their value, but you need to take expert advice in the light of how much you want to invest and how long for. It may be, for instance, that having several lesser stones will suit you better than a single one of very high quality, as it will give you greater flexibility in selling; but depending on supply and demand in the market, lower quality stones may be less readily marketable.

Tastes can also change. For example, colourless stones used to be preferred to coloured ones, but it is now the latter that fetch the highest prices. In all cases, it is essential to have a certificate from an independent assessor on the quality of the stone.

Like gold, diamonds used to prosper in times of high inflation, but have been less talked of in recent years. As well as market influences, they are subject to investment fads, so can experience sudden booms when prices reach unrealistic levels, as happened in the late 1970s, but can equally undergo long periods of disinterest.

WINE

Wine drinking has enjoyed increasing popularity in this country in recent years, leading to a growing interest in fine wines and corresponding opportunities for investment. Getting it right, though, can be tricky, as there are fashions in types, as well as acknowledged good and bad vintages.

The most popular wines among investors are claret and port. As these take some years to mature, prices and prospects will depend on the time-scale on which you are prepared to invest. If you are willing to tie up your capital for 10 years, say, you can go for a fairly young wine and wait for it to reach its prime; if you are taking only a five-year view, you may need to look at something older, which will be more expensive. You can even make your investment before the wine is bottled, through the wine futures market, in the hope that it will mature successfully to command a high price in years to come. However, there have been failures to deliver wine ordered this way, so it may be safer to invest at the point where it is first available for delivery. Generally speaking, you should expect to hold claret for at least five years before it becomes profitable, while port should be laid down for at least 20 years.

The minimum investment could be just a few hundred pounds, depending on what you choose, but around £5000 might be a more sensible starting-point. You should aim to buy in cases (12 bottles) rather than single bottles, as the latter tend to be traded only if they are particularly rare. Remember, too, that you will need proper storage conditions, which may require a certain outlay. In addition, you should consider specialised insurance, as a standard household policy may cover you only against theft and not, for example, accidental damage. Alternatively, some wine merchants offer storage facilities, including insurance. If you can arrange storage 'in bond' – in a customs-approved warehouse – so much the better, as this will avoid excise duty and VAT.

An alternative is a wine investment fund, launched in 1995. Specialising in Bordeaux, this gives you the opportunity to invest in 25 wines picked by the fund manager, for a minimum investment of £2500. There is a charge of 1.5 per cent to 2 per cent to cover insurance and storage costs, plus an exit charge of up to 2.5 per cent. Profits are not taxable, as wine is considered to be a depreciating asset, but the scheme is also not covered by the Financial Services Act, so you do not have the protection of the Investors Compensation Scheme should things go wrong.

There are numerous books available on wine, as well as occasional press articles, and Christie's and Sotheby's both hold regular auctions.

FORESTRY

One of the main attractions of an investment in forestry is that it attracts substantial tax concessions. For a start, commercial timber that is growing is free from both income and capital gains tax. The 1992 Budget also doubled the business property relief from inheritance tax, from 50 per cent to a full 100 per cent, on commercial woodland. This applies after the first two years of ownership and means that on the investor's subsequent death, there will be no liability to inheritance tax. With the tax rate currently at 40 per cent for assets outside the nil rate band of £234,000 (except property inherited by a spouse, which is exempt from tax), this represents a considerable saving.

The condition is that the woodland must be run as a commercial enterprise, which may mean you have to employ a qualified manager. The other drawback is that you can no longer claim tax relief on plantation expenses under Schedule D, as this has been phased out. This has removed the attraction of the traditional route into forestry, which was to buy bare land and plant it, offsetting the costs against other income for tax purposes, and then passing on the forest to your heirs as a long-term investment.

During the first 25 years of its life, a plantation incurs a good deal of expense in management and tending, while producing no return, as the trees are too young to be felled. Although the tax relief has been replaced by the Woodland Grant Scheme, this does not offer the same degree of financial support during the maturing phase, hence investors are turning away from new or young plantations towards those that are already mature enough to offer some felling opportunities and thus produce an income from the start. As a result, good-quality woodlands of an appropriate age are moving into short supply.

The current outlook for forestry as an investment is good, with timber prices on the increase. But while it is possible to buy part shares through a management company, it has to be remembered that this is essentially a large-scale, long-term investment rather than one of quick returns, and in many cases the tax advantages are a significant part of the appeal.

An alternative route is an investment fund. One launched recently will run for ten years and expects an initial tax-free return of 7 per cent a year, rising by up to 2 per cent each year. The minimum investment was £5000. The fund was open for a limited period only, so if you are interested in this type of investment you should be prepared to take up opportunities quickly as they arise.

THEATRE AND FILM PRODUCTIONS

You do not have to be rich to become an 'angel' – a sponsor of a theatre production – but you do have to be sanguine about losing money. There have been some notable successes but, for many productions, even commercial viability is a stiff target. By the time the initial cost and the running expenses have been met, ticket sales have to be very good for you to make a return – many shows fail to make enough even to recoup the original investment.

As well as being philosophical about losses, you need to be hard-headed in your choice of show or producer. Worthy causes are generally not the money-spinners; what matters is not what the critics say, but what the audiences think. The recommended approach is to back a successful producer, rather than choosing an individual production.

The Society of London Theatre operates a scheme on behalf of its members to put investors in touch with producers looking for backers. The minimum investment required is usually £1000 or £2000. An alternative to backing individual productions is a collective fund. The Gabriel Fund was launched some three years ago and units cost up to £5000 each. However, you pay only £1000 up-front and the balance will be called for only if the fund runs out of money and still has losses to meet.

You can also invest in films. Cromwell Productions was set up to provide a novel form of film finance. For as little as £500, you get not only a share of half the net profits and the full return of your money within a fixed time, but also the chance to be in the film yourself as an extra. Four such films have been released so far.

Because of the length of time it takes for a film to get from shooting to screening, you may have quite a wait to get your money back – you can expect it to be about two years before you see your first returns. But you will get a ticket to the première to see a glimpse of yourself and your name in the film's credits.

In the July 1997 Budget, the Chancellor gave the British film industry and its investors a highly attractive tax-break by allowing 100 per cent of production and acquisition costs to be written off for the purposes of income tax. This applied to low-budget British films and ran to July 2000.

Tax benefits are still available through the Enterprise Investment

Scheme, explained below, which several film-makers have used to raise money. There are also firms that specialise in this area, such as Matrix Securities, which has a division called Matrix Film that has been involved in film and television projects.

Information can be obtained from:

The Society of London Theatre
020 7836 0971
Cromwell Productions
01789 415187
The Gabriel Fund
020 7734 7184
Matrix Securities
020 7292 0800

ENTERPRISE INVESTMENT SCHEME

Just as there are theatre angels, so there are 'business angels' – private investors who provide finance for entrepreneurs. They help to fill a gap at the bottom end of the market, backing very small companies for which bank financing may be unsuitable or even impossible to arrange. In many cases, they will also contribute management expertise as well as cash.

The British Venture Capital Association produces an annual directory that can help you find a suitable venture to invest in. Another organisation that provides introductory services is the Local Investment Networking Company (Linc). It produces a monthly bulletin listing businesses that have undergone an initial screening for suitability. The subscription fee is £85 + VAT a year.

However, this is a highly risky area, because the companies are small and are likely to have no track record and no security for the funding. Two alternative routes into the venture capital arena are offered by recent government initiatives, which also carry tax advantages: venture capital trusts (VCTs), which are described in Chapter 8, and the Enterprise Investment Scheme (EIS).

The Enterprise Investment Scheme was announced in the 1993 Autumn Budget as the successor to the Business Expansion Scheme, which was phased out at the end of 1993. Dubbed 'Son of

BES', it has the same aim of encouraging investment in small, unquoted companies.

The scheme differs from its predecessor in certain respects. The maximum you can invest each year is £150,000, as against £40,000 for the BES, but income tax relief on the investment is limited to 20 per cent. This makes the scheme less attractive for higher rate taxpayers, who could get a full 40 per cent relief from BES investments.

In fact, the scheme as originally announced found few takers; during 1994, the total raised was only about £5 million and no scheme reached its maximum subscription level. This was addressed in the 1994 Budget, which improved the scheme with further tax concessions, while the 1998 budget raised the maximum investment from £100,000 to £150,000.

Investors may get 'rollover' relief on capital gains made from the sale of other assets if they reinvest the proceeds into an EIS. Although this only defers the tax – it will have to be paid eventually when the EIS shares are sold – it does mean that the up-front relief on the EIS investment can be equivalent to 60 per cent – 20 per cent income tax and 40 per cent capital gains tax relief.

Moreover, there is no capital gains tax liability on the EIS shares themselves. You must, however, hold them for at least five years to qualify for the tax benefits.

The scope of the EIS has also been extended to include property-backed businesses such as hotels, leisure clubs and housebuilding. In addition, schemes may offer a 'contracted exit', meaning that there is a guaranteed return to investors. This can cut the risk considerably, although any guarantee is only as good as the under-lying security – the company could fail and so might its guarantor. You should also remember that investments are locked in for at least five years, even if you are guaranteed an exit thereafter. But if you are a higher rate taxpayer and have money you will not need to access, this is an area worth considering.

Further information is available from:

Local Investment Networking Company (Linc)
020 7329 2929
British Venture Capital Association
020 7240 3846

ENTERPRISE ZONE TRUSTS

Enterprise zone trusts are based on enterprise zones, which are government-designated development areas around the country that attract special tax reliefs for construction. The trusts offer investors a stake in a portfolio of commercial properties, which should generate an annual income from rents.

Investments can be made during a trust's subscription period, with a normal minimum of £5000 and no maximum. Tax relief is available at your highest rate, but applies only to the portion of money used to buy or build properties, not to acquire the land. The Inland Revenue decides for each trust what proportion relates to land and is therefore disallowed for tax relief; on average, this is about 10 per cent, although it could be up to 30 per cent.

Besides the tax relief, a further attraction is that investments can be funded by borrowing that is itself tax efficient. You can borrow up to 70 per cent of your gross investment and interest on this loan will be set against the income earned for tax purposes. Hence you will need to provide very little, if any, money up front, while the income tax bill on your returns will be substantially reduced.

The income comes from rent on the properties, which is distributed to investors, less an amount to cover the scheme's costs. Several trusts offer a guarantee for an initial period, which will provide a set return if no tenants are found or if the rent drops below a certain level.

But these guarantees should be treated with caution. For one thing, the payments are fully taxable and no tax relief is given against them for interest on money you borrow to invest. Second, the value of the guarantee depends on the financial strength of the guarantor; there have been cases where schemes have collapsed. Third, the guarantee period is generally no more than five years and income thereafter will depend entirely on the rent received, which in turn will depend on the quality and location of the properties.

Enterprise zone investments also represent a long-term commitment, as tax relief is normally clawed back if investors pull out within 25 years. The exception is that after seven years, the trust may sell a lesser interest in its properties, thereby raising capital that can be distributed to investors.

While returns can look attractive, enterprise zone trusts should be viewed as high risk. The administrative costs can be high and the potential for capital appreciation is becoming more limited, as many zones are nearing the end of their 10-year life and the shortage of new investment opportunities is driving up prices. Hence it is well worth seeking advice from a specialist.

Enterprise zones are also under threat from European Union tax harmonisation. They are on a list of UK schemes under consideration by a committee of European finance ministers as potential 'unfair' practices that distort the single European market. This means new zones are unlikely to be created, although existing trusts will not be affected and there could even be new launches within existing zones.

LLOYD'S OF LONDON

Becoming a member of the Lloyd's insurance market has never been for the faint-hearted. The losses of recent years have only served to emphasise this: in 1989 they amounted to a record £2.06 billion. 'Names', as they are known, have had more than their fingers burned and the market has suffered considerable turmoil.

The primary feature of the market has always been that members have unlimited liability. To become a member, you must have minimum assets of £250,000 and this excludes the value of property that is your main residence. But in the event of losses, all your assets can be at stake, including your home and furniture. Underwriting profits and losses for any given year are not finally assessed for three years, so in the event of a disaster, there can be a long wait to discover the total extent of the damage.

There are currently over 100 syndicates. The standard procedure for joining has been that in addition to showing you had sufficient assets, you had to be supported by two existing members and satisfy the committee that you were suitable.

But the recent upheavals brought a radical rethink, as the market needed to put aside its difficulties and attract new money. In October 1993, Lloyd's members voted to allow limited companies to invest, to provide a back-up for underwriting syndicates. This has spawned a number of investment trusts, which provide a means for private investors to participate for as little as £1000. These are explained in Chapter 8.

A free guide to investing in the Lloyd's market is available from ShareLink (telephone 0121 200 4610). More information can also be obtained from:

Lloyd's of London
Lime Street
London EC3M 7HA
Telephone 020 7327 1000

ETHICAL INVESTMENT

Ethical investment is about knowing and approving of what your money goes into.

Although it may sound like a minority pursuit it is worth remembering that more than £1 billion of funds under management is now directed according to ethical criteria. If you add church-related pension and other funds whose investment is ethically guided, the figure may be four or five times that. Furthermore, the concept is nothing new. Having copied the idea from post-Vietnam America, British ethical investment vehicles have been around since 1983.

How to invest

Ethical investment options include unit trusts, pension funds, endowment policies and PEPs. In its *Money & Ethics* reference work – which, incidentally, is a must for anyone wishing to investigate the subject in greater depth – the Ethical Investment Research Service (EIRIS) analyses 42 funds that are run according to ethical criteria. EIRIS lists each of the funds, appraising them according to no fewer than 23 'corporate criteria'. It is worth listing them just to get a feel for the subject and whether they would be on your ethical do's and don'ts list. Those to be avoided are:

- ☐ sale and production of alcohol;
- ☐ testing of products on animals;
- ☐ gambling;
- ☐ production of greenhouse gases;
- ☐ health and safety breaches;
- ☐ operations in countries with poor human rights records;
- ☐ intensive farming and meat sale;
- ☐ Ministry of Defence contracts;
- ☐ production or sale of military goods;
- ☐ nuclear power;
- ☐ ozone depletion;
- ☐ pesticides;
- ☐ pornography and adult films;
- ☐ road building;
- ☐ exploitation of the Third World;
- ☐ tobacco production or sale;
- ☐ extraction, sale or use of tropical hardwood;
- ☐ water pollution.

EIRIS also lists five activities that investors may wish to support:

- ☐ provision of positive products and services;
- ☐ community involvement;
- ☐ disclosure of information;
- ☐ good record on environmental issues;
- ☐ good record on equal opportunities.

These two groups of issues place ethical investment securely in the twin camps of all that is morally 'right' and 'good' in the fullest, holistic sense and what is best practice in corporate governance. Shareholder power, participation and protest are certainly becoming red-hot issues and some may argue that they are the natural counterweight to the concept of limited liability and corporate short-termism.

Freedom to invest

But how far do you take this in deciding where to invest? Do you avoid all privatised utility stocks, for example, on the basis that you disapprove of the government selling off the family infrastructure silver? Do you avoid a raft of otherwise appealing emerging market investment destinations and the companies that are active in those emerging markets because of alleged or perceived human rights abuses? Would there be any companies or countries left to invest in if you did?

The point about ethical investment is that you are free to exercise your right to invest in those things you approve of and avoid those that you do not. There is an implicit recognition that beyond financial return, there are other values that should be taken into account when making an investment decision. Which they are is up to you. Of course, each time you set a criterion you narrow the range of investment options open to you.

Screened funds and returns

To take two funds as examples, the largest ethical fund in the UK excludes all but 18 of the UK's 100 biggest companies while another can select from only 400 companies worldwide because of the standards it sets itself. The technical term for this type of selective investment is 'screened funds'. Independent financial advisers and ethical fund investment managers can produce figures to show that this screening does not necessarily impair returns. Performance figures show that ethical funds, like any other, produce mixed results, but the best can match or beat non-ethical funds.

Risk

Depending on a fund's ethical selection criteria it may, however, have a higher risk profile. The argument runs that stringent criteria such as those listed above tend to exclude most, if not all, of larger, FTSE 100 companies. Investments tend to be in smaller and therefore higher risk stocks which can be vulnerable to price fluctuations and public relations accidents, especially if other funds themselves become disenchanted and start to sell their holdings in a significant way, so affecting share prices. This points to the importance of risk spreading within the fund, which, as we have seen, is restricted anyway owing to selection criteria: a kind of ethical-financial Catch-22.

There is still a deeply rooted folk-belief that if you invest with conscience and responsibility you have to accept higher risk and lower returns. However, the spread of shareholder pressure and higher degrees of corporate governance should eventually increase the range of companies that fit ethical criteria, and at the same time investors are likely to get more demanding in their performance expectations.

One development in response to concerns about performance has been the emergence of 'light green' funds. The criteria for choosing shares is positive rather than negative and investment is made in companies that have shown a positive social and environmental commitment. As a result, they may invest in sectors such as pharmaceuticals and banking, which would be avoided by traditional ethical funds but which have seen substantial growth recently.

Traditionalists claim that these funds are trying to take advantage of the ethical bandwagon without actually subscribing to the principles. But supporters of the funds say that they are likely to have wider appeal and, with more investors, can put greater pressure on large companies to clean up their act. They also extend the choices open to investors.

From next year, the government is to make it mandatory for pension-fund trustees to declare their ethical stance as regards their investment policy. Trustees' primary responsibility has always been to ensure that the members of the pension scheme get the best possible returns and this may not square with taking an ethical line. But it is arguable that it should be members' *interests* that they safeguard, which can include ethical concerns. At any rate, with an increasing range of investments available, it may be possible for trustees to incorporate ethical considerations without sacrificing performance.

NPI, which runs two ethical unit trusts, has launched the NPI Social Index, designed to measure the performance of ethical investments. The index is made up of 158 companies: 37 from the FTSE 100 Index, 36 from the next tier down, the FTSE 250 Index, eight investment trusts and the rest from the smaller companies sector. The selection aims to reflect the sector structure of the All-Share Index.

HSBC has also launched an ethical index, the HSBC Securities Ethical 100 Index. This comprises 100 of the most ethical companies from the FTSE 350 Index, excluding investment trusts. The constituents will be reviewed every year; new companies may be included if they improve their ethical rating, while any that drop out of the 350 Index will also be dropped from HSBC's.

Ethical banking

Choosing the right ethical fund may require a fairly compre-hensive study of all those available, but choosing an ethical bank is a little easier.

The Co-operative Bank led the way in 1990 by nailing its ethical colours firmly to the mast. It says, for example, that it 'will not invest in or supply financial services to any regime or organisation which oppresses the human spirit, takes away the rights of individuals or manufactures any instrument of torture'. Its policy goes on to cover, among other things, the sales of weapons, money laundering, animal experiments, factory farming and blood sports. The bank supplies a range of standard clearing bank services. Triodos Bank, a Dutch company with an operation in the UK, will only finance enterprises that have a positive effect on the community and the environment. It offers a high interest cheque account, postal savings accounts and a mini cash ISA, but not a current account.

In the end, ethical investment is largely a question of what you want it to be. If you are not sure just what would fit your conscience – and your pocket – a good way to start is to contact the Ethical Investment Research Service. It can cut short the process of research and help you to sift through the increasing amount of information that has become available as the concept of ethical investment has gained appeal.

Useful reading

- [ ] *The Ethical Investor*, Russell Sparkes, HarperCollins Publishers, 1995, £9.99.
- [ ] *Money & Ethics: A guide to pensions, PEPs, endowment mortgages and other ethical investment plans*, Ethical Investment Research Service, 1996, £12.50.

The Ethical Investment Research Service can be contacted on 020 7840 5700. It can carry out an appraisal of your portfolio and tell you which of your holdings may be ethically challenged.

Other contacts: Co-operative Bank 0845 7212212; Triodos Bank 0500 008 720.

INVESTING IN PROPERTY

Property has not looked an attractive area in which to invest since the major slump of the late 1980s and early 1990s. Any upward movement in prices has been eagerly hailed as a recovery but it is only now that there seems to be an upswing of any substance. However, with a lump sum to invest, you are well placed to strike a deal.

Domestic property

We all need somewhere to live. It still makes sense to avoid paying rent to someone else and, according to a recent survey, 92 per cent of home owners believe it is better to buy than to rent. Nationwide statistics show that 67 per cent of the housing stock is owner occupied. A lump sum investor does not need to borrow, so, apart from maintenance costs, council tax, insurance and the other usual bills, he can have a roof over his head for free.

The benefit of this should not be overlooked. A property that costs, say, £120,000 might carry a rent of around £200 a week – equivalent to £10,400 a year or 8.7 per cent of the purchase price. That represents an attractive return on the investment and the value of the house should also appreciate over time.

There is still one tax advantage in investing in a domestic property although they have slowly been whittled away in successive budgets: provided it is a main residence, any gain realised when selling the property is free of capital gains tax.

Aside from buying a property to live in yourself, you can also buy to let as an investment. Generally, you will want to set up an 'assured shorthold tenancy' – this is, in fact, what most tenancies are automatically these days. It is a contract for a fixed term, typically six months or a year. Thereafter it can be renewed, but the landlord has the right to repossess at two months' notice.

If you do not wish to manage the property yourself, you can get an agency to do it; many estate agents offer a letting service. The fees are of the order of 10 per cent of the rent to find a tenant and a running cost of 5 per cent to collect rents and manage the property.

Rental income is taxable, but you can claim costs against it, such as insurance, water rates if you pay them yourself and any agency letting fees. If you have a mortgage on the property, you can also offset the interest. Some lenders charge a slightly higher interest rate where property is let, generally 0.5 per cent above the standard rate.

Second homes and timeshares

The advantage of not having to pay rent extends, of course, to second homes and timeshares. In the case of second or holiday homes, use of the property is likely to be entirely in the hands of the purchaser throughout the year. The property can be rented out to produce income. Furthermore, it can be nominated as the main residence and exempted from CGT. The switch in nomination between homes is up to the owner in agreement with the Inland Revenue; careful consideration of the best option with a tax specialist is advisable.

Timeshares entitle the owner to the use of a property such as a villa, chalet or holiday apartment for a given number of days or weeks. But most can be exchanged with owners of the same or other timeshares so that you are not locked into taking the same weeks of holiday at the same place for the term of the timeshare. Ultimately, it is possible to sell on the timeshare although the price is unlikely to be predictable. All told, it is worth totting up what you would have paid if you had had to rent other holiday accommodation during the term of the timeshare ownership, and any profit can be a bonus. It must be said that, as with any other property investment, prices can go down as well as up and there is no telling which way they will go. Lastly, you should not forget to take into account annual maintenance charges and any other fees that may be payable. These can prove rather costly over the long term.

Commercial property

Although house purchase is the most obvious form of property investment, most of us also invest indirectly in commercial property through pension and life assurance arrangements. The main sectors of the market in which they invest are office buildings, retail outlets and industrial property.

The factors that are taken into account when fund managers invest can be useful in understanding their investment strategies and in making one's own property investment decision:

- the position of the property;
- the description of the property;
- the tenure of tenants;
- the lease terms;
- the identity of tenants;
- the amount and timing of rental income;
- the initial purchase price of the property;
- the total yield on the property.

These considerations will be taken into account when the fund manager invests in a piece of property, perhaps as a group of institutions buying an office block or trading estate. At the same time he may invest in property companies whose portfolios are made up of a spread of such investments or he may invest in property funds which in turn invest in a variety of different types of property in selected locations.

UK property, along with UK equities, has traditionally been a mainstay of insurance company investment. It has been considered long term and sufficiently reliable. However, confidence was quite severely dented by the aftermath of the property building boom of the 1980s, with projects such as London Docklands' Canary Wharf where boom was followed by bust within a short space of time. In the last year we have seen investors returning and buying in at lower prices. Some of this new activity has been funded by bank borrowings and rights issues. But despite a blizzard of statistics from commercial estate agents and property analysts supporting the idea that recovery is on the way, many investors have yet to be convinced.

Where pension plans allow for individual policyholders to pick which funds they wish to invest in, UK property may appear among the available options. Bearing in mind the above criteria, it is important for investors thinking of looking at the property sector to delve into details of the composition of the fund on offer and what properties their money would be funding, as well as to receive regular updates about broad market trends and reports about the sites themselves.

Unit trusts

Another way of investing in property is through a unit trust. A lump sum investment can be made from £1000 upwards. There are two authorised property unit trusts investing in commercial property in the UK, of which the larger is the Norwich Property Trust.

Its portfolio is split into five categories (not counting cash): offices, high street retail, retail warehouses, industrial and property shares. This last can be further broken down into ordinary shares, convertibles and convertible preference shares. Of the direct property held, the largest sector is generally offices and the largest geographic region, not surprisingly, is London and the south east.

As with any unit trust, the price of units can go up or down, but there is a further caveat, in that you may not be able to sell exactly when you want to; because property itself is not readily saleable, the managers of a trust can delay the repurchase of units. In practice, though, the cash and equity holdings provide a margin that should cover day-to-day transactions, unless there is a sudden stampede to sell. Normally, dealings take place daily and prices are quoted in *The Daily Telegraph* and the *Financial Times*.

13 | **Charitable Giving**

Giving to charity may not rank as an investment in the ordinary sense, but it can be regarded as an investment in the future of society. Moreover, with a little organisation – as opposed to simply giving to street collectors – it can be tax efficient.

The simplest arrangement is a payroll scheme, operated by an employer, that allows employees to make gifts directly from their salary. The money is deducted before tax and paid to an approved Agency Charity with which the employer has an agreement. The employees, however, have a free choice of which charities their money goes to and the Agency Charity simply passes it on, although it may make a small charge for administration. Before April 2000, there was an upper limit of £100 a month for payroll donations, but this has now been abolished. The government is also to add an extra 10 per cent to all payroll donations for the next three years.

If your employer does not offer a payroll scheme, you can use Gift Aid. Again, this has been made simpler, with the abolition of the previous £250 minimum and the need to complete a certificate. The charity needs only the donor's name and address and confirmation that he is a taxpayer for it to reclaim basic rate tax from the Inland Revenue. This means that donations can more easily be made by telephone – for instance in response to a television appeal – or even via the Internet.

In the 1998 Budget, the Chancellor announced an extension to the Gift Aid Scheme: Millennium Gift Aid. This will run until December 2000 and provides tax relief on gifts from £100 upwards. You may also donate smaller amounts and tax relief will still be added as long as you donate a total of £100 by the year-end. The money raised will go to a number of charities working in the world's poorest countries and donors may select both a region and any one of six categories of aid.

Another new concession concerns giving shares to charity. Donors can now not only avoid capital gains tax, but also cut their income tax. Suppose, for instance, that a donor gives shares worth £1000 to charity. The gift is exempt from capital gains tax and, at the same time, he will get income tax relief on the full value of £1000, worth £400.

The Charities Aid Foundation offers 'Personal Charity Accounts' for those giving through Gift Aid or covenants. The Foundation can reclaim tax on the gifts and also provides a 'cheque-book' of vouchers which you can make out to your chosen charities.

Further information on Gift Aid is given in the Inland Revenue leaflet IR113 and from the Gift Aid helpline on 0151 472 6038. The Charities Aid Foundation can be contacted on 01732 520000.

MAKING AN INVESTMENT IN A WORTHY CAUSE

Vicki Pulman
Charities Aid Foundation

Around 80 per cent of people in the UK make donations to charity. Few, however, are even aware of the full benefits available through the tax system, not just to the charities they choose to support, but to themselves. Overall, government has introduced three schemes for tax-effective giving, enabling both private individuals and corporate donors to make their charitable giving more effective.

Donations made from taxed funds through any one of these schemes enable the Inland Revenue to repay the basic rate tax of 22 per cent to the charity. If you are a higher rate taxpayer, you may reclaim the marginal rate of 18 per cent.

The schemes offer three very different methods of payment. These are by deed of covenant, payroll giving and Gift Aid. The *deed of covenant* is the oldest of the three and involves a contractual obligation to make regular donations over a period of four or more years. These payments can be made annually, monthly or in a lump sum, allowing the charity to subtract regular payments on its own behalf. Whichever method is used, tax is reclaimed and added to the total donation, increasing it by roughly one-third, at no extra cost to either you or the charity. There is no maximum amount payable under this scheme, although in order to cover the cost of administration, some charities may require a minimum donation.

Payroll giving was introduced by the government to encourage ongoing and regular gifts to charity. Since 1987, this scheme has enabled donors paying PAYE to make monthly contributions direct from their pay or pension at source, before tax is levied. The donor then pays tax at the usual rate but only on its remaining income. A donation, for example, of £50 per month made from pre-taxed income would cost you £39 in real terms and only £30 if you are a higher rate taxpayer. The real benefit, particularly to the charity, is in providing it with a regular source of income with which to budget and plan ahead.

Gift Aid is the most recent scheme and was introduced in 1991. It is the only scheme allowing single, one-off donations to be made tax effectively. As with the covenant, tax is reclaimed by the charity at basic rate. This would increase a gift of £100 to £128.20 and allows higher rate donors to reclaim the marginal rate of over £20 for themselves.

There is one condition when making donations through any tax-effective scheme: the money has to go to a charity either registered with the Charity Commission or recognised by the Inland Revenue as being charitable. Organisations such as scout groups, places of worship, schools and hospitals, while not being registered char-ities, are all considered to be 'charitable'. Despite the obvious benefits of these schemes, for many they lack the flexibility and the spontaneity essential when giving to charity. There is a way, however, in which you can respond to a radio or television appeal, send off a few pounds in response to an advertisement or even give to a local street collector – tax effectively.

A personal charity account scheme, operated by an agency such as the Charities Aid Foundation (CAF), enables you to pay your tax-efficient donation into an account rather than direct to a single charity. As a registered charity itself, CAF reclaims the basic rate tax on the donor's behalf and adds it to the amount already in the account, deducting a small administrative contribution. So, on an initial payment of, say, £120, a revised balance of around £150 is created at no extra cost to you. Higher rate taxpayers would be able to reclaim a further £28 for themselves.

Once the money is in the account, you are issued with a voucher book, similar to a cheque-book, and a CAF Charity Card, a debit card designed specifically for charitable giving. This helps you to support any charity or cause of your choice and in whatever amounts, either by writing out a voucher in the charity's name or by giving the charity your card details.

Where would your donation go? Take, for example, the balance of £150 used above (which has cost the higher rate taxpayer only £92): £50 could be used to support a local community group, £50 could go to a place of worship, another £50 could go to an international aid agency. It is entirely your choice.

An added advantage to using an account is that CAF will honour only those donations made to registered or recognised charities, thereby protecting the money from going to an organisation that is not bona fide.

If you have slightly larger amounts to distribute – a bequest under a will or investments that you wish to give to a charity free of capital gains tax – setting up a charitable trust may be an ideal solution. It can provide enduring support for charities and causes even beyond your lifetime and can help to develop close links with those supported on a regular basis.

Before pursuing this option, however, it needs to be given careful consideration. First, there are legal and accountancy fees to be considered. Trustees need to be taken on, decisions taken over trust fund investment and accounting, separate bank accounts need to be opened and annual reports, returns and accounts all need to be submitted to the Charity Commission. It can take anything from 6 to 12 months simply to get the trust up and running.

By using an agency such as the Charities Aid Foundation, a trust can be established almost immediately and, as it comes under the guardianship of CAF's own trustees, there is no need to appoint them independently. Another advantage is that there are usually no initial fees or legal charges and CAF will take care of all administration requirements on behalf of the trust holder. Initially, all that is required of the donor is a sum of at least £10,000 – £7800 plus tax reclaimed (or the commitment to reach that level within two or three years) – a name for the trust, which, within reason, is up to the donor, and a decision on the duration of the trust.

Once the trust has been established, it operates rather like a bank account. The capital is invested by CAF although the emphasis, such as high income or capital growth, is chosen by the trust holder.

The three investment funds operated by CAF are the Balanced Growth Fund, providing sustained capital growth and increasing growth of income, the Income Fund, which maximises income return with an element of capital protection, and the CAF Cash Deposit Fund, which pools investments to create a high rate of interest. The three schemes are designed exclusively for charities and trusts in a tax-effective way and are used by thousands of such organisations.

As with tax-effective giving, when it comes to distributing funds from the trust, donations may only be made to registered or recognised charities either by using a voucher book or by standing order. Capital can be added to the trust at any time, and tax effectively, and all rights and responsibilities of the trust can be passed on at any time to a successor of the trust holder's choosing.

Under the current schemes, it has never been easier to support the charities of your choice tax effectively, whether you give in a sustained and regular way, make your donations spontaneously and with flexibility, or whether you simply want to ensure that both you and the charities you support gain the maximum benefit from your donations.

Further information on Gift Aid is given in the Inland Revenue leaflet IR113 and on the Gift Aid helpline on 0151 472 6038.

For further information about the Charities Aid Foundation's Charity Account Scheme telephone 01732 520000; or to find out more about the trust service contact 01892 512244.

PAYROLL GIVING AND VOUCHER ACCOUNTS

With a cache of money to dispense or save as you please, you may wish to consider opportunities to give regularly to charity either as and when you like or through your salary. Payroll giving is a tax-free way to give from your pay. The voucher account system offers a versatile and flexible way to give to charity. Both schemes are administered by the Charities Trust.

Charities Trust is incorporated and registered as a charitable company to operate as a payroll giving agency in accordance with Sections 505 and 506 of the Income and Corporation Taxes Act 1988. Charities Trust aims to provide a high-quality payroll giving service, that is non-profit-making. The trust acts as a clearing house, sending donations to the chosen charities. Money is taken directly from the donor's pay with the benefit of tax relief. Any one of a quarter of a million causes can benefit. All contributions have to be distributed within 80 days of receipt and the interest obtained on deposit during that time helps to offset costs.

The administration fee is designed to cover the cost of the processing of the donor's requirements and the distribution to the selected charities. The fee is currently 5 per cent or 30p per donor per month, whichever is the greater. The breakdown of a single donation of £10 would be as follows: agency charge of 50p, cost to taxpayer of £7.50, charity receives £9.50.

HOW THE PAYROLL GIVING SYSTEM WORKS

A maximum of four charities per person is permitted. The minimum donation per charity is 25p per week or £1 per month. Donors can vary their choice of charity or stop giving at any time. A statement of donations can be provided to employers on request at the end of each tax year.

Two thirds of the world's blindness is preventable

Photo by: Colin Jones

With your help

Imagine you had a nine year old granddaughter who is blind.

One day you discover that in a country far away, there is a miraculous cure that will bring her sight back. But you can't afford it.

Sadly, for millions of families the world over, this is reality. Two thirds of the world's 38 million blind need never have lost their sight or could be cured. Human beings have the technology and the drugs. All that is lacking is money.

Will you help?

SEE is a charity which funds research in the UK into every cause of blindness: from childhood injury, to glaucoma to improvements in the treatment of diabetic retinopathy. In Africa and Asia, we support practical work such as eye camps to repair cataract and the treatment of river blindness.

Please help us by a donation, a deed of covenant or a legacy.

Save Eyes Everywhere

SEE (The British Council for the Prevention of Blindness)
Contact: Rachel Carr-Hill
12 Hanover Street, London W1H 1DS
Tel: 020 7724 3716
Reg. charity number 270941

Employers provide to employees a facility for a pre-tax deduction for charitable donations. Employers send those donations to Charities Trust monthly together with a list of donors. It is recommended that the donor code used is the employer's payroll number or National Insurance number. Donations are sent before the 19th of the following month in line with PAYE.

Employers should note that to achieve maximum tax benefits, they need to enter into a contract with an Agency Charity and register with the Inland Revenue. Charities Trust can undertake this on their behalf. Donors leaving a company's employment are entitled to request from the employer a statement of their contributions made during the tax year.

Employers may elect to match employee donations and/or pay their administration fees. To ease administration, personnel departments are advised to produce easy-to-follow forms to input for submission to Charities Trust and use constant donor/employee reference numbers. Inland Revenue regulations prohibit the return of any money withheld from employees.

VOUCHER ACCOUNTS

Alternatively, you can open a voucher account. The minimum monthly donation is £120 per annum – £10 per month. The maximum individual donation is £900 per annum. With the tax advantage, a £10 donation would cost only £7.50. The scheme gives you the flexibility to give to whomever you want, whenever you want.

The money is paid into a 'pot' and whenever you wish to make a donation, whether it be to the local hospice or a TV extravaganza, the money is paid out. A book of vouchers or a charity cheque-book is issued to you to enable this to happen.

A group voucher scheme runs alongside the individual voucher scheme. A 'group' is considered a minimum of five individuals. These contribute to a 'pot'. The minimum and maximum donations by the group are the same as for the individual's scheme: £120 and £900 per annum respectively. One employee is nominated to complete and return a group voucher account registration form to Charities Trust. An account number will then be issued.

In addition, each employee donating to the group completes a Charity Choice Form but nominates the group account number rather than a specific charity. Once the group or individual account is established, a book of vouchers will be supplied.

The vouchers are completed at the individual's discretion like a cheque book and forwarded to the charity. The charity will complete its section and return the voucher to Charities Trust for processing. (Remember that the charity must be or become registered with Charities Trust.) A statement of account is provided on a quarterly basis to the account holder(s). Statements show donations made (less an administration charge of 5 per cent maximum), vouchers issued and balance available to use.

Charities Trust can also offer personal advice to companies on how employers can save time and money, how voucher accounts can be set up, enabling irregular donations to be made to an assortment of charities. The trust is the second largest payroll giving agency in the United Kingdom. It currently handles over 800 employers and more than 100,000 donors. Funds are distributed to over 2000 charities.

For further information contact: Charities Trust, PO Box 15, Liverpool L23 0UU. Telephone: 0151 949 0044.

WILLS, LEGACIES AND CHARITABLE GIVING

Bernard Sharpe

Making wills is an age-old occupation. It is quite impossible to say when the first will was made, by whom and under what circumstances. There are of course copies of ancient wills still in existence or records of what they contain. The purpose of wills has, however, never changed as it represents the inalienable right of people to leave their lifetime possessions to whomsoever they wish. For some it also provides an opportunity to speak from beyond the grave and throughout history all manner of people have used their wills to express unflattering observations about their kith and kin.

Equally, some of the sentiments expressed in wills about friends, relatives and reasons for leaving money to charity are loving and heart-warming and depict the best features of human nature.

The style and nature of wills has of course changed down the centuries. Here is an example of a will by Joshua West of the Six Clerks' Office in Chancery Lane, made in the 18th century. He wrote:

> Perhaps I died not worth a groat;
> but should I die worth something more,
> then I give that, and my best coat,
> and all my manuscripts in store, to those
> who shall the goodness have
> to cause my poor remains to rest
> within a decent shell and grave.
> This is the Will of Joshua West.

With the passage of time the collection and storage of wills became more regularised and a system evolved whereby probate matters in England and Wales were dealt with by a mixture of almost 400 ecclesiastical and secular courts. Some of these, including the Prerogative Court of the Archbishop of Canterbury, were situated at the famous Doctors Commons near St Paul's Cathedral and it was there that the Principal Probate Registry was first located.

In 1857 Parliament passed The Court of Probate Act, which established the Principal Probate Registry and 40 District Probate Registries in England and Wales with effect from 12 January 1858. In October 1874 the great collection of wills stored in old Doctors Commons was transported through the streets of London in vans and wagons to Somerset House in the Strand into offices vacated by the Admiralty in the previous year. One hundred and twenty three years on, Somerset House remains the central repository for wills proved in England and Wales.

The case for challenging a will

In most respects the law in England and Wales provides the greatest freedom of choice for will makers in comparison with other countries. In other words, anyone from the age of 18 onwards can make a will disposing of their worldly goods in any way they choose. This of course can and does lead to injustices and where this occurs claimants have a right to challenge the will under the Inheritance (Provision for Families and Dependants) Act 1975. The basis of any claim is failure by the deceased to make reasonable financial provision for any person or persons who had some degree of financial dependence upon them prior to death. In other words, the plaintiff can claim compensation for the loss of benefit out of the estate.

The legal position is that claims should be made within six months from the date of grant of representation (probate) but the court can extend this time limit in very special circumstances. In order for the Act to be applied the deceased must have died domiciled in England and Wales. Currently the classes of persons who may challenge a will under the 1975 Act are:

- ☐ wife or husband of deceased;
- ☐ former wives or husbands of deceased who have not remarried;
- ☐ a child of the deceased;
- ☐ any person (not being a child of the deceased) who, in the case of any marriage to which the deceased was at any time a party, was treated by the deceased as a child of the family in relation to the marriage;
- ☐ any person (other than those above) who immediately before the death of the deceased was being maintained, either wholly or partly, by the deceased;
- ☐ for deaths on or after 1 January 1996, a new category: persons living with the deceased in the same household and as the husband or wife of the deceased, during the two years immediately prior to the date of death (Law Reform (Succession) Act 1995).

The first Act of this kind was introduced in the 1930s since prior to that date a will in England and Wales could only be challenged on the basis that the legator was not of testamentary capacity – in other words, he was not considered to be of sound mind, memory and understanding. This was a very unsatisfactory state of affairs since in order to gain redress for any injustice created by the will the plaintiff could only in effect allege that the deceased was of unsound mind. This could be deeply distressing when the testator or testatrix was a loved relative. It still remains a fact that wills are occasionally contested on the basis that the deceased did not have testamentary capacity, but in most cases wills are now challenged under the 1975 Act.

In Scotland the position is markedly different. Under Scottish law a will can be challenged on a number of grounds – for example, if the person were insane when it was made, if children were born after the will was made, if the person had been improperly influenced by another person when making the will. The 1975 Act referred to earlier does not apply to Scotland in that there are inbuilt rights to protect the immediate family. Basically, whatever the will says, a surviving husband, wife or children can if they wish, after 'prior rights' have been satisfied, claim further 'legal rights' to a proportion of any property excluding house and land.

The amounts designated under 'prior rights' are changed from time to time but the current provision is as follows.

Prior rights

These are the surviving husband's or wife's rights to (a) the house (up to the value of £110,000); (b) furniture in the house (up to £20,000); (c) a payment of £30,000 if there are children, £50,000 if there are not.

Legal rights

After prior rights have been dealt with, a surviving husband or wife and children have certain 'legal rights' to a proportion of the 'moveable estate' – that is, all things such as money, shares, cars, furniture and jewellery.

Where there is an intestacy (no will) and any prior or legal rights have been dealt with, the remainder of the estate is given to surviving relatives according to a strictly laid-down sequence – for example, any children have first claim; if there are no children, half goes to the parents or parent and half to the brothers and sisters; if there are no children or parents, all goes to the brothers and sisters and so on. In the event of there being no qualifying relatives in the case of an intestacy, the estate will pass to the Crown.

Because of the complexities in the law relating to claims and contested wills, it is imperative that plaintiffs, defendants and lay (non-professional) executors seek legal advice from qualified solicitors.

Despite these ways and means by which disputes over wills can be resolved, it is important to remember that the overwhelming majority of wills create no problems at all and the intended beneficiaries receive their bequests as the will maker intended.

Why make a will?

Let us now consider the reasons why people make wills. As already stated, anyone over the age of 18 in England and Wales is eligible to make a will, whereas in Scotland girls from the age of 12 and boys from the age of 14 are able to make wills. Some people make a will at quite an early age, perhaps because they are involved in a dangerous job, pursuit or hobby or serving in Her Majesty's forces. Long-distance travel or going abroad as a family often motivates people to make a will. Another strong reason for making a will is marriage or partnership or buying a house. It is also very important for people to make a will when their children are born, both to provide financial security and to deal with guardianship issues. Divorce does not totally invalidate a will except where it affects the provisions made for the former husband or wife. As life moves on, the marriage or partnership of children may motivate parents to make wills, as may the birth of grandchildren. The problems associated with the ageing process are often the main reasons for making wills, such as illness, the death of loved ones and the general desire to put one's affairs in order. Experience of dealing with an intestacy is another strong motivator for making a will. Moral – don't make life harder for the loved ones you leave behind.

Above and beyond all else, it is important for people to realise that the only way to ensure their worldly possessions pass to the beneficiaries of their choice is to make a will. It is often presupposed that there is no need to make a will because the immediate family will benefit anyway, which is to some extent true where the estate is of modest size. In the case of high-value estates, it has been known for husbands or wives in particular to find that the provisions under the Intestacy Rules do not sufficiently cater for their needs and it may then be necessary in England and Wales to seek further and better provision under the 1975 Inheritance Act.

Tax considerations

For some people tax planning is important and anyone wishing to make special arrangements to reduce or avoid tax should seek expert advice. Bequests to a surviving husband or wife are totally exempt from inheritance tax, as are gifts through wills to charities. Other beneficiaries, such as children, are liable to pay tax on any inheritances they receive in excess of the inheritance tax threshold. With effect from 6 April 2000 the inheritance tax threshold was raised to £234,000 from the previous level of £231,000. For estates over £234,000 a flat rate tax of 40 per cent is levied on the excess unless it passes to exempt beneficiaries as mentioned earlier.

There are other ways of reducing the burden of tax on estates but because of the unique nature of each person's affairs it is always advisable to obtain professional advice on the legitimate ways in which this can be done. While many solicitors have knowledge in this field, it is sometimes better to consult accountants, who probably have the greatest skills in this area of tax planning.

At the moment, for instance, we have what is generally known as the seven-year rule. This relates to any personal gifts made during a person's lifetime in excess of the annual or other specific exemptions, such as gifts on marriage known as 'potentially exempt transfers'. These transfers are subject to inheritance tax only if the person who makes the gift dies within a seven-year period from the time of making the gift. Tax is reduced on a sliding scale depending on how many years have elapsed before the donor's death as shown below:

Years before death	Percentage of full tax charge
0–3	100
3–4	80
4–5	60
5–6	40
6–7	20

The wealth factor

It is impossible to say how many people place a high priority on tax planning when making their wills but, to judge by the wealth statistics produced by Smee & Ford, the vast majority of people who die each year do not leave large estates. For instance, in 1994 there were approximately 544,000 adult deaths in England and Wales. Of these, fewer than half (247,491) left estates worth over £5000. The probate value of these estates was £17.66 billion; 53,409 or 21.6 per cent died intestate, the cumulative value of their estates being £2.02 billion. The 194,082 will makers together left £15.64 billion. Furthermore, detailed analysis indicated that 85 per cent of the will makers had estates worth between £5000 and £125,000, suggesting that the great majority could be described as cash poor but asset rich. In other words, for most of them their house would have been their most valuable possession. Just under 15 per cent of will makers had estates valued between £125,000 and £1 million. People leaving estates in excess of £1 million totalled 690 or 0.4 per cent of all will

makers. Fourteen millionaires died intestate and of course their estates would be distributed in accordance with the Intestacy Rules.

Professional involvement

Although available evidence indicates that relatively few will makers take financial advice from accountants when making their wills, it is very important that they consult a solicitor who will be able to give sound legal advice, particularly when complicated provisions are required. The research carried out by Smee & Ford reveals that the majority of will makers still appoint lay executors only but in most cases these executors engage solicitors to obtain the Grant of Probate and carry out the subsequent estate administration on their behalf. Many will makers appoint non-professional executors because they believe it will reduce the cost of administering their estates but, for the reasons stated above, legal charges are incurred by the employment of solicitors who will require a written undertaking from the lay executors that their proper professional fees will be deductible from the estate. When solicitors are themselves appointed executors their charging clause will automatically be written into the will. All the main banks provide a will-making and probate service but have only a very tiny percentage of the executorship market, possibly because of the fact that their charges are for the most part higher than the fees charged by solicitors.

It is of course quite feasible for people to make home-made wills or use the standard forms that can be obtained from stationer's shops. Providing people observe the basic legal requirements, such wills are perfectly valid and raise no problems in implementation. Even so, the best advice is to consult a solicitor, who will be prepared to give prospective clients a quote for making their will. The cost of a solicitor-made will is not nearly as high as some people believe. In some cases it can be less than £50, with special deals for joint wills made by husbands, wives or partners.

Legal requirements

The basic principles for making a valid will are that it must be in writing and must appoint executors. The attestation clause must follow the legal requirement that the testator and two witnesses be together and sign the will in the presence of each other. In the case of Scotland, only one witness is now required, but there the testator is required to sign each page of the will, whereas in England and Wales the testator need only sign the attestation clause on the final page along with the two witnesses. Although it is possible to have up to four executors, one is sufficient, but on balance it is preferable to choose two people such as a solicitor and a younger adult relative or close friend. Remember, a will may be declared invalid if it has not been signed and dated by the testator in the presence of the witness or witnesses, who must also sign the will. Witnesses do not need to know the contents of the will they are witnessing, nor should they be beneficiaries, since being a witness or a spouse of a witness could invalidate any gift bequeathed to them if the will is made in England and Wales. In Scotland it is preferable not to have the will witnessed by a beneficiary but this will not invalidate the attestation or (as in England and Wales) the gift. On the other hand, an executor may be named as a beneficiary in any will.

As indicated earlier, the sole purpose of making a will is to dispose of one's lifetime possessions and to decide on the list of beneficiaries who are to inherit your estate. There are three main types of legacy. The first is a specific gift such as a car, house, item of jewellery or other household effect. If at the time of death the gift described in the will cannot be found or identified, it will fail. The second type of legacy is a pecuniary (cash) gift of any size (for example £1000). The third type of legacy is what is called a residuary bequest, which is all or part of the balance of the estate after all debts, taxes, expenses and other legacies have been paid. With the passage of time, pecuniary legacies will lose value because of inflation and legators may therefore wish either to index-link their cash gifts to family, friends and charity or divide the whole estate into shares or percentages so that all classes of beneficiaries will gain if the value of the estate increases between the will being made and the time of death.

Charitable giving through wills

Despite the growing incidence of divorce and the increasing numbers of people who live alone, the strong allegiance to family and other loved ones is still reflected in the provisions of wills, but there have always been a minority of legators who make charitable bequests. Although this amounts only to about one will maker in seven, Smee & Ford estimate that in England and Wales alone charitable will makers collectively leave £1 billion to their favourite causes each year. It is the second most productive form of voluntary income for charitable organisations and any diminution in this source of funding will have very serious implications for most of the UK's leading charities. To illustrate this point further, the following charities among many others receive over 50 per cent of their total voluntary income from legacies: the RNLI, the Imperial Cancer Research Fund, the Cancer Research Campaign, the Guide Dogs for the Blind Association, Barnardo's, the RNIB, the Salvation Army, the RSPCA and the British Heart Foundation. A number of smaller charities are also heavily dependent upon legacy income, including the Dogs' Home, Battersea, which every year receives more than 90 per cent of its income in the form of legacies.

It may well be that far more people could be influenced into leaving charitable gifts, bearing in mind the tax benefits to both the giver and the receiver. Charities have been influential over the years in promoting the concept of will making since there is no provision for charities under the Intestacy Rules. No will equals no charitable bequest.

It is to be hoped that with the passage of time and continuing growth of individual wealth more people will see the wisdom of making a will and not allow the law to have the final say in their affairs. I began this article by quoting an ancient will and I will end with a few lines from a very recent will:

> O, grant me, heaven, a middle state,
> Neither too humble, nor too great,
> More than enough, for nature's ends,
> With something left to treat my friends.

Bernard Sharpe is Director of Consultancy with Smee & Ford Ltd, having previously worked in the charity sector for over 20 years, promoting and administering legacies for the RNLI and SCOPE.

14 Where to Go for Professional Advice

One question often asked by investors is where to go to get reliable financial advice. In practice, there is no shortage of people or organisations willing to offer advice, from stockbrokers to solicitors and accountants, banks and various kinds of intermediary. The services offered also cover a wide range, from advice on specific types of investment, such as life assurance plans or stocks and shares, to overall financial management, including tax planning and long-term strategies as well as day-to-day affairs.

As well as scope, services differ in terms of independence, cost and the type of client they are aimed at. Traditionally, for example, stockbrokers, merchant banks and accountants focused on the top end of the market, so-called 'high net worth individuals', while smaller investors dealt mainly with insurance brokers and agents or the local bank manager.

These two extremes have now come much closer together. The top end has spread downwards, as stockbrokers have made efforts to enlarge their appeal and appear more user-friendly. Some are even advertising on commercial radio in order to spread the message to a wider audience. At the same time, smaller firms of advisers have been expanding the range of services they offer, moving up the scale from simple life assurance into the realms of investment and, in some cases, tax planning.

There are perhaps three main reasons for these changes. In the first place, the substantial growth in home ownership before and after the Second World War has meant that far more people are now inheriting property. In many cases, they already own their own homes, so the inheritance translates into a sizeable capital sum – even despite the 1990s fall in property prices. This creates a need not only for investment advice, but also for tax planning; the nil rate band for inheritance tax of £234,000 can easily be surpassed where the estate includes a house.

Redundancy, sadly, is another source of increased demand for advice. Again, there are two sides to this. First, the redundancy payment may be a sizeable sum that needs careful investment, particularly if the redundancy happens fairly late in life and the person is not expecting to find another job, or not at the previous level. Second, the tighter job market has encouraged younger people to set up their own businesses, with a consequent need for advice on matters such as tax and pension arrangements.

Third, the spate of privatisation issues over the last few years has enticed many first-timers into the stock market, some of whom have then caught the bug and gone on to other share dealing. A good number, of course, have not stayed in the market, particularly as some issues gave exaggerated opportunities to take a quick profit. But this in itself encouraged the growth of cheap share-dealing services; while the issues could be bought very easily through application forms in newspapers, selling was more of a problem and 'no-frills' services sprang up as a convenient solution.

THE FINANCIAL SERVICES ACT

In addition to these social changes, a major influence on the development of financial services, and the cause of much upheaval, has been the Financial Services Act, which became law in 1988. This was founded on the principle of self-regulation by the industry rather than statutory control by the government.

Nevertheless, it has still spawned a substantial amount of bureaucracy and one suspects that vast acreages of forest must have been expended on producing rule-books that are continuously needing to be updated for amendments, and which are so complicated that further reams of paper are devoted to clarification of what it all might mean. The majority growth area in the industry has been the compliance departments of financial services companies, which are responsible for ensuring that all these rules are followed.

It has now been decided, after much debate, that statutory control is needed after all. As a result, the Financial Services Authority (FSA) was set up in 1997, as a replacement for the Securities and Investments Board (SIB), which had previously supervised the whole show.

The creation of the FSA is part of a general crackdown on the industry, which is seen in some quarters as being contaminated with bad practices and over-high charges. Already the PIA has taken action on pensions that has prompted companies to move away from the traditional 'front-end loading' structure, under which charges are heavily weighted towards the early years of a plan, to level loading, where they are evenly distributed throughout the term. The Cat standard on ISAs is another attempt to encourage lower charges and a similar concept is to be applied to stakeholder pensions. And in his 1999 Budget speech, the Chancellor proposed that the FSA should draw up 'league tables' that compare the costs of certain products, such as pensions. These are due to come into effect by the end of 2000, although many people – including some at the FSA itself – are not keen on the concept.

The FSA took over from the SIB as the main part of a fairly complex regulatory tree. At the next level down are the Self Regulatory Organisations (SROs), which take their authority from the FSA and carry out the day-to-day tasks of regulation. Prior to 1994, there were four of these bodies: the Financial Intermediaries, Managers and Brokers Regulatory Association (Fimbra); the Life Assurance and Unit Trust Regulatory Organisation (Lautro); the Investment Management Regulatory Organisation (Imro); and the Securities and Futures Authority (SFA).

In July 1994, a new SRO came into operation: the Personal Investment Authority (PIA). This is responsible for retail investment services and is in effect an amalgamation of Fimbra and Lautro, plus Imro members who deal primarily with private clients.

The PIA was originally conceived as an answer to funding problems experienced by Fimbra, particularly in relation to the Investors' Compensation Scheme. It was felt that a single regulator would be more cost-effective and financially sound; it would also offer a measure of control to life assurance companies, which had been repeatedly asked to subsidise Fimbra while having no say in how it was run. The creation of the PIA was also seen as an opportunity for raising regulatory standards.

In addition to the SROs, there are also Recognised Professional Bodies (RPBs). These cover professionals who offer investment advice and management services as part of their business, such as solicitors, accountants and insurance brokers. The Law Society, the Insurance Brokers Registration Council and various accountancy bodies act as RPBs.

Anyone who gives financial advice must currently be authorised through one of these various organisations. The PIA covers independent financial advisers, life assurance companies and their agents, and unit trust groups, while investment managers dealing mainly with institutional clients continue to come under Imro and stockbrokers are governed by the SFA.

Anyone who offers financial advice without being authorised is breaking the law, unless it is on a casual, one-off basis and unpaid. This was once explained to me by a regulator as follows: if you are in the pub one evening and a friend asks you for some advice, you may obviously offer your opinion. But if you hold court at the bar every night, offering advice to all and sundry and perhaps accepting a few drinks in return, that would, strictly speaking, be against the law.

Once the Financial Services and Markets Bill comes into effect, which could be sometime in the autumn of 2000, the FSA will take over the functions of the other authorities and become a single 'super-regulator'. Just as with the creation of the PIA from Lautro and Fimbra, the single regulator is expected to be a simpler and cheaper operation than the current one. There will, for example, be a single Handbook of Rules and Guidance, replacing 14 separate rulebooks that have been in issue in the past. The FSA is also planning to promote public understanding of the financial industry, working in conjunction with consumer bodies and educational authorities. Overall, it will aim for a strategy that is consistent across the whole financial services sector, rather than dealing separately with the various areas, such as banking and insurance. It will also take a proactive line, following the adage that prevention is better than cure.

POLARISATION

Authorised firms must display on all their literature, stationery, business cards and so on which of the regulatory bodies they belong to. In addition, they must make it clear whether they are offering advice in a wholly independent capacity, or as the representative of one particular company.

This distinction, which is known as polarisation, was one of the main planks of the Financial Services Act when it was first drawn up. Before then, it was quite common for some advisers to recommend products supplied by more than one company, but without professing to cover the entire market. For example, they might limit their suggestions to just a handful of companies because they lacked the resources to research all of them. Alternatively, they might act in the main for a single company, but occasionally recommend others if the required product was not offered by that one company.

The powers that be decided that this could prove much too confusing for the customer, who would not be sure whether the advice he was getting was genuinely free range or in fact limited to a small sector of the market. So they came up with the principle of polarisation, under which an adviser must be either completely independent and able to offer the products of any company in the market, or tied exclusively to one company and barred from offering the products of any other. Since then, there have been occasional proposals to modify the principle; for example, to allow 'multi-ties', under which an adviser could represent several specified companies, but so far it has not been changed.

To be independent, the cardinal rules laid down were 'know your customer' and 'give best advice'. The former still holds: advisers must complete a fact-find on their clients, covering circumstances such as age and tax position, the range of their financial needs and other relevant factors such as attitude to risk.

The 'best advice' principle has since been toned down to 'good advice'. The adviser is not expected to have a crystal ball to show which product will produce the best results at the end of the day – which could be 20 years hence – but he must select the most appropriate for his client from all those available, in terms of both the type of product and the track record of the company on charges, past performance and so on.

In practice, this means that the adviser may focus on particular companies if they are seen to be the market leaders. For example, if he identifies one company as being good for endowment policies, there is nothing to stop him recommending it to several different clients, but he must be prepared to justify his choice to inspectors from his regulatory body, who will make periodic visits to check that the rules are being satisfied.

While this is basically a sound concept – and what any good adviser should be following anyway – there are certain drawbacks in practice. First, advisers may be tempted to stick to big name companies, the choice of which would not be queried, rather than face having to justify a recommendation that might be based on gut feeling as much as hard facts.

Second, the considerable costs and pressures of being independent have meant that a large number of advisers have simply given up and become tied, so the availability of independent advice has shrunk considerably. It is arguable that the quasi-independent advice that existed before, for all its faults, at least gave investors a degree of choice.

Those tied to one company may work as part of a direct sales-force or be self-employed but acting as an appointed representative. Either way, they can offer only the products from that one company's range but, within that, they are still expected to recommend the most appropriate product. The obvious drawback is that the company may simply not provide the type of product that would best suit the client, in which case he may be persuaded into a poorer substitute.

In practice, the competition between companies to attract and retain good-quality representatives does influence the product range, although it is still true that any single company is unlikely to be a market leader across the board. Naturally, both independent advisers and representatives will argue fiercely for their own merits: the former point out that they are free to select the best product on the market for any given need, while the latter claim that the closer relationship they have with the company can work to the client's advantage. The truth is that there are good and bad in both sectors; what really counts is honesty and competence.

For banks and building societies, polarisation presented a difficult problem. On the one hand, they did not want to give up offering independent advice, as that might mean losing their more discriminating (and more valuable) customers, but on the other, the branch network represented an excellent outlet for business from an associated operation.

Midland, Barclays and Lloyds already had associated life and assurance and unit trust companies and a number of others have set up subsidiaries since: among them, NatWest Life, Abbey National Life, Woolwich Life and Halifax Life. In fact, 'bancassurance', as it is known, is becoming a growing force in the market and represents considerable potential competition to traditional operators because of the huge opportunities afforded by high street outlets.

Of the major banks, National Westminster was the only one to retain independent status at the outset, which it has since given up, while among the top-ten building societies, only Bradford & Bingley offers independent advice. To some extent, though, banks and building societies have cut across polarisation by offering tied advice through their branches and independent advice through a separate arm. But where they have associated operations of their own, these would not normally be recommended through the independent side; the rule for that situation is that the recommendation would have to be 'better than best advice', which in practice would be almost impossible to prove.

However, the rules could be set to change again. Periodically, the principle of polarisation has been reviewed, with suggestions of one or another form of 'multi-tie' – a system whereby an adviser could be tied to more than one company. One of the most cogent arguments in favour is that some companies do not offer all types of product, so their tied agents cannot provide a comprehensive service to their clients. Multi-ties would allow them to mix and match products from several providers to achieve a full range. But critics argue that after years of polarisation, investors have come to understand the difference between tied and fully independent advice and blurring the boundaries would simply cause confusion.

A suggested compromise solution is what is termed 'white labelling'. Under this, providers label other companies' products as their own just as some supermarkets' own-brand products may actually be manufactured by one of the major names in the food industry. Again, the idea has its supporters and its detractors. Those in favour see it as less likely to cause confusion than multi-ties, because advisers would still be polarised into the tied and independent camps, while still allowing providers to fill in gaps in their product arrays. Those against – including many independent financial advisers – believe it would simply muddy the waters and that any departure from polarisation would be a retrograde step.

With so many developments in the market, it is difficult to be categorical about what sort of advice is available from where. What follows is therefore just a basic guide to current sources and the services they offer.

MERCHANT BANKS

Merchant banks still tend to operate very much at the top end of the scale, offering investment services mainly or wholly for six- and seven-figure portfolios. These would be based on UK equities and gilts and also on overseas investments, either directly into equities or, particularly for smaller markets, through the medium of unit trusts and other pooled funds.

Commonly, they provide services on a discretionary basis, which means that they will take the decisions without previously referring to the client. You do, of course, have the chance to specify your aims and requirements; for example, whether you are primarily seeking income or capital growth and the degree of risk you are prepared to take.

The firm will take care of all the paperwork, but you will be kept informed of all the transactions and in addition will receive regular reports and valuation statements. The management fee will generally be based on a percentage of the portfolio value on an annual basis.

STOCKBROKERS

At one time, stockbrokers were generally regarded as inhabiting a rarefied world of high finance that had little to do with the man in

CHARTWELL direct

SAVE at least 5% on your With Profit Bond

Choose your With Profit Bond, then buy it through Chartwell.

We rebate at least 5% commission and reinvest this in your Bond.

JUST LOOK AT THE SAVINGS:

YOUR INVESTMENT	YOU SAVE
£5,000	£250
£10,000	£500
£15,000	£750

All investments attract the full allocation rate.

Why pay full price?

Call **01225 446 556**   www.chartwell-direct.co.uk

Chartwell Direct, 9 Kingsmead Square, Bath BA1 2AB
E-mail: enquiries@chartwell-investment.co.uk

Is your investment advice in *your* best interests?

Check it out with our
FREE GUIDE

CHOOSING AND USING A FINANCIAL ADVISER

Before you try to choose from the mass of financial advisers that are available on the market you really need to decide what you want the firm of advisers to do for you. This will depend on your level of knowledge and how much planning you actually require. If you know what it is you require then you may not need to pay for advice. This may sound obvious but how do you avoid paying when most investments have a cost for advice built into them in the form of commissions? The answer is that you use a discount broker.

What is a discount broker (execution-only service)?

Discount brokers, or execution-only services, are authorised as independent financial advisers and regulated by the Personal Investment Authority. It may sound like a contradiction, but a discount broker is simply an independent financial adviser that does not give advice.

A discount broker will be able to deal with the same investment companies and life assurance companies as an independent financial adviser.

Investment companies and life assurance companies reward dis-count brokers and independent financial advisers in exactly the same way for introducing business to them, and that is by the payment of commission. In many cases a large discount broker will receive more commission than an independent financial adviser because, due to the high levels of business they transact, they are in a stronger bargaining position when commission rates are negotiated.

Because discount brokers do not give specific advice, they do not have to pay for the services of an adviser, and so should operate on lower margins than an independent financial adviser.

Benefits of using a discount broker

The benefit of investing through a discount broker is that they will not take all of the commission due to them; sacrificing some commission to benefit the investor. This commission will either be reinvested in order to increase the investment or will be rebated by cheque to the investor.

If the investor does not use a dis-count broker but deals directly with the investment house or life company then they will not receive any of the benefits of the commission. The investment company will simply keep this commission for themselves.

For further information on how to use a discount broker telephone Chartwell Direct on 01225 446556 or visit the website at: www.chartwell-investment.co.uk.

However if you decide that you would benefit from financial advice then you need to be aware how your adviser earns his pay and you have the choice of paying a fee or working on commissions.

Fee Based Advisers

In many cases, you will pay for the 'advice' you receive through a commission loading on the price of the product(s) you buy. The commission, which should be disclosed to you, may form all or part of the commission based adviser's income.

Now, it is hardly stretching the bounds of credulity to suggest that at least some advisers who are remunerated in this way will have one eye on how much they'll be getting for selling a product, with the other cast vaguely in the direction of the client's actual needs.

But what would be the attitude of a 'fee-based' adviser who is paid only for the provision of advice,

and nothing for the products their clients obtain as a result of that advice? Here it is reasonable to assume that the adviser is more likely to be objective in the selection of products. In this case the outcome would depend on the professional expertise of the adviser rather than their need for income.

The ideal scenario for any client is to have the services of an adviser who:

- Will take the time to gain an overview of their entire personal situation and aspirations before searching the universe of financial products/services to find the rights ones for you.

- Will only advocate buying and selling of investments/products when such activity fits in with your aims.

- Is not compromised between product providers and clients by being paid by the providers. The adviser is paid by you, so the adviser puts you first.

That's the deal. We believe that independent financial advisers (IFAs) who work on a fee basis are more likely to come close to this ideal than commission-based salespeople. For further information telephone 01225 321710 for a free copy of Chartwell's Fees versus Commission book or visit their website on www.chartwell-investment.co.uk.

the street. In recent years, though, the mystique has been all but dispelled. For one thing, Big Bang brought greater potential for competition between firms, stimulating the wider publicity of their services. For another, potential clients are no longer just the upper classes whose families have placed business with the same broker for generations. With privatisations, all kinds of newcomers have been drawn into share-buying and most stockbrokers are keen to attract this new business.

As a result, whereas choosing a broker was once largely a matter of personal recommendation, a number now advertise their services and provide information on what they offer. For example, the Association of Private Client Investment Managers and Stockbrokers produces a directory in which members set out brief but alluring guides to the facilities they provide. All this is very welcome, as it makes the choices much clearer.

Most brokers offer a range of services, from the very basic to the fully comprehensive, as follows.

1. *Dealing or execution-only service.* This is for people who simply want the broker to buy and sell shares, generally without any advice being given. Because there are no added frills, this is generally much cheaper than management facilities.

2. *Discretionary or portfolio management service.* This is suitable for those who have an overall idea of what they want, in terms of income or growth and degree of risk, but do not want to take part in the decision process. The broker will take full responsibility for managing the investments, but the client will be kept informed of the transactions carried out and will receive regular valuations and reports. While some brokers only offer this type of service to wealthier clients, many are happy to take on quite small portfolios and there may be no fees above the dealing commission.

3. *Advisory service.* This may cover dealings in individual shares or the whole of your investment portfolio. Unlike the discretionary service, the client takes responsibility for decisions; the broker will offer advice, based on the client's needs and objectives, but no transactions will be carried out without reference and express permission. Although some brokers specify a minimum portfolio size, which might be anywhere between £20,000 and £75,000, others are happy to consider any amount.

THE DILEMMA OF LONG TERM CARE

Thanks to advances in medical science and improved standards of living, we can all look forward to a longer and healthier life. However, as a consequence, it is also more likely that we will need some form of help and assistance during old age.

The traditional solution of care being provided from within the family unit, is becoming increasingly impractical. The rising divorce rate, greater mobility of family members and the fact that women are increasingly likely to pursue careers, are just some of the reasons for this social change. When these factors are combined with the growing numbers of elderly people as a proportion of the population and their increased dependency in later life, the consequence is a growing demand for professional care both at home and in residential establishments.

Successive Governments have failed to address the consequences of this trend, by establishing an acceptable funding strategy. At present, all but the most financially vulnerable are required to meet some or all of the cost from their own resources. For many, this situation implies that the need for care will result in a reduction or indeed the complete erosion of their children's future inheritance. It also suggests that fiscal prudence during our earlier life, will count for nothing whilst those who have been less thrifty will have the assurance that the State will provide.

The problem is further compounded by the structural inequality of the system. If

our care need requires treatment in hospital then this falls within the remit of the National Health Service and is free to all. However, if our requirements can be met at home or in residential or nursing homes, then the provision of our care is the responsibility of the local authority and is subject to financial means testing.

Consequently, it is hardly surprising that this issue raises such strong emotions and that so often our attitude to the whole subject of long term care is tainted with feelings of resentment and unfairness. Sadly, these views are further aggravated by many quarters of the press and media, who seek to focus on the more sensational aspects of care provision.

Since the report issued by The Royal Commission in early 1999, there has been a growing expectation that Government will announce major reforms to the care system. However, in the meantime, thousands of individuals and families find themselves having to deal with a system fraught with complexity and difficulty.

Perhaps the greatest problem faced by the public is the lack of easily accessible information. Without a basic understanding of the system and the way in which it will impact on an individual's circumstances, then clearly any attempts to plan for or manage the position is likely to prove ineffective.

All too often, people's perception of the care system is inaccurate and based on hearsay. Therefore the most important first step is to obtain an understanding of the basic principles of the system and to appreciate how these are likely to affect an individual's particular position. This is fundamental whether planning ahead or dealing with an immediate need.

Knowing the circumstances under which the value of property will be excluded from the financial assessment, realising that some state benefits are not means tested and appreciating that there are different State systems for funding support, especially where property is involved, are all critical issues.

A lack of understanding can often cause a panic reaction when the prospect of a care need actually arises. The gifting of property and assets is a typical response, often without realising the consequences and appreciating that such action may simply not be necessary. Depriving oneself of assets in order to avoid paying for care is simply not an effective strategy. This is one aspect which creates a great deal of confusion as many people believe that after seven years, such gifts are exempt. However this seven year rule is only relevant for inheritance tax planning and has no bearing on care funding.

Such transfers of assets can present enormous problems, bearing in mind that to have any effect, they must be made without reservation. Consequently it is important to take into account events which may befall the recipient of such gifts. Death, divorce or bankruptcy may well have devastating consequences.

There are however a number of legal measures which can be taken to protect assets. These would include changes to the way in which property is jointly owned and modifications to the provisions of our Will.

The simple fact is that a care need does not necessarily result in erosion of the estate

Once the system and relevant rules are understood, the ability to plan for care becomes much more effective. After utilising the system to best advantage, it may still be that savings are required to help fund care but there are a whole range of facilities available, specifically to assist in this process.

Most people do not realise that it is possible to "insure" care costs at the time the problem arises. This enables a care recipient to precisely limit the effect on the estate and to guarantee a minimum future inheritance value for the family. Significant progress has been made in this area over recent years and the range of facilities available enables virtually all circumstances to be catered for.

However, the precise options of funding for care remains a highly specialised area and advice in this field should only be obtained from suitably qualified and independent organisations who possess a detailed knowledge of care.

With understanding and appropriate guidance, the dilemma of funding for long term care can be resolved. It is possible to accommodate the desire for the very best healthcare and at the same time maintain the desire for wealth to pass to the next generation.

4. *Comprehensive financial planning.* In addition to investment management, this would include advice on any other financial needs; for example, retirement planning, school fees, tax planning, mortgages, life assurance and general cash management. In fact, it could go right down to advice on bank and building society deposit accounts and some brokers also offer banking facilities themselves.

Now that standardised commission scales no longer exist, costs can vary from one firm to another. As a rule, those based in the provinces are likely to be cheaper than those in London, simply because they have lower overheads, and with modern communications technology, location should not have any impact on the quality of service. If you are using an advisory service, it may be more convenient to choose a local firm; for a discretionary service, this is not particularly necessary, although you may need to make the occasional visit to update your objectives.

ACCOUNTANTS AND SOLICITORS

Traditionally, accountants have focused on tax affairs, while solicitors have touched on financial matters only indirectly, through business such as conveyancing and wills. Nowadays, however, the distinctions are becoming blurred and accountants in particular may offer overall financial planning services, generally on a fee basis.

Solicitors are becoming more involved in investment business and there is now a trade association for those who specialise in giving financial advice – the Association of Solicitor Investment Managers. A directory of members can be obtained free by telephoning 01892 870065. Work is undertaken on a fee basis, as solicitors are required by the Law Society to disclose and repay any commission earned.

INDEPENDENT FINANCIAL ADVISERS

Independent financial advisers will generally come under the auspices of the PIA, but that, and the fact of independent status, are

CHELSEA FINANCIAL SERVICES

When investing a lump sum, whether for income or growth, the main consideration will be the return you wish to achieve. The underlying charges payable within the investment play a crucial part in this. Chelsea Financial Services was the first Discount Broker in the UK. The major discounts that they offer ensure that their clients make the most of their money – right from the beginning.

There is a wide range of choice for a lump sum investment and there are many factors to consider when making that choice. Attitude to risk, your tax position, a need for income or capital growth, perhaps an ethical approach, the length of time that you wish to hold an investment – these are just some of them!

Chelsea Financial Services offers discounts on a variety of products to suit most peoples' needs, including Unit Trusts and OEICs, ISAs, Investment Bonds and Venture Capital Trusts. They also offer big discounts on PEP and ISA transfers. This cuts the costs significantly. The original investment choice will rarely remain suitable for the very long term. Chelsea provide a PEP and ISA Appraisal Service, at no extra cost, to enable their clients to consider adjustments when they are required.

The amount of tax payable within or on encashment of an investment is important too. ISAs appear at the top of the selection list here because of their tax status. An ISA is merely a tax wrapper for a variety of investments, including cash, insurance, shares and unit trusts.

The maximum investment is restricted to £7,000 (for this tax year) because it is tax free. There is a massive choice of funds available for this. Chelsea Financial Services offer discounts of up to 5.25% on lump sums invested in funds with companies such as Invesco, Henderson, Aberdeen and Jupiter. This means a saving of £367.85 on a £7,000 investment – a significant amount.

Investors often save the maximum allowed in this way to build up a tax free portfolio of unit trusts, OEICs, investment trusts and shares. This has many uses. It may be the method of saving used to repay a mortgage – the tax status enhances the growth within the plan, there is no tax on encashment and the ability to encash ISAs at any time without penalty means that the mortgage loan may be reduced earlier than planned, if they have achieved an impressive performance. This means that the interest payments for the mortgage loan can be reduced. If your ISA portfolio is achieving a higher return than the interest rate that you are paying on your mortgage loan then it is not logical to repay the loan early.

A portfolio of ISA investments is often used to supplement income in retirement. Pensions are relatively restricted. Of course, there is tax relief given on every premium paid and a portion of the plan paid out as a tax free cash sum. However, the earliest age for taking a pension income is 50 and the government are looking to raise this. You have no access to the major portion of the fund saved, which must be used to purchase an annuity which produces the pension income.

ISAs are flexible. They may be set up initially for growth then for income – all tax free. The risk profile can be altered at will. The capital is accessible at any time, regardless of age or the term of the investment. The discounts given by Chelsea Financial Services ensure that any changes made to the ISA portfolio are made at a low cost, maintaining the value of the investments.

If you have used up your £7,000 annual ISA allowance then you can invest in plain Unit Trusts or Open Ended Investment Companies (OEICs). These can also be bought on behalf of children. Chelsea Financial Services typically offers a 3% discount on these, with 4% on funds managed by Soc Gen, Perpetual and Mercury. On a lump sum investment of £50,000+ even bigger discounts can be negotiated.

Investment Bonds are an attractive investment because of their tax treatment. The basic rate taxpayer has no further tax liability as this is payable within the Bond itself. Higher rate taxpayers can defer encashment of the bond until they no longer have the higher rate tax liability. Also, 5% income can be withdrawn from the bond tax free. Chelsea Financial Services will typically discount these investments by 4%. If the investment is £100,000+ then this is negotiable up to 5.25% – that is a saving of £5,250!!!

Investment Bonds are useful for Inheritance Tax Planning, where 101% of the value of the fund is paid to the estate on death. The plan can be written in Trust, when the value of the plan is paid directly to the named beneficiary. This way the value of the estate can be geared to stay below the Inheritance Tax threshold which is currently £234,000. There are different types of Trust available and sometimes legal advice is appropriate.

There are many types of Investment Bonds available, some for Income, others for Growth, some cautious, others are risky. Many have varying degrees of safety attached. Some examples are the Prudence Bond, a With Profits bond managed by Prudential for growth and the Canada Life Platinum Income Bond which pays an income of 11% per annum for 3 years, guaranteeing return of capital relating to performance in a stockmarket index.

Venture Capital Trusts (VCTs), as their names suggests, are not for the cautious investor. They are popular for deferring Capital Gains Tax and for their other tax breaks. The shares must be held for 3 years to qualify for the initial 20% income tax relief. Chelsea Financial Services will refund 50% of the commission received on these lump sum investments.

Many people assume that the cheapest route for investment is to go direct to the investment company, cutting out the middle man. Wrong! Going direct means that you often pay the full charges which the provider hangs on to – Chelsea Financial Services is happy to rebate those charges, working on the principle that it is better to earn a little from a lot of people.

more or less the only things that any one may have in common with any other. In other respects, this group has enormous diversity, ranging from one-man bands to large firms and offering a wide variety of services.

In the first place, there are different categories of authorisation, depending on the type of business carried out. At the lower end, the adviser will not actually handle your money; you simply make out your cheque direct to the company supplying the product. Firms that do handle clients' money have to undergo more rigorous checks designed to ensure that they are not likely to make off with it.

New entrants to the industry must undergo training before they are allowed to give any advice. This includes passing an examination, commonly that leading to the Financial Planning Certificate, which tests knowledge of regulation and products. They must also be supervised for a period of time before they are fully qualified to give advice.

Once qualified as competent, advisers must undertake a minimum amount of ongoing training as continuing professional development. There are also additional examinations that are required for certain specialist activities, such as discretionary portfolio management, broker fund management and dealing in options and warrants.

The Financial Services Act has led to greater costs for independent advisers and a considerable burden in time and money to comply with the morass of rules. One response has been the establishment of networks linking together anywhere between a dozen and several hundred advisers. Through either centralised or decentralised administration, a network can take over much of the burden of compliance with the rules, leaving advisers to concentrate on their main business, and may also offer technical support and training. Generally, network members will deal with their clients in the normal way, but they may also cross-refer for specialist products, which may be an advantage for the investor.

The range of services offered by independent advisers can include any or all of mortgage arrangements and related products, life assurance, pension planning, school fees planning, unit trusts and investment trusts. In the last two categories, some firms provide portfolio management facilities on a discretionary as well as an advisory basis. However, they do not normally offer advice about individual stocks and shares or get involved in sophisticated tax planning techniques.

The majority operate wholly or mainly on a commission basis, but some are fee based or may offer the client a choice. The organisation IFA Promotion runs a telephone service that can supply investors with the names of three independent advisers in their local area.

INSURANCE BROKERS

Insurance brokers are members of the Insurance Brokers Registration Council (IBRC). In addition to general insurance, such as motor and household, they may also deal with life assurance, pensions and a certain amount of investment business. In the case of those who are authorised only by the IBRC, this last is currently limited to a maximum of 49 per cent of total business, but a number of insurance brokers are also members of the PIA, and hence are not subject to this restriction.

CHOOSING AN ADVISER

In addition to the above categories, financial advice is also offered by banks and building societies, although, as mentioned above, the majority of these act on behalf of one particular provider and can only offer its products. Similarly, the appointed representatives and direct salesforces of life assurance companies can offer advice within the range of the company they represent. Unit trust groups may also offer portfolio management services within the scope of their own trusts.

All advisers must clearly notify the investor of their status, whether they represent one company or act as an independent. The Financial Services Authority maintains a central register of authorised firms, so if you are in any doubt, you can check whether a firm is authorised and the types of service it is allowed to provide. The information can be obtained by telephone or via the Internet.

In principle, independent advisers offer the widest choice, because they can select any product on the market. But if you are happy to deal with one particular product supplier, a tied agent can offer equally valid advice and, by virtue of his relationship with the company, may be better placed to sort out any problems that arise.

TYPES OF SERVICE

Discretionary

With a discretionary service, you are effectively handing over all control to the adviser. At the outset, you will, of course, set out your basic requirements, your investment aims and the degree of risk you are prepared to accept in trying to achieve them. But thereafter you must trust the adviser to carry out your wishes faithfully and effectively.

On the other hand, there is the advantage of speed of action. Since the adviser is not having to refer decisions to you for approval, he can act immediately on opportunities that might otherwise be missed.

Advisory

Advisory services give you complete control, while you still have access to professional advice. Of course, if you are simply going to agree to everything the adviser suggests, you may as well give him discretion and have done with it. But an advisory service can also provide a useful learning process, so that you gradually come to take a more active role.

Since every transaction will require your prior authorisation, it is important that you should be accessible to your adviser. Equally, he should be readily accessible to you whenever you need advice or to deal.

Execution-only

Execution-only services are aimed at those who are confident that they know what they want and do not want to pay extra for added frills. Since no advice is being given, the choice may be largely cost

Our core business is
investment management
and we manage funds for;

- private clients
- trustees
- charities
- pension funds

We are committed to providing high quality independent professional advice with the aim of helping our clients to achieve their financial objectives.

We have a proven record demonstrated by the succession of performance awards for the BWD Rensburg Unit Trusts. We have also received top awards for the overall quality of our service in a recent independent survey.

For further information on our award-winning services contact: Martin Cooke

BWD Rensburg Investment Management
100 Old Hall Street, Liverpool L3 9AB

Telephone 0151 227 2030 Facsimile 0151 227 2444

Email: infoliverpool@bwd-rensburg.co.uk

Web: www.bwd-rensburg.co.uk

BWD
RENSBURG
INVESTMENT MANAGEMENT

BWD RENSBURG INVESTMENT MANAGEMENT

INTRODUCTION

One hundred years ago the personal wealth in the United Kingdom was held by a relatively small proportion of the population. Most people lived in rented accommodation and savings were very modest.

The twentieth century has seen a much wider dispersal of wealth and in recent decades more and more people have had money to invest. There are many reasons why this has happened and perhaps the most important of these has been the spread of home ownership. This has resulted in an accumulation of capital which has then passed down to the succeeding generation. Other factors include the greater prevalence of pensions and the consequent lump sum receipts on retirement and also the growing maturity of life assurance policies often taken out to provide mortgage protection.

But the recipient of these lump sums is faced with a problem – the ever-widening range of financial products.

IMPORTANT CONSIDERATIONS

Before setting forth into this jungle, it is vitally important to draw up a plan and in so doing many considerations need to be taken into account. The starting point must be the age and family situation of the investor. Younger people's circumstances and objectives are likely to change more rapidly and therefore flexibility and accessibility will be important. Older people's objectives may be more clearly defined and may also involve estate planning.

The investor's overall financial position will be important in determining an appropriate strategy. Someone who is already wealthy is likely to be less interested in income and may be more prepared to take risks. On the other hand a person with lesser resources may wish to boost income or even repay borrowings.

ATTITUDE TO RISK

Attitude to risk is a most important consideration and is an area where misconception often arises. For example investments in gilts (government securities) or building society accounts are sometimes mistakenly thought of as risk-free; but whilst capital may be protected, its 'real' value, especially during periods of higher inflation, will diminish. Investment directly into shares or through collectives such as unit or investment trusts have produced good returns in the past twenty years but must be regarded as longer term investments because of the shorter term fluctuations in value. In this vast array of investments and investment products there are great variations in the degree of risk involved and no investor should ignore this.

TAXATION

Taxation is a major consideration when investing but the importance will vary depending upon the circumstances of the individual. Over the years governments have introduced a variety of incentives to encourage saving. Often, however, tax advantages may require investments to be 'locked-in' for a minimum period and this will reduce flexibility which for some investors may be an important consideration. Sometimes more attractive tax concessions may be available where an investment is inherently more risky. Certainly an investment should always be justifiable in investment terms rather than just as a means of securing tax advantages.

PROFESSIONAL ADVICE

Once objectives have been established and attitude to risk considered a further important decision is faced – whether to seek professional advice or whether to look after one's financial affairs oneself. With the growth of the Internet more people may be tempted to make their own decisions but the very growth of the Internet presents a bewildering array of financial products and financial services providers. Furthermore many people do not have the time or inclination to get involved in the detailed management of their affairs, preferring to entrust this aspect to professional advisers.

CHOOSING AN ADVISER

Prior to 1986 there were no controls over who could describe themselves as a financial adviser; anyone could put up a brass plate and whilst there were many professional and well-established firms there was also an abundance of firms and individuals totally focused on selling the highest margin products.

The Financial Services Act 1986 was the first comprehensive regulatory system in the UK. It prohibits the "carrying on of investment business" except by those authorised or exempted by this Act. Currently the Financial Services and Markets Bill is being considered by Parliament. It aims to consolidate existing legislation and extend and encompass almost all areas of the financial services market place in particular the protection of the consumer.

Legislation therefore provides a protective umbrella; but legislation does not mean that all those so authorised can advise on all aspects of investment. For example it is important to distinguish between the direct salesmen and the independent financial adviser. The direct salesman acts as an agent for the company that employs him whilst the independent financial adviser acts as the agent of the client.

Within the independent sector there is a wide variety of firms; some specialise in particular segments of the market such as pensions or estate planning whilst others have a broader spread of capabilities. Because of the interconnections between various aspects of a person's financial affairs it is more usual to start with an all-round review.

In selecting an adviser people should look at such matters as image and reputation, continuity of service, qualifications of staff, transparency of fees and independence.

MOVING FORWARD

The starting point for a relationship between adviser and client is likely to be the completion of a financial data questionnaire; this will present a complete picture of the financial circumstances and will provide the adviser with an informed basis from which he can discuss the financial objectives and offer possible strategies. Only then will the adviser and the client begin to look in detail at the range and variety of possible investments.

As we look forward into the new Technological Age, some investors may be inclined to take all their investments decisions through the World Wide Web but many more will want to build a human relationship with a professional adviser whom they can trust.

based but, if you plan to deal actively, you need to be sure that you can place an order easily and that it will be carried out quickly. Also, some execution-only share-dealing services do offer a few additional facilities, such as company reports or recommendations, and may also deal with the paperwork; for example, looking after share certificates and providing composite tax vouchers at the end of the financial year.

COMMISSION VERSUS FEES

The commission versus fees issue has always been a sensitive one and has become more so lately. Since the start of 1995, all independent advisers and insurance company salespeople have had to disclose what they stand to earn from a product sale before the client signs the application form. This includes not only commission but, for company salespeople, any relevant additional benefits provided by the company.

As there is no longer a maximum commissions agreement, companies are free to pay whatever levels they choose, which means there is the potential for advisers to be biased in their recommendations. In practice, rates are still based on the old scales and the differences between providers tend to be small. A more important issue is possible product bias, as products with similar functions may carry quite different rates of commission. In particular, if an adviser has spent considerable time checking a client's circumstances and requirements, he may be reluctant to recommend something like National Savings Certificates, which carry no reward.

Commission disclosure, however, will not prove whether a product is good value for money. That depends on a number of factors, including the overall level of charges, the service provided and the total returns one might expect. To judge impartiality, an investor would need to know not only the levels of commission on all the possible alternative products, but also their relative merits in different circumstances; without that knowledge it would be difficult to prove a case of commission bias.

The obvious solution would be to move to a fee basis for all advice. But while this would increase independence, it is no guarantee of good advice. There is also the key question of whether people would be prepared to pay realistic fees. For those who are, there are a growing number of advisers who work on a fee basis or offer clients the choice. But this route is likely to prove more expensive for small investors, for whom percentage commissions can offer very good value.

MAKING COMPLAINTS

If you feel that you have been badly treated by a company, or given inappropriate advice, the first step should be to take it up with the company itself, explaining why you are not happy and what action you expect. Always keep copies of any correspondence and also make a note of any telephone calls – when they were made, who you spoke to and what was said.

If you are not satisfied with the response, the next stage is to take your complaint to the appropriate SRO. Advisers and companies must indicate which SRO they are authorised by.

If you believe you are entitled to compensation, and this is not forthcoming from the adviser, you can take your case to an ombudsman. There are now ombudsmen covering each sector of the financial services market: banks, building societies, insurance, investment and pensions, plus a PIA ombudsman.

However, just as the FSA is to become the single regulatory body, there is also to be a single, centralised ombudsman. It will have compulsory membership and be regulated by the FSA, and is due to come into force in the autumn of 2000.

This should avoid the current problem investors have of not knowing which of the eight ombudsmen to take a complaint to. It will also mean equal powers in all areas, whereas the current ombudsmen may differ, for example, in the amount of compensation they can award.

But there are drawbacks. A 'super-ombudsman' could become a bureaucratic monster compared with the smaller, more user-friendly offices there are at present, with long delays and backlogs of cases. The new scheme will also be more formal in its procedures, with hearings that can be attended by lawyers, and this may scare off the very people it is intended to protect. Finally, it will cover only the firms that are regulated by the FSA, which could exclude some mortgage lenders, for instance.

In some cases, you may be able to make a claim from the Investors Compensation Scheme. Claims should be made within six months of a default being declared and the maximum for any individual claim is £50,000. The main criteria for eligibility are that:

- ☐ you are a private investor;
- ☐ the firm involved is fully authorised;
- ☐ the firm cannot pay out claims;
- ☐ the firm owes money or was holding investments on your behalf;
- ☐ your claim relates to business regulated by the Financial Services Act.

But the Scheme cannot help in the following cases:

- ☐ the firm is not fully authorised;
- ☐ the firm has gone into liquidation but has not been declared in default;
- ☐ the firm is still in business;
- ☐ the business was conducted before 18 December 1986.

Bear in mind, too, that you cannot claim compensation simply on the grounds of bad performance if you have been fairly advised and warned of investment risk.

The various ombudsmen publish guides to their services, which are provided free of charge to investors. Product providers – whether life assurance companies, unit trust groups, banks or

Monitor Your Investments

Most quality weekend broadsheets bring you a mountain of investment opportunities – some of them worthwhile, many of them a waste of time. Only time will tell which funds will do a good job for you. A potentially expensive mistake many investors make is buy a PEP or ISA then lock it away for years without paying attention to what the fund is actually doing.

This can be costly – the difference between a good performer and a mediocre fund can run into thousands of pounds. At least once a year you should analyse how your funds are performing, relative to the rest of the market.

This doesn't mean you should adopt a policy of switching between managers on a regular basis – if you do this a lot you can expect to be penalised in charges. However, if you can see that one of your funds has been a disaster it may be beneficial in the long run to make the switch.

Several specialist IFAs (brokers) exist to help you monitor your portfolios. Very often, you will be able to obtain a monitoring service without paying a fee. This is because many funds pay an ongoing "trail" commission of 0.25% or 0.5% of the fund value each year to the broker who is looking after your account. If you bought your fund through a broker that doesn't offer a monitoring service it may be worthwhile to switch your agent. The new agent takes the trail commission and, in return, provides you with a free monitoring service. The trail commission is paid from the annual management fee of the fund. It is not an additional cost.

The standard of service can vary widely. Some brokers offer their clients a printout of past performance tables, and, perhaps a graph. This is all very nice but you can get this for free yourself using the internet. There is also a big question mark over whether past performance presented in this fashion is of any use to investors – the phrase "Past performance is not a guarantee of future profits" will be familiar to most readers.

The better brokers will employ analysts whose job it is to research funds, sectors and general news to build a full picture. The analysts will look at consistency and volatility as well as performance. The theory goes that a fund that has a disciplined investment process is more likely to achieve above average results in the future. You can't get this information from past performance alone.

Expect to receive "Alarm Bells" or "Red Alerts" that keep you up to date with fund manager departures or bad performance. Several firms also provide online valuations and research notes through their clients-only web site. In addition to giving you a health check on your existing funds this can give you a head start when you are selecting new investments.

Another sign of a good monitoring service is the offer of discounts when you switch or buy new funds. Look out for discounts of 3% or more of the sum invested. If a broker suggests a switch but takes the full commission there could be a question mark about his motives.

The monitoring services represent a sensible halfway house for most investors who hold more than one fund. Without having to pay a fee, the investor can tap into the knowledge and experience of fund analysts. This can, in turn, build up your own knowledge so that in the future you can be better placed to sort through the broadsheets, separating the worthwhile offers from the junk.

building societies – can also supply information on their complaints procedures, but if you have any doubts, further guidance is available from the Public Information Office at the SIB.

USEFUL CONTACTS

The Financial Services Authority, Public Helpline: 0845 606 1234; www.fsa.gov.uk

Personal Investment Authority Ombudsman, Helpdesk: 020 7712 8937; Inquiry line: 020 7712 8700

The Investment Ombudsman: 020 7390 5000; www.imro.co.uk

The Insurance Ombudsman: 0845 600 6666; www.theiob.org.uk

Office of the Banking Ombudsman: 020 7404 9944; www.obo.org.uk

Office of the Building Societies Ombudsman: 020 7931 0044

Pensions Ombudsman: 020 7834 9144

SFA Complaints Bureau and Arbitration Service: 020 7676 1000; www.sfa.org.uk

IFA Promotion: 0117 971 1177

Index

Index of Advertisers